IF YOU TURN TO LOOK BACK

A MEMOIR AND MEDITATION

TOM HAZUKA

IF YOU TURN TO LOOK BACK

A MEMOIR AND MEDITATION

TOM HAZUKA

woodhall press

Woodhall Press | Norwalk, CT

Woodhall Press, 81 Old Saugatuck Road, Norwalk, CT 06855
WoodhallPress.com

Cover design: Jessica Dionne
Layout artist: TBD

Library of Congress Cataloging-in-Publication Data available
ISBN 978-1-954907-66-9(paper: alk paper)
ISBN 978-1-954907-67-6(electronic)

First Edition
Distributed by Independent Publishers Group
(800) 888-4741

Printed in the United States of America

This is a work of creative nonfiction. All of the events in this memoir are true
to the best of the author's memory. Some names and identifying features have
been changed to protect the identity of certain parties. The author in no way
represents any company, corporation, or brand, mentioned herein. The views
expressed in this memoir are solely those of the author.

TABLE OF CONTENTS

Cawdor picked up the Indian-wrought stone. "There were people
      here before us," he said, "and others will come
After our time. These poor flints were their knives,
    wherever you dig
          you find them, and now I forgot
What we came up here for."

—Robinson Jeffers
"Cawdor"

The past is a foreign country: they do things differently there.

—L.P. Hartley
The Go-Between

IF YOU TURN TO LOOK BACK

Caminante, no hay camino
Se hace camino al andar
Y al volver la vista hacia atrás
Verás los pasos
Que nunca más volverás a caminar.

Traveler, there is no road
You make your own road as you wander
And if you turn to look back
You'll see the steps
That you will never walk again.

—Antonio Machado
"Caminante, No Hay Camino"[1]

---

1 This is actually Hugo Buitano's memorized paraphrase of the poem, which I like better than the original.

PREFACE

"We Are in Pain"

When my Chilean friend Hugo Buitano sends me email, the "subject" line is usually blank. But not on September 12, 2001. "We Are in Pain," I read next to his name. Four short English words, though we always correspond in Spanish. I hesitated before opening the message, sure of the cause of that pain, pain shared by people worldwide after the horrors of the day before. Suddenly I realized that those same four words, which made me feel a trifle better, as sympathy cards are supposed to, would have panicked me on another day. Instead of knowing the words referred to terrorist attacks, I would have assumed they meant bad news for my friend or his family. My heart would have thumped like crazy; I'd have gnawed on my lip as words crawled onto the screen that I didn't want to read.

But it wasn't another day. It was the day after 9/11. The day after the United States joined Chile in having that date seared into the national consciousness. On September 11, 2001, terrorists hijacked planes and crashed them into the World Trade Center and the Pentagon. On September 11, 1973, the U.S. government and the CIA helped General Augusto Pinochet stage a bloody *golpe de estado*, overthrowing Chile's democratically elected government and establishing a military dictatorship. One event seized the horrified attention of the world; one event was little noted outside the region. The American tragedy resulted in over 3,000 deaths. The American-assisted tragedy led to more deaths than that, though not all at once. Torture and assassination work more slowly than huge flying suicide bombs. Instead of making the slaughter a grisly public spectacle, whenever possible the murders were committed at night, behind walls, out of sight, bodies dumped in remote mass graves or flung into the Pacific Ocean from helicopters.

I don't remember what I wrote back to Hugo. I doubt that it was eloquent. Probably I rambled, for coherence was in short supply during those days. A seed was planted, though, an idea that grew clearer in the coming months. Life is short; time rushes by. I knew that; everybody knows that. But only in certain moments is that knowledge truly real.

Twenty-one years had slipped past since I left Chile. I was twenty-one when my Peace Corps group arrived in Santiago in 1978. The numerical symmetry was probably neater in my mind than in reality, but so much of human reality is *in* the mind that I can't be sure. Twenty-one meant less in those days of eighteen-year-old drinking ages. Twenty-one was just a number. But so is nine; so is eleven. Just numbers until they're not, until circumstances give them new significance. Do lottery players avoid nine and eleven or use them, figure their bad luck is bound to turn around? Call 911. 9/11. September 11. *El once de septiembre.*[2]

I could have returned to Chile earlier, years earlier. Sure, it's expensive to fly to South America and I wasn't rich—for an American, that is, for a citizen of what my Chilean friend Ronnie Ferreira laughingly calls Gringolandia. But I could have done it. I had managed to go to Europe on a graduate student's stipend, after all, and travel to Portugal with my wife Christine. I didn't do it, that's all. I had other priorities, places I hadn't seen. But when I went back to South America to visit Brazilian friends in 2002, and later read the hurt and disappointment in Hugo's email that I hadn't visited him in Chile, I knew next winter's destination.

It was time for both of us.

2 September 11, 1857 was the date of the Mountain Meadows Massacre, when Mormon fanatics murdered about 120 members of a wagon train passing through Utah en route to California, after showing a white flag and promising the settlers mercy if they set down their arms and surrendered. On an entirely different note, the Beatles' Magical Mystery Tour bus trip started on September 11, 1967.

CHAPTER ONE

The Politics of Goodbye

"Time has no division to mark its passage, there is never a thunderstorm or blare of trumpets to announce the beginning of a new month or year. Even when a new century begins it is only we mortals who ring bells and fire off pistols."

—Thomas Mann, *The Magic Mountain*

December 24, 2003, flying into Arica through summer haze. We're heading north over the Pacific, hugging the Chilean coastline to our right, the baked brown Atacama Desert said to be the driest place in the world. Scores of mummies have been found there, preserved by the arid climate. Some are over 10,000 years old.

In twenty minutes, I'll be on the ground, seeing my old friends.

Our Lan Chile flight route has been roundabout ridiculous. From New York to Lima, Peru, then south to Santiago in central Chile before changing planes to backtrack 1300 miles north to Arica (with a stop in Iquique). Arica, the last Chilean city before the Peruvian border, is where I lived for nearly two years in the Peace Corps, from 1978-80. Maybe capitalism rules and there are solid business reasons for no direct flights from Lima to Arica. Just as likely, though, is lingering resentment from the 1879 War of the Pacific, when Chile captured Arica from Peru and annexed Bolivia's entire seacoast, landlocking the country. Compared to ancient mummies, that war wasn't just yesterday, it was less than an hour ago. Which is the way many people feel now. When a country's ego is bruised, it doesn't heal quickly. When a country's ego is stroked, it doesn't relish giving up the feeling, or the territory.

Through the scratched Plexiglas window, I take photos I know won't be clear. I hope that doesn't turn into a metaphor for this trip. My heavy Canon AE-1 is a relic, the same camera I had when I left Chile in 1980. But not the one I'd come to Chile with, or even the next. My Canon Ftb was stolen in Santiago in 1978, a few weeks after I arrived; its replacement was ripped off in Arequipa, Peru, in '79. So, I have no photos of Cuzco or Machu Picchu, none of La Paz or Lake Titicaca. I think about that loss sometimes, how great it would be to have pictures of those days. But I was traveling Peace Corps-style, backpacking with barely enough money to get by. I consoled myself—still do, ineffectually—that travelers through the ages had no cameras, that only recently has a photographic record of a trip become an expectation. Humans are creatures of their era; we assume that our temporary reality is what *is*.

Nowadays, as a card-carrying (literally) member of the middle class, I would break out the plastic and, grumbling, buy a substitute. In 1979 I window-shopped in Arequipa, checking out cameras that cost two and three times what they did in the States (ditto for film and developing). I was furious at myself for getting fleeced by a Peruvian guy I'd stupidly trusted so as not to be seen as an Ugly American. But overwhelming the anger was sadness that so few people here could afford my camera, and guilt that through no merit of my own I was an American who took such objects for granted. Third World cheap beer, food and hotels? I was all for that. But paying outrageous camera prices like Chileans or Peruvians? Not if I could help it. I'd never thought of myself as spoiled, and didn't like the idea, but living in South America forced me to admit it was (and is) true. I had to wait a while, but my parents sent me new cameras via the U.S. Embassy's diplomatic pouch.

Excitement mixes with unreality as the kilometers fly past. How have twenty-three years disappeared since I left here? Disappeared. *Desaparecido.* I think of *In the City of the Disappeared,* my novel set in Chile during the Pinochet dictatorship. The book is dedicated to my Chilean friends, Veronica Inostroza and Hugo Buitano, but also to *"los desaparecidos que nunca conocí"*— "the disappeared ones I never met"—the thousands of people who vanished during the *golpe* and its aftermath, murdered by Pinochet's troops. What must it be like for friends and family separated for decades by barbed wire in Korea, or Berlin before the Wall fell? Or the final goodbyes of emigrants in the days before airplanes or even steamships, knowing they almost surely would never see these people again? My experience is nothing compared to that. Nothing.

Yet this is something.

I feel my wife Christine's chin on my shoulder. She's thrilled about this trip, her first time to Chile, but for her it's just an adventure. The weight of history isn't behind every step, that inevitable comparison between past and present that you make, and see, and feel, whenever you return somewhere that matters to you, that's still part of you. The ghost of who you were still haunts the place. But *who* you were, that bygone stranger wearing your skin, is no more. For the ancient Greeks, "nostalgia" meant "home pain." What we miss, though, is not just home (except as the body is home to the soul), but the self we've grown out of. The self we've left behind, whether we wanted to or not.

A traveler can have many homes, or none. Arica is one of mine. I feel nostalgic; my heart beats faster as the plane swoops lower, curving east toward the coastline. The Pacific is almost painfully blue.

What will my friends look like? Still on time's good side? How much has been transformed since I left? I think about other arrivals I've made over the years, and quickly see that they mean little without the flip side of leaving. The power of showing up depends on the context of what was left behind. I left for the Peace Corps from Logan Airport in Boston on January 4, 1978. It was thirteen degrees outside; a month later the Northeast would be paralyzed by a massive blizzard that I would read about in the middle of South American summer. At the gate, my mother cried. My father, my two youngest brothers and I had moist eyes, but played our roles as men and the tears didn't spill over as we shook hands. What would our goodbyes have been like if I'd been going to war, instead of to teach kids how to play baseball? I turned around once in the tunnel and we smiled for each other, waved one last time. A tear slid down my cheek and I wiped it away, casually, as if I had a speck of dust in my eye.

I watched the East Coast come and go as we flew to Miami, where I would meet my group for three days of "staging" (Peace Corps bureaucratese for "orientation") before going to Santiago. Not until right now, as I write this so many years later, have I

8

ever wondered about my family's ride back home to Connecticut that frozen winter day. Did anyone have much to say? Or were they as silent as their son and brother six miles in the sky, staring and staring out a window at clouds and shifting, elusive slivers of the earth?

It's too late to ask Dad. Too late to ask what the send-off from his family was like when he left for World War II in 1942. Too late to sing him "My Father's Smile," the song I wrote about the expression on his face that October day in 1980 when I returned home unannounced, after two years and nine months in South America.

Christine takes my hand. "What are you thinking about?"

Our tired eyes meet and we share a smile. I'm wired on lack of sleep and warring emotions.

"More than I can say," I tell her, and turn back to my past on the other side of the scratched window.

The plane lurches as we descend. "We'll be on the ground shortly," the pilot says in Spanish, which I understand, then in heavily accented English, which I do not. In Miami for Peace Corps staging (over twenty-five years ago; I can't help it, I keep doing the math) I had felt something bordering on shame that I couldn't understand the Spanish all around me: in shops and restaurants, on the street. It never occurred to me to be resentful, to think "Hey, this is America, speak English." The point wasn't to hunker down with a self-righteous identity and expect others to conform. The point was to expand your identity, become as much a citizen of the world as possible.

That's the idealistic part. On a practical level, we had to learn Spanish quickly or be up *mierda* creek trying to do our jobs in Chile. Like our daughter Maggie had to learn Portuguese when she spent her junior year of high school in Brazil. On our way

9

back from taking her to the airport, we were silent till Christine started crying.

"Try to be happy for her instead of sorry for yourself," I said, my voice breaking. "She's off to have an amazing experience." I thought of the day before I left for Chile, when I'd confided to my friend Jay Clark that I wasn't sure what I was getting myself into.

The look on his face set me straight. "Give me a break," he said. "What you're getting into is the time of your life."

He was right, of course. The Peace Corps experience *was* the time of my life. Sometimes in South America I'd think about what a luxury that was, and how lucky I was to have it. I think about it still. I was twenty-one when I went to Chile in 1978. If I'd been that age in 1942, I'd probably have spent that part of my life as a soldier, like my father and so many of his generation. I might not have lived to *have* another part of my life. If I'd been a little older, I'd have faced big decisions about Vietnam. Enlist? Canada? Prison? Wait for the capricious draft lottery gods to decide my fate? Instead, my friends and I were lucky enough to avoid those decisions, though we grew up with the war. It was the bitter backdrop to our childhood. Eating dinner with machine guns blasting on TV in another room, bleeding soldiers loaded into jungle helicopters. Cops beating demonstrators at the Democratic National Convention, Nixon lying about peace with honor, Paris peace talks stalled over the shape of the conference table.

When we landed in Santiago in '78, for nearly four years I'd been old enough to be a soldier. But I was in that first charmed group of American boys who knew that wouldn't happen. The draft was gone. I'd spent those four years studying at Fairfield University, not building airstrips in North Africa and Europe like my father. I read the words of dead white men, for the literary canon was still quite traditional; Dad saw the bodies of dead

10

white men, for the U.S. Army was still segregated. I joined the Peace Corps to help people and see the world, and wound up living in a dictatorship. Dad returned home after helping people defeat dictators, and what he had seen of the world landed him for months in a V.A. hospital with what in those days was called a nervous breakdown.

We swoop across the border of sea and sand, above waves like white lines of coca *pasta base* that had ruined some of my Chilean friends. Seconds later, wheels touch the runway. Even now as I write this, my heart is beating faster. The heart remembers. That might sound Hallmark; it certainly doesn't sound cool. But unlike the me who first arrived in Chile, I don't care about cool: I care about true. And it's true that the heart remembers.

Squinting in the December sun, we walk down metal steps to the tarmac at small Chacalluta airport. The warmth is delightful after the chill of New England. I force myself to move slowly, to take it all in before it's gone. Well, not *it*, but my moments in it. "Photo op," I say, and snap Christine smiling below BIEN-VENIDOS A ARICA on the single-story terminal roof.

Amazingly, our bags are the first to emerge. That's never happened to me before. "A good sign," Christine says.

"Definitely," I say. "Now, let's hope all our stuff's still inside." (That might sound like an Ugly American remark, but you'll soon see why I said it.)

Out in the lobby I scan the crowd, see no one I know. Could Hugo possibly have the date wrong? We head outside, threading through a flock of *taxistas*.

"Taxi, *señor*? Taxi? Taxi *al centro*? Taxi? Taxi?"

"No, gracias. No. No."

There's a patch of grass and some palm trees, kept alive in this land too dry for anything to grow without irrigation. Cactus

11

wouldn't have a chance here. Compared to the Atacama Desert, Arizona is the Amazon.

Suddenly I see Hugo's wife Any, her beaming face. "Hola, Gringo, how great to see you."

I hug her first, then Hugo. My short, wiry friend takes a step back, strong hands gripping my shoulders. His smile is as big as my father's on that long-ago October day.

"Welcome back, Gringo," he says in English. "Welcome home."

CHAPTER TWO

Sweet and Right

"...but the rain
Is full of ghosts tonight, that tap and sigh
Upon the glass and listen for reply..."

—Edna St. Vincent Millay
"What Lips My Lips Have Kissed"

It was a different world the first time I landed in Chile, on January 7, 1978. Military dictators controlled most of Central and South America. I vaguely knew that, but I knew lots of facts. Jimmy Carter was President of the U.S., for example, and Elvis Presley had died last summer. T-shirts proclaiming that Disco Sucks spoke the truth, though I did enjoy *Saturday Night Fever*. I would never buy a used car from Richard "I Am Not

A Crook" Nixon. Wearing Gerald Ford's WIN buttons did not "Whip Inflation Now." The Yankees just won the World Series for the first time in fifteen years. To be honest, my sheltered self probably cared more about gasoline prices climbing to eighty cents a gallon than about military dictators.

Our Braniff DC-8 touched down in sunny, smoggy Santiago after an overnight flight from Miami. The ten-hour trip had been uneventful except for two things, one personal and marvelous, the other public and sobering. First, Catherine Connor sleeping with her head soft on my shoulder had eased the cramped discomfort of the seats. Second, the discovery during a stopover in Lima, Peru, that Marco Mahoney's hand-tooled leather bag had been stolen from inside his luggage. This was Marco's second tour in the Peace Corps, and he had worked for months making the bag with a craftsman in his village in Ecuador. The theft felt like a warning to all of us: watch yourself, Dorothy, you're not in Kansas anymore. Keep your guard up. But what could Marco have done differently, outside of never letting the bag out of his sight?

In my novel *In the City of the Disappeared*, I cribbed from reality to describe main character Harry Bayliss's arrival: "On the bus to Santiago from the airport he saw a *Tome Coca Cola* billboard and felt both scornful and reassured. He saw a two-wheeled donkey cart and snapped a picture. He laughed with proper irony at a wrought-iron factory sign that read 'American Screw (Chile).'" Those things happened, even the screw factory sign that seems so conveniently ironic that it had to be invented. The more I learned later about the *golpe de estado* and U.S. complicity in it the more the irony increased—though it was harder and harder to laugh. Forty minutes later, when the bus arrived at our destination, more irony: the *centro de capacitación* where we would be studying Spanish for the next ten weeks was right across the street from an army base. A billboard proclaimed the motto of the Chilean military: POR LA RAZON O LA FUERZA. By Reason Or By Force.

At the moment I was more excited than scared, and more tired than either. From the start I had been different from the other sixteen members of my training group (twelve of whom were women). Yes, most of us were in our early twenties. But all except me would be working in health-related areas, the kinds of jobs you'd expect a Peace Corps Volunteer (PCV) to have. Only the kid from Connecticut was there to be a baseball coach, a guy whose meager qualifications were four years of high school baseball and a quick cut from his college team. Peace Corps people lived in mud huts, right? They helped people with, according to the bureaucratic catchphrase of the time, "basic human needs." Baseball was beautiful, baseball was fun, but woefully deficient in the basic human needs department. Was this whole thing a joke? Spending two years of my life teaching America's national pastime under a military dictatorship with a curfew and a censored press? When my Peace Corps recruiter had mentioned on the phone a position that "with your sports background might appeal to you," and read the job description about a baseball coach in Chile, my first thought was, "Are you kidding? The Peace Corps does *that*?" Skeptical but intrigued, I asked him to mail the information.

I had already turned down one assignment. When a Peace Corps job opens up you can apply for it, but if you're not interested, no problem. You can't be forced to accept a position, just as you have the right, although it's certainly not encouraged, to bail out before your two-year hitch is up. The Peace Corps is not the military, though I did take the required physical with a bunch of recruits at an Army facility. Waiting for the hearing exam, a guy told me he hoped to be stationed in Panama, where his cousin said the dope was killer. The officer on duty obliquely

15

suggested, wink, wink, that we reply "no" to the questions about whether we had ever used drugs, had a homosexual experience, or been a member of the Communist Party.

I wanted to go to a country where I could learn Spanish, though I expected to end up in Africa using the French I'd taken every year since seventh grade. Then my first potential posting came through, and it involved neither French nor Spanish.

It was in rural Afghanistan.

I did some research, which in those pre-internet days meant going to the library and sorting through card catalogs. The results were sobering. Afghanistan was one of the poorest countries on earth, with a 10% literacy rate. Life was rough and short. Most PCVs there contracted intestinal amoebas and parasites. The Pashto, Dari or whichever of the twenty or more tribal languages I might learn would be of little use anywhere else. In short, Afghanistan was no place for wimps, and the payoff would be questionable. So, I chickened out quick, thus missing the chance to witness a major historical event: the Soviet invasion of Afghanistan in 1979. I confess to feeling zero regret over this lost opportunity. As it turned out, I would see some of the aftermath of another revolution in 1979, when PCVs from Nicaragua transferred to Chile after the Sandinistas took power and expelled them for being representatives of imperialist and capitalist America. Never mind any good work they were doing, or Nicaraguans who would be hurt by their leaving. Dogma, dogma, *über alles*.

Americans can't claim much high ground on this issue. Anti-communist dogma has led to U.S. support of some truly vile people: Pinochet in Chile, Videla in Argentina, Stroessner in Paraguay, Somoza in Nicaragua, Noriega in Panama. That's only a partial list of the rogue's gallery of the 1970s, thugs propped up by U.S. money in the name of freedom while they oppressed their citizens, fattened their bank accounts—and of course kept their countries open for business with, and sometimes exploitation by, American companies.

Uncle Sam simultaneously funded our Peace Corps Spanish lessons at the *centro de capacitación*, and the training of future Central and South American death squad members at the School of the Americas in Fort Benning, Georgia. Of course, creating killers wasn't the school's stated objective; students were supposed to learn to fight the bad guys, not *be* the bad guys. But when "bad" is defined as anyone who opposes the government, or who even *might* oppose it, civil liberties and democracy are at grave—shallow grave—risk.

I didn't know any of this as we stepped off the bus to meet our Chilean families, with whom we'd be living for the next ten weeks. Like most people, I had never heard of the School of the Americas. I had never heard of Operation Condor either, the clandestine arrangement among South American military governments (with the U.S. as a tacit partner) to share information and work together to quash dissent. Freedom anywhere is a threat to autocrats, but freedom next door is the most dangerous, because it's harder to kill people's hope when the promised land is in sight. Cubans on their rafts trying for Florida, East Germans tunneling under the Berlin Wall—people will risk their lives for freedom if they can feel it nearby, no matter what obstacles are in the way. All I knew as we stepped off that bus to meet our families was that Pinochet was in charge, and that Peace Corps Volunteers had to steer clear of politics. The rule was absolute, we were told during staging in Miami. Get caught messing with politics and you're on the first plane home—the infamous "Braniff Award." We had all laughed about that. And over beers, some of us wondered who decided what "politics" meant.

Are discussions about politics, "politics"? We would soon discover that Chileans continually talked about politics (at least in private), the way starving people talk about food. When something you take for granted is wrenched away, getting it back can become an obsession. And when that something is part of your identity, if you have always seen yourself as a free person living in a democracy, what is your self-image now? Who are you? Are you diminished by events? Embarrassed by reduced circumstances, but trying to keep up appearances, like someone throwing a lavish party when the credit cards are maxed out and the banks about to foreclose?

"All politics is local." People all over the world know about the U.S., though many Americans are distressingly ignorant about anything beyond the latest tabloid scandal and *American Idol* winner. It's too simple to blame this myopia solely on laziness and smugness. Yes, lack of curiosity is a factor. But the U.S. is a political, economic, military and cultural colossus. It's easy for Americans to ignore the rest of the world until trouble intrudes: planes hit the World Trade Center or your job is outsourced to India. Other countries don't have that luxury. They pay attention to the U.S. because U.S. actions affect them. When they benefit from those actions, they're usually appreciative, but they resent being bullied or patronized.

I wish I could remember the first time a Chilean mentioned the CIA to me. It was not at the party that first day in Santiago at the training center. When we met our host families that afternoon for a gringo-style barbecue with *hamburguesas* and such, it was time for laughs and halting communication in Spanish, not politics. Some of the families were hosting a PCT (Peace Corps Trainee) for money, others for experience or curiosity or all of the above. At the moment, we had no idea about anyone's motivations. We simply met the people from another world under whose roofs we'd be living for ten weeks, shook their hands and smiled a lot, hoping for the best.

It was eighty-five degrees. The hulking *cordillera* behind the military base was a hazy silhouette in the thick, brown smog. We poured wine from five-liter *garrafas* and with the sun warm on our faces, we toasted to friendship, we toasted to life and possibility and adventure. *"Salud, salud"*—yes, yes, to your health as well. We felt exhausted from the trip, but alive, so very alive.

And no one mentioned the CIA.

CHAPTER THREE

Sea A Tranquility

"Without heroes we are all plain people and don't know how far we can go."

—Bernard Malamud, *The Natural*

"Meet Chato Rojas," Hugo says, patting the rump of an ancient red Suzuki in the airport lot. "He looks like hell and runs worse, but has been a good friend over the years."

"'Chato' means 'short,'" I tell Christine. "So, the car's name is Shorty Rojas."

She smiles. "Hugo, do you have a nickname for everything?"

"Only stuff I love. You should hear the ones I have for your husband."

"Maybe later," I say. "After enough drinks so she'll forget them."

21

We stow our bags in the trunk, which needs several slams to latch. Hugo seems a bit embarrassed about driving a rattletrap, though when I was in the Peace Corps, he couldn't afford a car at all. It's strange to see two naked posts below the windshield till I remember that wipers aren't needed in Arica. I wonder how Chato Rojas got so rusty in a desert. Maybe the salty sea air.

Engine laboring, we chug fifteen minutes into town, shimmering Pacific off to our right, Arica's iconic El Morro hill looming up ahead. Soon we're traveling on streets and through neighborhoods that I've never seen before, where Arica has expanded much farther out into the desert. Bizarrely, some of the two- and three-story apartment buildings have balconies facing inland toward the dry hills rather than the ocean.

"Where do all these people work?" I ask.

Hugo shakes his head. "*No tengo idea*. Arica's economy is terrible."

I talk mostly Spanish with Hugo in the front seat, while Any and Christine speak English in the back. Christine knows only basic Spanish, but Hugo and Any are English teachers, and noticeably more fluent than they were twenty-three years ago.

We circle a roundabout, past a billboard in the shape of a bottle advertising Arequipeña beer from Peru. Hugo deadpans, "Try not to get too shaky, Gringo. Many of his friends are waiting for you at the house."

I turn around to Christine. "I wanted to spare you the grisly details of Hugo's drinking problem, but you're about to see the ugly truth."

"Sounds good to me," she says, and everyone laughs.

Hugo slaps my knee. "How the hell did you ever convince such a woman to marry you? Bribe? Hypnotism?"

"Animal magnetism," I say.

"I don't know," Christine says. "It probably *was* hypnotism."

22

After the laughs wear away, the sense of hyper-reality and unreality returns. Somehow, I'm actually back in Arica after so many years, but outside of the ocean, the desert and the Morro, almost nothing is familiar. Suddenly Hugo points across my body, out the passenger window, and says something totally unexpected.

"*Allí está la cancha de béisbol.*" There's the baseball field.

My eyes follow his finger and my sense of dislocation deepens. Down a dusty gray slope stands a backstop made of netting draped over metal poles maybe twenty feet high. It looks rundown, but permanent, unlike anything that existed when I lived here. There's a weathered sign on top of it advertising Aguadelzar, whatever that is, and I see bleachers—but then we've passed. It's out of sight.

"Amazing," I say. "A real baseball field."

Hugo shrugs. "I don't think anyone uses it. Have you seen them playing, Any?"

She hesitates, obviously thinking of my feelings. "Not that I've noticed. But I don't really pay attention."

Like all of South America except Venezuela, Chileans love soccer and hardly know baseball exists. For decades I had asked Hugo in my letters how my baseball programs were doing, and he'd never mention it. Finally, one time when I inquired yet again, he wrote, "Gringo, I have no idea, and I don't care. Ask one of the baseball people if you want to know." But that wasn't an option. I hadn't kept in touch with my baseball friends.

Hugo hangs a left at the Pollisimo chicken store, then a quick right, and stops inches in front of a barred metal gate. He hops out to unlock it, pulls inside and locks the gate behind us.

"Welcome, my friends," he says in English. "Home sweet home."

The single-story house dwarfs the one I'd known downtown. Three bedrooms instead of one, two bathrooms, an office, dining room and small back yard. Pieces of the past inhabit the living room. Shelves of antique glass bottles, a boxy black camera on a tripod, and a manual typewriter that looks like Hemingway might have used it. On a whitewashed brick wall hang dozens of metal anachronisms: old-fashioned keys, sconces, signs, tools (many that I can't even identify), all covered with a patina of age. But these relics were born yesterday compared to Hugo's Chinchorro artifacts. He dug them up years ago in the nearby Azapa Valley: a comb, nearly intact bowls, a wooden spoon, an arrowhead. I touch the comb and feel a connection to…I don't know, maybe everything.

I think of the 1976 Bicentennial coin set I've brought for Hugo, uncirculated and shiny in its clear plastic case.

"Me gusta mucho su casa," I tell my friends, and they smile with pride.

Soon we're sitting in the back yard, on white plastic patio furniture. There's no humidity, no mosquitoes. It's 7:00 P.M. on Christmas Eve; summer has just begun in South America. The New England winter we left behind yesterday feels nearly as unreal as it does to be sitting here. Christine and Any are drinking white wine. True to his word, Hugo pops the cap off a liter bottle of Arequipeña. He says he prefers it to the Chilean brands and it's no more expensive, or from my perspective is just as cheap—about a buck a bottle.

Four glasses clink in celebration. Hugo reaches over and softly pats my head. "Is it snowing in Connecticut?" he asks, dead serious. It takes me a second to realize he's commenting on my new gray hairs that are spreading like dandelions gone to seed. Meanwhile, Hugo's seven years older than I am, but there's not a single white *cana* in his black curls.

"No seas pesado," Any says.

"She told him not to be obnoxious," I translate for Christine. "Good luck with that one."

We all laugh. "I think the snow will melt away in Arica," I say.

Hugo claps my shoulder. *"Eso es, Gringo. Eso es."* As he pours the rest of the first bottle of beer he asks innocently, "So, do you still work for the CIA?"

Christine looks puzzled. "CIA?"

Any rolls her eyes. "It is a joke," she says. "Hugo thinks he is funny, but no one else does."

"I don't know," I say as Hugo fills our glasses. "I laugh at him all the time."

"Salud," Hugo says, and four glasses rise again.

CIA references were common during my Peace Corps days, even from my friends. Only the tone changed. Though usually delivered with a smile, that smile could be friendly or accusatory, and almost always held at least the trace of a challenge. The speaker, after all, was Chilean; I was American. The speaker lived under a dictator who had overthrown an elected president. I represented a country that gave constant lip service to democracy, yet had undermined democracy by helping Chile's dictator rise to power. Only four years removed from the murderous days after the *golpe*, was it paranoid to be suspicious of people like me? Or was it realistic?

The first time I heard the CIA mentioned in Chile I thought I was expanding my vocabulary. What did it mean, this Spanish word that sounded like "SEE-ah"? When you're learning a language in another country you spend a lot of time nodding, smiling and pretending to understand more than you do—at least I do. Suddenly my linguistic light bulb turned on. OK, I get it: Chileans make an acronym from the letters CIA.

Sheltered and ingenuous as I was, at first, I found the CIA remarks to be ridiculous, even borderline insulting, like sitcoms with an irritating laugh track. The CIA infiltrating the Peace Corps? Give me a break. Yet when I learned more...well, who knows, maybe they did back in the bad old days. It was conceivable, at least. In 1978, though, no chance. No way any of my fellow trainees was a CIA agent. But any decent agent *would* be impossible to spot, right? Isn't that their job, to go undercover and gain people's confidence? I didn't believe it for a second. But....

Living in a dictatorship breeds suspicion. Censorship brings cynicism. The Chilean nightly TV news program, *Sesenta Minutos* ("Sixty Minutes") was called *Sesenta Mentiras* ("Sixty Lies") by most of my friends. *Hoy vamos bien, mañana mejor* ("We're doing well today, tomorrow even better.") was the government slogan, and evidence to the contrary was neither welcome nor acknowledged. Rarely did an evening pass without footage of Pinochet's wife Lucy kissing children at hospitals or orphanages. The irony that her husband had likely created some of those orphans seemed to escape her.

Welcome to Chile in 1978.

Sometimes bombs would go off. Most explosions happened late at night in the street with no one around. Proof that the Communists were still active, said the government and the newspapers, proof that *Su Excelencia* General Pinochet was forced to maintain the State of Emergency to safeguard the people. Maybe the bombers *were* members of the MIR (*Movimiento Izquierda Revolucionário* /Leftist Revolutionary Movement) or other Marxist groups. Maybe, as I heard numerous Chileans claim, the bombs were set by the military to keep people scared and provide a pretext for continuing the repression. Maybe both, at different times. Even when a house blew up, you didn't know what—or whom—to believe. The government claimed that a terrorist accidentally caused the blast while making a bomb. Many of my friends assumed the military had framed and murdered the man.

26

All I knew for sure was that I wanted no part of explosions. Late one night in Arica, a loud blast woke me up. I lay in bed, heart pounding, wondering if it was a dream and knowing it wasn't. I waited for another explosion that never came, hoping I was safe in my little room. Many had not been. As a man from the northern desert city of Tocopilla told me: "Everyone in Chile may seem free and able to do what they want, but you never know when that knock on the door in the middle of the night might come."

Arica's local newspaper, *La Estrella* (*The Star*), gave the explosion large red headlines the next day, though there had been no damage. (The color was not symbolic; the tabloid's front-page headlines were always big red letters.) The leftists were still out there, the paper said, and vigilance was the eternal price of liberty. No matter who had set the bomb, after that I stayed alert on my tipsy late-night walks home from Hugo's place, always crossed the street if I saw a bag or bundle on the sidewalk and picked up my pace to get past it in a hurry. Commie bomb or fascist bomb? As if that would matter as the shrapnel ripped my flesh. I just wanted to stay in one piece, not become the collateral damage of some zealot's desperation.

Desperate times call for desperate measures. Everyone has heard that line. The sentiment is so easy to agree with, yet so fraught with danger. It was essentially Hitler's platform, after all. It was the rationale for Pinochet's *golpe* in 1973, and the CIA's complicity in it. In 2006, the Pentagon dropped from its new detainee policy the part of the Geneva Convention that forbids "humiliating and degrading treatment." In other words, almost anything is acceptable to get the bad guys—even if we're not sure someone *is* a bad guy. Hey, the argument goes, if you've done nothing wrong you have nothing to worry about.

Tell that to the dozens of Death Row inmates released after new evidence showed they were wrongfully convicted.

Tell that to the families of people killed while struggling for freedom, whether in Tiananmen Square, or Tunisia, or Mississippi in 1964.

Tell that to the relatives of Charles Horman and Frank Teruggi, young Americans living in Chile who were imprisoned in Santiago's National Stadium shortly after the *golpe*, then murdered.

Most fear has to be learned. As a group of gringos in our twenties we were appalled when a lively party at the Peace Corps training center stopped dead shortly after midnight. The directors wanted to give everyone ample time to get home before the 2:00 A.M. *toque de queda* (curfew). None of the Chileans complained; they resented it, I'm sure, but they knew the reality. But for the gringos, it was a new reality. We had been in Chile for six days; this was the first time I truly felt the pressure of the military thumb. Sure, it was only the demise of a party, not a pre-dawn knock on the door from the DINA (*Dirección de Inteligencia Nacional*), the secret police. But we had been having fun with our friends and Chilean families, laughing, dancing, speaking Spanish, drinking wine. We were living our lives, doing what we wanted. But none of that mattered. The heavy hand of the authorities, unsmiling men with guns, was there even when they weren't. And you knew they were never far away.

We were incredulous at first. Surely, you're not serious? For one thing, it's not even close to 2:00 yet. But Elisa, the center's *directora*, was not fooling around. We were her responsibility, and the Chileans all knew how much you didn't want problems with the police. We young, naive gringos saw only the injustice of our fun being cut short. This is wrong! This is messed up!

None of our hosts disagreed. But that's the way it is, they said. You're not in *los Estados Unidos* now.

This incident might seem trivial, but it was a lesson, the beginning of learning new fear. A few weeks later, on my twenty-second birthday, after a party at someone's house, PCTs Beverly Tucker, Jocko Vertin and I found ourselves on the street with twenty-five minutes till curfew. I had a bottle of wine in one hand, my guitar case in the other. Jocko and I had been jamming for much of the night, with Mike Welsh on harmonica. Here's what my journal says came next:

> We nipped a cab, took Bev home, then cruised to my house (and I mean cruised—this guy was blowing red lights like mad in his haste to beat the *toque*). Just to be ridiculous we hung out on the bus bench in front of the house, killing that bottle and flaunting curfew. It was a trip watching cars scream by at 1:55, trying to make it home in time. If I were a native that would piss me off to no end. I'm not exactly thrilled as it is.

What the journal doesn't say is that we kept the gate to the yard open with our guitars inside. And the first time headlights approached us in the quiet neighborhood after two o'clock, we two brave outlaws retreated behind the gate and pushed it shut.

Earlier that night I'd been carrying my guitar like Woody Guthrie, a free man ramblin' down the road. We had played Woody's song "Hard Travelin'" and it sounded pretty good.

Now, on the first day of my twenty-third year on earth I stood—yes, I suppose I hid—behind a heavy wooden gate topped with thick iron rods, watching the empty street in the spaces between the bars. A prisoner, safe on the inside.

CHAPTER FOUR

The Gringo Advantage

"If the unexamined life is not worth living, the unexamined past is not worth possessing."

—Brendan Gill, *Here at the New Yorker*

Christmas Eve continues, South American style. Hugo makes a blender of pisco sours as darkness falls. Daughter Francisca (Panchy) shows up with her boyfriend, Juan Marcos, providing the biggest time-shock yet. The cute toddler who couldn't pronounce r's and called me "Gingo" is now a lovely twenty-six-year-old law student—two years older than I was when I left Chile. We eat dinner at 10:30, downright early compared to the 2:00 A.M. meal Christine and I had shared with our Brazilian friends the year before. Partly that's because in Brazil we exchanged gifts before

31

dinner, and it's tradition for children to go outside at midnight to look for Papai Noel (Santa Claus), allowing the presents to appear while the kids are gone. In Chile, the gifts come after we eat: "Just a few," my journal states, "not the American idiocy."

Christine says goodnight at 1:15, and the conversation switches to all Spanish. I swim in the familiar warm sea of Chilean *castellano*. Mine is rusty, but still fluent, a linguistic bicycle I doubt I'll ever forget how to ride. By 2:00 A.M., though, I'm beat from the long trip, the excitement, the socializing. Wisely declining Juan Marcos's offer of a piscola (pisco and cola) nightcap, I join Christine in Hugo and Any's bed. Despite our protests, they'll be sleeping on a mattress in the office.

"I love your friends," she says sleepily.

"They're your friends now too. You know how South Americans are."

"You were so lucky to come here. And I was so lucky to meet you." She kisses me and falls back to sleep almost as soon as her head touches the pillow.

I *was* lucky, both to meet Christine, and eight years earlier to be sent to Arica. The Peace Corps had balked about sending me 1300 miles north, by far the most distant PCV from headquarters in Santiago—and therefore the farthest from supervision. But the Chilean Baseball Federation, with my Santiago housemate and former PCV David Osinski as intermediary, convinced PC country director Gene de la Torre that: 1) the project was worthwhile, and 2) I was not likely to snap and do an imitation of Kurtz in *Heart of Darkness*, or otherwise bring discredit to the organization. Helping people is obviously the Peace Corps' mission, but every PCV soon learns that it's also a government bureaucracy, and bureaucracies value toeing the line and avoiding risks. De la Torre occasionally made noises about coming to Arica to check up on me. I thought for sure he'd take

32

the chance to visit the northern beaches, stay in the best hotel, probably time the trip to escape Santiago winter for a while. To my surprise, though, it never happened. I'm probably the only PCV he didn't visit.

Which was fine with me.

I was twenty-two (then twenty-three, then twenty-four) and on my own, a sometimes lonely or scary situation but for the most part a lovely bit of exhilaration. Especially since I was only on my own for the freedom part of the equation. I knew that every month my Peace Corps living allowance would magically appear in my bank account. Outside of the summer before my senior year in high school, when I'd worked forty hours a week as a custodian at Westbrook High for the $1.60 minimum wage, it was the first time I'd had a regular salary. I'd had a regular income, mowing lawns with my friend Jay, but the pay varied depending on weather and how much work there was. Now I knew I could expect around $220 a month, a figure that with Chile's steady inflation rose from 7,200 pesos in April '78 to over 9,000 pesos by mid-1980. I also received 8,200 pesos after training as a one-time "settling-in allowance." (In Chile the $ sign applies to pesos, but I'll use it only for dollars to avoid confusion.)

Some friends back home were incredulous. "You've got to be kidding me. You live on two hundred-twenty bucks a month?" Well, my rent at various places ranged from 1,400 to 2,100 or so pesos a month. My only other necessary expenses were food and transportation (especially in sprawling Santiago, where I often spent several hours a day on buses or in taxis). The *menu* (*prix fixe* meal) at low-end restaurants in Arica, even with a couple of beers or glasses of wine, was only 60-90 pesos ($1.50-$2.25). So, it really wasn't all that tough to get by. Besides, I was a Peace Corps Volunteer. Luxury wasn't supposed to be part of the equation.[3]

Neither was guilt, but suddenly there it was: our tiny paychecks put us around the 40th percentile among Chilean workers—plus we got free health benefits. I had friends with families who were somehow scraping by on 4,000 pesos a month. The *empleo mínimo* wage was even worse. *Empleo mínimo* involved menial labor such as sweeping sidewalks or picking up litter, funded by the government at essentially starvation wages. Our PCV salary was triple or more the *empleo mínimo*. Meanwhile, Pinochet's government cynically used the *empleo mínimo* program to lower unemployment figures. *Empleo mínimo* was a job, right? Not one that could keep you alive for long, but a job. So, the many thousands of people desperate enough to work for the pittance did not show up in the official unemployment rate of about 16%.

I met many Chileans who had lost their manufacturing or professional jobs and became taxi drivers. A *colectivo* taxi driver I knew in Arica was unfortunately typical. (*Colectivos* travel a set route for a single price, carrying up to four passengers at a time.) Hector worked an *empleo mínimo* job all morning, then spent eight hours driving his cab to make 300 pesos—less than ten bucks. Assuming he took one day off a week—though I wouldn't be surprised if he didn't—he was working ungodly hours to earn

---

3   Unlike food and other basic necessities, luxury goods, especially imported ones, often cost far more in Third World countries than in the U.S. In 1979, a box of four pressureless Tretorn tennis balls (still white in those days, and my Jack Kramer racquet was wood) cost a hefty $10. They were like rocks but lasted for weeks, especially on clay courts, a better deal than $6 for a can of three pressurized balls. Public courts were also rare, so tennis was largely for those who could afford club memberships. That included me. From my Peace Corps salary, I paid 1,000 pesos a month ($25) for access to the clay courts at the El Paso, one of Arica's best hotels.

the same money I got as a PCV. And unlike Hector, I wasn't married with three small children.

The distinctions didn't stop there. We also got a month of paid vacation each year, which nearly everyone used for traveling—adventure subsidized by Uncle Sam. Not that I think it was wasted money. Far from it. Each one of us was a mini-ambassador for the U.S., and I firmly believe that the vast majority of folks PCVs encounter in their travels come away with a positive opinion of Americans. Just as important, PCVs return to the U.S. with new experiences and perspectives, still Americans but also citizens of the world. Which is a very good, and for lovers of the bottom line, very useful thing for our society.

For PCVs, coming home to the States has financial rewards as well. You get a readjustment allowance to smooth your transition back to U.S. society. Set at $75 for every month of service when I started, before long the figure was bumped to $125. (As of 2022 it's $375; $475 for PCVs who, like me, served more than 24 months.) I was given three grand when I left the Peace Corps in 1980, plenty to travel on for three months before heading home, with a fair chunk left over to actually readjust with. So, my $220 salary was actually far heftier, because it included an approximately 50% automatic savings plan. Counting the readjustment money, as a supposedly self-sacrificing Peace Corps Volunteer, I was easily in the top half of Chilean wage earners.

Did I feel guilty? A bit. Leafing through my journals from those years I found this phrase more than once: "I'd feel guilty if it would do any good." Far more than guilty, I felt lucky. Extremely lucky. Through no merit of my own I happened to have been born in the country that sponsors the Peace Corps, giving me this tremendous opportunity. Sure, I still had to embrace that opportunity, but the point is that it was there. A Chilean kid fresh out of college like me had no Peace Corps to join. That kid simply didn't have as many options.

Here's a story about gringos and options. In December of 1978, nine weeks after I'd moved to Arica from Santiago, some coaches and I took a group of kids to play a friendly baseball game in Iquique, 300 kilometers to the south. A crazy-long trip for one game, but that's life in the Atacama Desert: Iquique is Arica's closest Chilean neighbor of any size. We got steamrolled, 28-5, but considering it was the first time our guys had even played with stealing allowed, they did fairly well (they even briefly led 4-3 in the third inning). A reporter from *La Estrella de Iquique* showed up at the game and promised a prominent article in the paper. That was good news because baseball was (and still is) an exotic, little-known entity in Chile and we jumped at any chance for publicity.

The problem, as I discovered the next day, was that the Iquique *Estrella* was hard to find in Arica. After all, Arica had its own local *Estrella*. I checked several newspaper kiosks without luck, kicking myself for forgetting to look until noon, when any stray copies were more likely to have been sold. There had also been a fairly strong earthquake in Iquique a few hours after we'd left the evening before, which might have interfered with delivery. Finally, one kiosk vendor directed me to the newspaper distributorship, in a downtown building half a dozen blocks away. The boss there had a single copy of the Iquique paper—which wasn't for sale. He let me read the article, though, and asked why I was interested. We got to talking. Suddenly, the paper that wasn't for sale was slid back across the counter to me.

"Take it," the man said. "No charge."

I was delightfully amazed. *"Un millón de gracias, señor."*

"Nada. Feliz Navidad."

36

That night I spent Christmas Eve with my friends Lucho and Pitina Varas and their family. I told them about the Good Samaritan who'd given me the newspaper.

Lucho grinned and clapped me on the shoulder. *"Amigo,"* he said, pouring me more champagne, *"eso es la ventaja de ser gringo."* (Friend, that's the advantage of being a gringo.)

At the moment I didn't do much but smile, take another drink and enjoy the midnight rabbit supper. Only later did I think it through and realize how much truth Lucho's light-hearted comment contained. I certainly had no idea that twenty-three years later, in a new century, the Gringo Advantage would bring me back to Chile, courtesy of a grant from my union and my university to do research for this book.

But even the Gringo Advantage has a downside, a dark side. To avoid hassles about the Vietnam War, a war she detested, when Christine traveled to Europe in 1970, she told people she was from Canada. A similar situation resulted with the war in Iraq. Before the war, some Brazilian friends—conservatives who had voted against leftist Lula da Silva for president—asked me in astonishment, Bush isn't crazy enough to go to war without proof, is he?" All I could say was that I sincerely hoped not. After the invasion, people the world over blamed Bush and the U.S. for tragically misguided policies, and American travelers sometimes found themselves judged guilty by association.

In the wrong hands, the Gringo Advantage devolves into the Ugly American. The Ugly American is a stereotype, and Americans certainly have no monopoly on crass behavior, but since I'm an American, it's the stereotype that most affects me. Humans tend to lump people together in catchall categories—and to dislike it intensely when others do the same to them. I've received freshman composition essays describing the three types of students at the writer's high school: bookworms, jocks, and stoners. (One time a student added a fourth classification—"the Mexicans"—and I'm still trying to recover.) Each group gets a mostly negative portrait. When I ask the writers which group was theirs, suddenly those three limiting categories aren't enough, for of course the stereotypes don't apply to them. I'm reminded of "freedom fries" politicians who rightly decried broad-brush Al Qaida denunciations of Americans, yet had no trouble calling the French "cheese-eating surrender monkeys." Homer, the pathetic patriarch in the TV's *The Simpsons*, sadly and succinctly described the phenomenon: "I like it better when they're making fun of people who aren't me."

As I mentioned earlier, my fear of being an Ugly American cost me a camera. On August 7, 1979, I slogged through multiple layers of infuriating Chilean bureaucracy to finally receive a simple *salvoconducto* pass allowing me to travel to Peru. (That's the abridged version; the ordeal was a multi-day process.) Because of the wasted hours, by the time the *colectivo* taxi got me to Tacna, Peru, the 2:00 P.M. bus to Arequipa was full, so I had to wait for the next bus at four. No big deal, just a bit of an inconvenience. If you can't handle that, pal, you might as well stay home.

I had no idea how the chain of events was linking together. Here's my journal's version of those events:

Tues. Aug. 7—...Pretty good ride to Arequipa, but absurdly lengthened by the number of checkpoints. Two customs checks, and 5 (!) times we foreigners (several Argentinians, a German and an older American) had to descend and have our names recorded in a ledger. Absurd waste of time. No wonder these countries get nowhere when the govt. spends what money it has on creating obstacles for the people. Added 2 hours to what should have been a

6-hour trip, and we didn't arrive till midnight.... I walked the dark streets, littered with sprawled sleeping bodies, asked directions a few times (this would be a tough trip w/ out Spanish) but found all the hotels full. Met a Peruvian from Lima who'd been on my bus, and we finally rented a triple room for the price of a double at Hotel San Juan de Dios, overlooking the road next to the terminal. Noisy? Rock hard beds and pillows? Light flowing in at 6 A.M.? Yes on all counts. But from the terrace you have a splendid view of El Misti, Chachani and Pichu-Pichu [volcanoes]. My companion and I BS'd a while—their accent certainly is different from Chile's. So far, I'm extremely impressed w/ Peruvian folk in general.

Wed. Aug. 8—That last statement should definitely put me among the frontrunners in the 1979 famous last words competition....

That morning I went to the terrace to wash socks and hang them to dry. I knew, absolutely knew, that I should take anything valuable with me. No way I should trust some stranger I'd shared a room with out of desperation and convenience. But we'd had a pleasant talk. He really seemed like a nice guy. If I took my stuff with me, I worried that I'd look like an Ugly American who thought Peruvians were thieves. I left for five minutes and washed my socks, the sun warm on my face in the morning chill at over 7,000 feet. The perfect, snow-capped cone of El Misti had me composing poems in my head.

When I returned to the room, the nice guy was gone. So was my camera.

I wasted two days of my vacation trying to get it back. First, I reported the theft at the P.I.P. (Policía de Investigaciones del Perú). Two German girls were there; their purses had been slit and cameras stolen at Arequipa's notorious train station. The policeman practically yawned in my face as he tossed me a form to fill out. I knew a fair amount about the thief from our talk in the room, so I asked the cop to check the passenger list from the bus company. Isn't that why they have all those security checkpoints that stop the bus every few miles? But he couldn't be bothered. Even after a long day of detective work when I'd narrowed the list of suspects to two or three, he refused to follow up. Maybe if I'd bribed him, he would have put in some effort, though I doubt he would have succeeded. After all, of my final six suspects from the bus, two of them turned out to have used false names on the passenger manifest.

I was getting an education, at least. The cops were not just incompetent, although they certainly were that. But perspective is everything. Why should they bust their tails trying to find some gringo's camera? What's in it for them? The gringo probably doesn't think of himself as rich, but the mere fact that he's traveling in Peru and owns (well, owned) a nice camera makes him wealthy as far as most Peruvians are concerned. A cop is far from likely to own such a camera, or to have money enough to travel to the U.S. The gringo victim feels violated; meanwhile, most locals don't shed a tear unless a bad reputation starts to hurt business. It's a type of Robin Hood syndrome: "So what if some gringo needs to buy a new camera, one that I'd never be able to afford in my life. He's just going to go home to a California mansion like I've seen on the TV shows. I'm sure the thief needs the money a lot more than he does."

The motivation is probably psychological as well as financial. Stealing a camera or a backpack could be a form of "sticking it to the man." People like to see someone too big for his britches get taken down a peg, get taught a lesson. The problem is that getting taken down a peg doesn't necessarily lead to learning a damn thing.

The Gringo Advantage also means relative immunity. Americans have never had to live under a military dictator. We've gotten inklings of what it would be like (the suspension of *habeas corpus* during the Civil War; police brutality from the Civil Rights Movement to Black Lives Matter; National Guard shootings at Kent State in 1970; Donald Trump's attempts to undermine the 2020 election), but no war has been fought on U.S. soil since Lee surrendered to Grant in 1865. We have endured two major attacks—Pearl Harbor and 9/11—both of which led to curtailment of civil liberties: concentration camps for Japanese-Americans during World War II, and the Orwellian-named Patriot Act in 2001.

I can guarantee that the Patriot Act made life edgy for Peace Corps Volunteers. Local people would ask Volunteers their opinions on issues like the war in Iraq, torturing prisoners, and locking them up for years without being charged. A necessary first step to being a successful PCV is gaining the trust of the folks you'll be working with, and the Peace Corps is predicated on the goodwill of the United States. Volunteers represent our government in direct, visible ways with foreign citizens. If the ethos and credibility of the U.S. are damaged, the Peace Corps mission is compromised. PCVs have tough enough jobs without needing to overcome that hurdle.

I got a taste of this problem from Chileans' questions about the CIA. But although the CIA had helped Pinochet overthrow Allende, that was five years earlier under Nixon. In my Peace Corps time, the late '70s, Jimmy Carter had made human rights a cornerstone of his presidency. The effectiveness of Carter's foreign policy could be questioned, but not his intentions. Most Chileans saw Pinochet as the enemy, with the U.S. as a sometimes bumbling, but generally (now that the Vietnam War was over) benevolent presence.

In the Peace Corps, I assumed the Gringo Advantage meant I couldn't get in huge trouble, at least if I stayed out of politics. In 1973-74, maybe, during Pinochet's Caravans of Death, but not now. In fact, by the time I left Chile in 1980, I naively believed that *desaparecidos* were a thing of the past. Repression, sure, and lack of civil rights, but I didn't think anyone was actually getting disappeared anymore.

Later, though, I heard three stories that changed my mind. If even a peripheral observer like me knows of three incidents, logic says that's only a tiny fraction of the reality. It's not as if most of this stuff got in the papers.

The first story is from my PCV friend Neil McFadden, who had a similar opinion about *desaparecidos* until an encounter with the Arica police left him wondering. In his words, here's what happened:

It was Saturday night, March 21, 1981. I was heading home when a camouflage green army bus chugged up the street. A man was running alongside the bus, which beat him to the corner. Two *pacos* [cops] jumped out and began kicking this pathetic dude in the doorway of a store. I crossed the street yelling, "*Basta! Basta!* ["Enough!"] A third cop asked me, "*Estas reclamando?*" ["You complaining?"] and escorted me into the bus. I thought he might want a witness or something.

The bus was full of whores, drunks, and tourists experiencing the Saturday night Arican festivities. When we reached the jail we were separated by gender; the women were taken upstairs, I think. We were interviewed, and our valuables placed in plastic bags identified with our names. I began to get nervous and realized that I was not there to be a witness. I figured that my watch and pesos were history. We stood at attention in a large room, and were searched but not asked to remove our clothes.

After a roll call we were escorted into a holding cell about 8 by 12 feet. With twenty of us jammed in there only one man could sit on the floor at a time. In a corner there was a funnel-like contraption for relieving oneself. By now it was probably 2:30 A.M. It was difficult to determine why we were being detained. Pinochet had just taken office on March 11 [for the first time as an elected president, though the referendum was a joke], and this may have been part of a nationwide show of force. In another part of the building, we heard one or two women scream. God knows what was going on there.

Eventually a uniformed officer came to the door of the cell and read off the roll call. As we answered and all were accounted for, we assumed that freedom was soon to come. The officer left. We waited and waited and nothing happened. It was a ruse. This scenario went on for hours. The roll call was read four different times by different *pacos*, seemingly just to make sure no one slept (as if we could, standing up). Finally, after one roll call we were walked out of the lockup and allowed to retrieve our valuables.

At the main entrance everyone scattered like roaches from a lit kitchen. Not having learned my lesson, I turned to a *paco* posted at the door and asked why we had been detained.

"You can go now," he said. "It's a free country."

It was Sunday around noon. I was glad to see the sunlight.

In 2006, an out-of-the-blue call from someone I had never met came to my office at Central Connecticut State University. It was Suzanne Kolb, Associate Professor of Environmental Science at Antioch College, and still active in South America as director of Antioch Education Abroad's Brazilian Ecosystem Program. She had seen my novel *In the City of the Disappeared*, and the book's Chilean setting and baseball element made her wonder if I were a member of her Peace Corps training group, writing under a pseudonym.

That possibility might seem far-fetched until you learn that her PC group, which came to Santiago in October of 1978, included a pair of baseball coaches: Neil McFadden and Bob Maurer, who would become two of my best friends. Neil, you've met during his night in jail. Bob was in his late fifties, an amazing guy who had been a college professor for thirty years. Philip Roth, Bob's student at Bucknell University, was so impressed that Roth dedicated his novel *Our Gang* to him, and the poem "For Robert Maurer" appears in Stuart Dischell's book *Good Hope Road*.

Early in our conversation, I asked Suzanne about the rumors of CIA involvement with the Peace Corps. She said that she'd suspected Bob and Neil might be agents. "I mean, *baseball* coaches? Come on!" When I broke the news that I had been one of those coaches, we laughed and decided that the CIA presumably would have arranged a better cover.

I doubt that any PCV was better prepared than Suzanne for life in post-*golpe* Chile. Before leaving the U.S., she had attended meetings of Chilean exiles in San Francisco. Obviously, those exiles detested Pinochet, and she heard numerous

44

behind-the-scenes stories, many of the horror variety. She also learned that one of the first casualties in life under a dictatorship is trust: there was widespread suspicion that CIA moles were monitoring the exiles' meetings.

Suzanne was appalled at how casually most of her training group treated life in Santiago, at least at first. Many cavalierly assumed that gringos were immune from the bad stuff. Some acted as if they weren't even aware that bad stuff had occurred. "I wanted to scream at them that it's not the movies here," Suzanne told me. "The government has a file on every Peace Corps person from the moment you step off the plane."

After training, Suzanne worked with fishing co-ops in Caldera, a small coastal town in the desert nearly 600 miles north of Santiago. She soon got a lesson in oppression. Why not brighten up one of the co-op buildings near the water? she suggested. Let's paint a mural—a sunrise, seagulls, a pretty beach scene. Instead of the enthusiasm she'd expected, people said they'd be carted away if they did such a thing. The government would interpret the painting as a protest. Suzanne figures the co-ops were somewhat suspect with the government from the start, given the military's paranoia of anything even remotely Communist.

Despite knowing the risks, she eventually got involved with politics, more heavily involved than any other PCV in Chile that I know of. Maybe more accurately, she got involved with certain compelling, charismatic people, with politics as an inevitable corollary given Chile's traumatic circumstances. Foremost among them was Nano, "a pretty serious student dissident" at the Universidad Católica in Valparaíso, a major port 75 miles west of Santiago. Through him, Suzanne began to attend clandestine anti-government meetings.

Political activity was grounds for dismissal from the Peace Corps—that fact was drummed into us during training. Under

Pinochet, it was also grounds for arrest. For Suzanne, conscience and curiosity trumped worry about the Braniff Award. She said people at the meetings had an enormous hunger to talk to foreigners, hoping they would spread the truth about Chile back in their home countries, and that maybe external pressure would help curb Pinochet's repression. Dozens of Chileans expressed similar sentiments to me, never at secret meetings, but always in whispers and usually behind closed doors.

Nano introduced Suzanne to families of the murdered and the disappeared. In Copiapó, a city fifty miles southeast of Caldera, there was a field with an unmarked mass grave where victims of the *golpe* were buried. *"Vamos a ver a los niños"* ("Let's go see the children") was Nano's code phrase for visiting the place. Sad flowers were strewn around the field, left by people in quick visits after dark. It was too dangerous to do it in the daylight. Ironically, though, once flowers were in the field, soldiers didn't remove them, for that would have been a tacit admission that the field was more than just an empty lot. Nano and Suzanne would sit on a bench with their backs to the graves in order not to get caught, casting occasional surreptitious glances and thinking, thinking. When a soldier sauntered by with his gun slung over his shoulder, eyeing them, they would all pretend they didn't know why each other was there.

In Santiago, Nano took Suzanne to visit relatives of Violeta and Nicanor Parra. Violeta had been a popular singer and song-writer, a leader of the *Nueva Canción* ("New Song") movement that emphasized music about the poor and the dispossessed. After the *golpe*, many of these singers were persecuted, and their songs banned. Parra is best known for her haunting ballad "Gracias

A La Vida" ("Thank You to Life").[4] She committed suicide in 1967, six years after Ernest Hemingway and in the same fashion, with a shotgun. Her brother Nicanor was a poet known for his self-styled *"anti-poesía"* ("anti-poetry"). Nano and Suzanne were invited to stay for dinner, sharing what little the family had, although the Parras lived in a *callampa* (slum) in such poverty that their house had a dirt floor.

On another trip to Santiago, Suzanne went with some Peace Corps friends to a soccer game in the National Stadium. Like most of the world, Chile is mad for *fútbol*, and this was an international match (possibly versus Uruguay, though Suzanne can't recall for sure). Latin American military dictators for years had exploited soccer to whip up nationalistic fervor and distract citizens from the grimness of their lives. The most egregious example is Argentina, World Cup champions in 1978. The nation celebrated—except for thousands of people murdered during the government's anti-Communist "Dirty War" that began in 1976 and didn't end until 1983.

This soccer game wasn't Suzanne's first time in the National Stadium. She's a runner, and once while in Santiago had asked a guard for permission to use the stadium track. Somewhat to her surprise, the guy said yes. Minutes later, though, changing alone in a locker room, a wave of horror washed over her. All she could think of was the atrocities that happened at the stadium in 1973. The screams still seemed to echo off the walls. Heart thumping, sweating more than she would have if she had run, she hastily put her street clothes back on and got out of there.

---

4 Internationally, the most popular recordings of "Gracias A La Vida" are by Joan Baez and Argentine singer Mercedes Sosa, but my favorite is an austere version with Violeta accompanying herself on charango, an eight-string instrument (sort of an altiplano mandolin) with a body made from an armadillo shell.

When goals are scored in soccer, spectators often leap to their feet and throw up their hands. When Chile scored this time, some people used the chance in the glorious confusion to fling anti-Pinochet pamphlets into the air. After the game, Suzanne noticed a pamphlet on the concrete and knelt to pick it up. Suddenly a pair of shiny black army boots stepped into her field of vision, pointed at her. Terrified, she dropped the paper and pretended to tie her shoe. She turned and walked off slowly, faking nonchalance but fearing the grab from behind that fortunately never came.

Suzanne returned to the States in 1981 and started grad school at SUNY Stony Brook. But Chile was still in her blood: during Christmas vacation she took out a student loan and flew back. She spent the holidays in Caldera, had a fine time with friends there and elsewhere for a few weeks, then headed to Valparaíso for a couple of days with Nano and his family before she had to leave.

She accompanied Nano to a meeting of student dissidents. The students asked her to take a letter home to her university, a letter that essentially said, "We exist." Suzanne agreed to do it, though she warned them nothing was likely to result. They understood that, but she felt their desperation, their overwhelming need to try to connect with the outside world, "almost like reaching through the bars of their cage."

Suzanne and Nano left the meeting in broad daylight. They strolled to an outdoor market and bought vegetables. It was a busy part of town: plenty of traffic, people on the sidewalks. Suddenly two unmarked cars screeched to a stop next to them. "La CNI!" Nano whispered (*Centro Nacional de Información*, successor of the reviled DINA). They were jumped from behind, wrenched in chokeholds. Carrots and tomatoes spilled onto the sidewalk. Suzanne says she'll never forget the faces on passersby who saw the kidnapping: a quick shock of recognition before they looked away, walked away, terrified and impotent.

Hands cuffed behind them, hoods pulled over their heads, Suzanne and Nano were shoved into the back of a car, pushed down onto the floor. The car sped off. A long ride followed, full of crazy turns. Suzanne is sure the frequent changes of direction were to ensure they had no idea where they were taken. It might have been miles away, though it's just as possible that the car eventually doubled back and ended up close to where they were assaulted.

Suzanne was sure they were going to be killed. The kidnappers placed gauze under their handcuffs—not for humanitarian reasons, but to leave no marks on the skin, no evidence of mistreatment. In the midst of this horror, Suzanne salvaged what she calls "the proudest moment of my life." Thinking she was about to die, helpless on the floor of an automobile, somehow she had the presence of mind and the courage—my word, not hers—to gently stroke the back of Nano's neck with her cuffed hands, "to show him love and console him." She fully expected that would be her last meaningful gesture on earth.

At the prison—or wherever they were taken, for she never saw a thing—Suzanne and Nano were separated. Unseen hands fumbled under her hood; cotton was stuffed over her eyes and in her ears, gauze wrapped around her head before the hood was removed. Still handcuffed, she was shoved belly-down onto the wooden floor.

She's not sure how long she was kept prisoner. It's impossible to track time under conditions of complete darkness and complete fear. Probably she was there one night. Several times she heard roosters. She wouldn't eat or drink, worried it might be drugged. "I have a flight to catch," she kept saying, to alert the guards that people were waiting for her, that she would be

49

missed if she didn't arrive. Once, someone kicked her to shut her up. She figured her best chance was to keep talking.

When she was released, the hood was draped over her head before the blindfolds were removed. Again, she was forced to the floor in the back of a car. Again, she was taken on a long, circuitous drive, this time to Nano's house. Someone slipped off her hood. She wouldn't look at her captors; she never looked at them. She couldn't handle knowing who had done this.

"We need a front door and a back door," she heard an agent say (in Spanish, of course). She interpreted this to mean they were worried about an ambush. "Go in," they told her. "Act like nothing has happened."

The house had been ransacked. It looked like a movie set. There was no sign of Nano's wife or anyone else. Suzanne collected her stuff and came out. Though her scheduled flight wasn't for several days, they said they were taking her to the airport. She was leaving right now.

"But my passport's with a friend in Santiago."

"Tell him to bring it to the airport."

They stopped en route so she could call from a pay phone. As Suzanne nervously talked to her friend Kiko, a guard's thumb dug into the inside of her elbow.

Kiko was uneasy; this didn't make sense. They were supposed to spend some time together in Santiago. Her flight wasn't today.

Suzanne knew there was no way her voice sounded normal. "Please, just bring me the passport. I need to go."

Kiko was a non-political person, which maybe explains why he was concerned but clueless when he met her at the airport. "Who are they?" he asked about the two guards flanking her, each with a thumb pressing hard into her arm, body language screaming, "Get rid of this guy."

50

"They picked me up hitchhiking." That was what they had told her to say. Kiko almost surely suspected the truth, but what could he do? Suzanne was ushered into a special room, where airport security stole the film from her camera, a roll of 36 memories almost—as Murphy's Law dictates—completely exposed. The CNI agents escorted her the whole time. When they took her to the plane, she realized it had been held up for her. She was the last passenger on, by far. Everyone stared at her as she walked to her seat traumatized and alone, still wearing the bathing suit and shorts she'd had on when they were kidnapped. She hadn't combed her hair since she was arrested. The nine-hour flight to New York felt a lot longer. She might never see Nano again. He was probably dead.

Suzanne's story doesn't end there. The letter the students gave her had been confiscated by the CNI, but she wanted to publicize what had happened to her, hoped to broadcast it as widely as possible. Maybe that would help the anti-Pinochet cause, or at least wake up some Americans to what was going on in Chile. There was a chance the publicity might even save Nano's life. Her writer friend Dennis promised to check with his media connections, to try to drum up some interest. It was news, right? Potentially even the sort of sensational, lurid news that attracts headlines and TV time.

Sure enough, a day or two later Tracy Holmes from *Newsday* called. *Newsday* is the largest newspaper on Long Island, so Suzanne was thrilled. Her story was going to get a big audience. It even had the "local girl victim of foreign abduction" angle to catch people's attention. She met Tracy at a diner for lunch, and Suzanne gave her all the details. She dared to hope.

Suzanne called Dennis with the good news. Suddenly his voice sounded the way hers probably had to Kiko when she asked for her passport. "'Tracy Holmes'?" he said. "Suzanne, think about it. Dick Tracy? Sherlock Holmes?"

Dennis checked with *Newsday*. No Tracy Holmes worked for the paper.

Suzanne's heart sank. Paranoia set in. For days afterward she felt she was being followed. Possibly even worse, "Tracy" had gone to Suzanne's parents' house on Long Island and asked her mother, "How do you feel about your daughter getting kidnapped in Chile?" To that point Suzanne had only told her brother, not sure how to break it to her parents. Her mother called, frantic with worry, and Suzanne tried to reassure her. In the decades since then her family has never mentioned it to her again, but Suzanne still feels guilty about her mother not knowing and getting that dreadful surprise.

Suzanne's story eventually appeared in *The Progressive*, an obscure left-wing journal with a miniscule circulation. To this day, she can't understand why *Newsday* or other mainstream outlets weren't interested, and wonders if the CIA leaned on editors to squelch it. Suzanne exhibited symptoms of post-traumatic stress disorder; she felt fearful and paralyzed, which required months of therapy to overcome.

Time passed. Suzanne knew nothing of Nano's fate, and assumed the worst. Then in 2005, over twenty-three years later, a short, exploratory e-mail arrived at her work address: Nano, making a tentative overture to get back in touch. Suzanne was thrilled to learn that he was alive, and enthusiastic at the prospect of reconnecting with her friend. But soon doubts crept in. Elements of her PTSD symptoms returned, not full-blown, but undeniable. With great regrets and profuse apologies, Suzanne had to ask Nano to leave one of the most important friendships of her life forever in the past.

The third story doesn't come from a personal source. I was in graduate school at the University of Utah when it happened and heard nothing of it at the time. But the only American *desaparecido* is Boris Weisfeiler, a naturalized U.S. citizen from Russia. Remember that *desaparecido* means "disappeared" in the sense of "missing person." Other Americans were murdered in the *golpe*, but we know their fate; they're not *desaparecidos*. Weisfeiler, a Penn State math professor, disappeared while hiking alone in southern Chile—in 1985, over eleven years after the *golpe*.

The official, highly dubious explanation was that this experienced backpacker had drowned while crossing a shallow river. Weisfeiler's body was never found, though his backpack was—in the river, supposedly, minus camera, passport, plane ticket and money. According to a U.S. State Department memo, though, the backpack had been dry when recovered. All evidence points to Weisfeiler being taken into custody by a Chilean Army patrol, possibly because he had strayed too close to Colonia Dignidad ["Dignity Colony"], a secretive enclave founded by German immigrants in 1961. Colonia Dignidad was essentially a city-state unto itself in the outback, with a reputation among Chileans for weirdness and insularity.[5] German was spoken there, not Spanish. Local people, including the authorities, were afraid, or at the very least wary, of the place. Many Nazis were harbored there, most of whom were still alive in 1985. No one got in unless invited, and in the likely case that the army turned over Weisfeiler to the colony, no one got out either.

Boris Weisfeiler had become a U.S. citizen in 1981, and according to his sister Olga (who is convinced he is either in

---

5 In 2005 the founder and leader of Colonia Dignidad, ex-Nazi Paul Schäfer, was found in Argentina, extradited to Chile, and convicted of sexually abusing over two dozen children in the colony. He died in prison in 2010 while serving a 20-year sentence.

Colonia Dignidad, or more likely died there), "He felt protected by having an American passport." In other words, he felt secure in his Gringo Advantage. But Weisfeiler didn't fit the gringo prototype. He was a Jew with a Russian accent, apprehended alone by soldiers of a rabidly anti-communist government, near a fenced-in community of Nazi sympathizers. It was 1985; the Soviet Union still existed, as did Ronald Reagan's rhetoric about the "evil empire." Out there in the sticks, in the essentially lawless frontier, possibly Boris Weisfeiler wasn't gringo enough for the advantage to save him.

Would the same fate have befallen a more typical gringo—me, for instance?

It might be part of my Gringo Advantage that this remains a nice, safe, rhetorical question. Or it might just be the luck of the draw. In a book like this you do a lot of searching and ask a lot of questions. You try to be honest.

To be honest, I've discovered that only someone stronger than I am always wants an answer.

CHAPTER FIVE

Misma Mierda, Distintas Moscas

"The beggars have changed places but the lash goes on."

—W.B. Yeats, "The Great Day"

My second day back in Arica is Christmas. After a late-morning breakfast of Peruvian Nescafe with bread and butter, ham, cheese and avocado, Panchy, Christine and I ride with Juan Marcos on a tour of the city in Any's parents' car. We take streets that didn't used to be here, through neighborhoods that didn't used to be here, to a road that didn't used to be here, over the Morro down to the ocean, both of which in human terms have been here forever. We roll north toward town along a coastal road that before noon is literally in the shadow of the Morro; to the south, the road dead-ends into ocean cliffs within a few miles. Juan Marcos takes the short causeway to Isla Alacrán (Scorpion Island), site of the Arica Yacht Club (which I've never been inside) and a Spanish fort wrecked by an earthquake and tsunami in 1868. We climb on the ruins, take pictures. Christine and I smile to see a café on the island called Rolling Coffee El Gringo.

We drive to the summit of El Morro. There's a small museum chronicling Chile's bloody taking of the hill from Peru in 1880, a cannon presumably from that period, a monument to the Unknown Soldier, and a towering statue of Jesus Christ with open arms that supposedly celebrates Chilean-Peruvian amity, though Chileans like to point out that Jesus's holy backside faces Peru. As we stroll around up here in the sunshine, the main thing I notice is how much Arica has grown. The city spreads out from the deep blue ocean below us to misty brown mountains in the distance. With a wide-angle 28 mm lens I need to take four photos to complete the panorama.

At three, we return for a festive lunch at the house, then at five Hugo, Any, Christine and I take Chato Rojas to old friends Jorge and Veronica Ferry's place in the Azapa Valley. We swim in their pool, Neil Young cranked on the stereo in a nearby cabana. Jorge always loved Neil Young, though he hardly understood a word. Now he breaks out a bottle of Chivas Regal and pours liberally; I stick to beer and don't regret the decision. We head home at seven and Christine and I catch a short siesta.

After dark, Juan Marcos cleans and seasons the backyard grill with a raw onion, and soon is sizzling various cuts of meat and chorizo over the coals. Jorge and Veronica come by, and a Christmas feast ensues at 10:30. By one o'clock everyone except Hugo and me has either gone home, gone out or gone to bed.

"I'm still thirsty, Gringo," he says. "You're not going to make me drink alone, are you?"

"I'm not *that* rude." I pull up a chair at his round kitchen table while he extracts an Arequipeña from the *refrigerador*. Beyond the bars of the slightly ajar window the warm December air is heavy and still. Occasionally someone passes by on the dark sidewalk, so close I could reach through the bars and touch them.

Hugo fills our glasses, leaves the sweating bottle on the table. For the first time in twenty-three years, we're alone together, drinking and talking deep into the night the way we used to. It feels so familiar it's strange. *Tanto tiempo*, I think. So much time. Yet somehow here we are again, old friends Gringo and Cabezón (Big Head).

"*Oye*, Hugo, what do you think of Michelle Bachelet?" Bachelet is a Socialist pediatrician whose father, an Air Force general and member of Allende's government, was arrested during the *golpe* and died of a heart attack after severe torture. Bachelet and her mother were also tortured before she went into exile, first in Australia, then East Germany.[6]

Hugo flicks his hand in the air, the Chilean gesture of disgust. "*Qué me importa?*" ["What do I care?"]

"Would you vote for her?"

"I don't vote for anyone."

"Are you serious?"

"I don't vote anymore."

"Not even to vote against someone you can't stand?"

"It doesn't matter. Politicians are all scum, out to line their pockets. Nothing ever changes. *Misma mierda, distintas moscas.* Do you know what that means?"

Same shit, different flies. "It's not hard to figure out," I say.

Hugo holds up his glass. "Then it's not hard to see why I don't vote."

---

6 In 2006 she was elected Chile's first female president.

My friend's across-the-board cynicism is disappointing. It seems an easy way out, despite any negative experiences that created it. Not that I don't know Americans—some of whom I respect—who feel the same way. But cynicism and apathy in the U.S. are nothing new, and both lead to the same result: low voter turnout. The current situation in Chile, however, stands in stark contrast to the 1970s, when people frequently (though almost always privately) talked politics, even to a young gringo from Connecticut who didn't necessarily know anything. Maybe most Chileans today are simply talked-out about politics. What's left to say? The biggest debate is whether Pinochet should be put on trial, or if that would cause more upheaval to the country than it's worth. Many Chileans just wish the bastard would die and render the question moot.[7]

"Did you vote for Allende?"

"*Claro.* And he turned out to be weak. He allowed himself to be led by Cubans and other outsiders. If not for Allende's failure there would have been no *golpe*, no murders and *desaparecidos*. Gringo, you have to understand, by 1973 things were so bad that most Chileans *wanted* the army to take over. During parades people would throw corn at the soldiers and squawk like chickens, calling them cowards for not doing anything."

"You too?"

Hugo takes a long swallow of beer. He nods. "*Yo también.* I didn't throw corn, but I wanted the *milicos* to act. Just set things in order, then after six months return Chile to democracy. Pinochet could have been a hero and a patriot if he did that. Instead,

---

7 Pinochet finally died on December 10, 2006. He was 91.

the *conchasumadre*[8] grabbed power and sucked the public tit as long as he could."

That reminds me of a poster in my office, acquired in Chile though I don't remember how: a drawing of an obese Richard Nixon in a Stars and Stripes dress, offering his ample right breast to a pint-size Pinochet sprawled in his lap—but grasping a huge pistol in one dangling hand. It's sobering to realize that Pinochet actually started with more popular support than Allende, who was elected with only 36% of the vote. Pinochet was a Machiavellian politician, not simply a thug. He had sucked up to Allende during his presidency, to the point that Allende appointed him leader of the armed forces. Surely, they had eaten dinner together, had shared the customary Chilean hug. I wonder about their last meeting before the *golpe*, when and where it was, and what kind of actor Pinochet had been to hide from his boss—his friend?—what was about to happen.

My second glass is already empty. That means two things: these stories have made me nervous, and Hugo introspective. It's unheard of for him to be anything but an incredibly solicitous host, never allowing my glass to drop below half full.

"Ah, gringo, *perdón*." Hugo pours me the rest of the bottle and goes for another.

"*Gracias*, Hugo. *Oye*, what do you know about Pinochet stealing from the government?" I've read that Pinochet has stashed millions in money-laundered accounts.

"Stealing from *us*, you mean? All I know is that I'm sure it's true." He holds the bottle like a microphone and breaks into a high, reedy voice, a spot-on imitation of Pinochet. "*No robé ni un peso—puros dolares!*" ["I didn't steal a single peso—just dollars!]"

---

8 This strong epithet has no direct English equivalent. "Son of a bitch" more or less conveys the intent.

We laugh, but it's laughter with an edge. For a while neither of us speaks. Silence is not uncomfortable between Hugo and me. We both often live apart from others with our thoughts, and sometimes we sit together with them. My eyes are heavy, but know I won't be going to bed soon. Who knows how many years will pass till we see each other again?

I think about our outing today, driving around Arica like tourists. *Am* I a tourist now? I suppose I am, a voyeuristic tourist of my past. But I still feel like I'm part of this place. After all, so much of Chile—the Chile of a quarter-century ago—went into creating who I am now. I get a similar feeling when I go to my hometown of Westbrook, Connecticut, and find more new houses carved into the woods, see the taming of the wild land that wasn't truly wild but had seemed that way to a younger me. The ageless woods of childhood turned out to be just temporary trees between the land's former days as pasture and its reincarnation as two-acre lawns.

Our lives are full of surfaces, necessary but deceptive. When I was a kid, my father hired a backhoe to dig out rocks in the lawn. Only the gray granite tips stuck out of the grass, dangers to mower blades and kids playing tackle football, and I was amazed when the machine, after quite a struggle, left three hulking chunks like asteroids next to gaping holes. The hard little landmarks I'd grown up with had been like the visible fraction of an iceberg, or the Hawaiian Islands, apexes of massive underwater mountains barely jutting above the sea. I learned about the unreliability of visible surfaces that day, though it took me years to realize that it applied to people as well.

One of the rocks had served as third base in many a ball game with my three brothers, creating a slightly asymmetrical diamond but you knew that base wasn't going anywhere. For the other bases we'd sometimes use stones from the wall around the property, undoing some forgotten mason's expertise from a century or more ago. After the game we'd return the stones to the wall, more or less to the same spots but without the expertise. It never occurred to us that it was disrespectful, just convenient. The man I am now sees so much that is convenient *as* disrespectful, as lazy, as wrong.

On the surface, Chile has changed considerably since I left in 1980. The population has grown from eleven million to sixteen million. Arica's population has doubled, to nearly 200,000. There's more stuff to buy here now, a lot more. When I was in the Peace Corps, color TVs had just come to the country; today we saw a McDonald's and a Blockbuster downtown.

How much has *my* surface changed? My light brown hair (which to my amusement many Chileans had called *rubio*—blond) is shorter, darker, and getting grayer by the day. I weigh the same as I did in those days, around 165, though at one point in Arica I'd dropped to 158. Three decades' worth of lines are etched on my face, but they're not extreme. Looking at old photos I feel as if my face was almost *too* fresh and smooth, impossibly young. I remember a related feeling back then, and growing several ratty beards in a vain attempt to look more mature, or more like an artist. For I had started to write songs, inspired by the ghost of Woody Guthrie—or at least my romantic image of him.

I grew the first scrubby beard in Santiago after our ten-week training period ended. Everyone else in my group had gone south to their assigned sites, but I stayed in Santiago to work on various baseball projects until we figured out the best place for me to go. Eventually it came down to Arica and the famous seaside resort city of Viña del Mar, only two hours from Santiago. Arica won, a decision that changed my life.

At night I'd often take a bus to Veronica Inostroza's house. We'd met during training, when I had lived with her mother,

Violeta. Vero's late father Jorge wrote numerous historical novels and had been Chile's bestselling author. Even today, virtually every Chilean has heard of *Adios al Séptimo de Línea,* Jorge's novel about the War of the Pacific, when Arica was taken from Peru and became part of Chile. I was fascinated by the parade of friends who showed up at Veronica's house, night after night: poets, writers, actors, musicians, interesting people of all stripes. But most of all, I was fascinated by her.

No one called before coming over. They couldn't—money was tight and Vero had no phone—but I doubt they would have anyway. It was a tremendous chance to hang out with exciting people, improve my Spanish in the bargain—and after a while, to stay overnight. Veronica was my first older woman, thirty-one to my twenty-two. Eventually, she was my second broken heart.

I'll never forget Vero's words the day I showed up with that mangy scruff on my face. She was all smiles.

"Ahora tu eres un poeta de verdad!" she said. ["Now you're a true poet!"] I took her—and myself—seriously, though now I'm sure she was just trying to make me feel good. To be fair, the beard wasn't that much worse than Fidel Castro's, or Bob Dylan's.

These days, after years of wearing a beard I'm clean-shaven again. Why? Because the same guy who once wanted to look older now dislikes the gray encroaching in his beard like Arica into the desert. *Am* I the same guy now that I was at twenty-two?

Call it the same ego.

Hugo taps my foot with his under the table. "Gringo, I know you never thought a macho like me would say this, but I'm tired. Ready to call it a night?"

"Bien, I'm tired too."

My friend flashes the grin I remember so well, and stands up. "It's settled, then—we'll only have one more bottle!"

I certainly don't need any more to drink, but at least I don't have to walk empty streets to my room on unsteady legs, with a baseball game to umpire the next morning. Warren Zevon has a song called "I'll Sleep When I'm Dead," and right now that seems as wise a philosophy as any.

Hugo pours with a flourish, and once again we clink glasses.

"To old friends and Arica," I toast. "It's great to be back—even if it kills me."

CHAPTER SIX

A Finite Window

What a gulf between the self which experiences and the self which describes experience.

—Edmund Wilson, *I Thought of Daisy*

The next day, in the early afternoon Christine and I take a *colectivo* taxi downtown. She wants to see the landmarks of my past, and I want to show her. We get out at the corner by the Insituto Chileno-Norteamericano, where I first met Hugo. He taught English classes there at night after working all day in a public school, both for dismal pay. I used the Instituto as my mailing address, and would borrow books in English from its tiny, wildly eclectic library. For that reason, and no other, I can truthfully say I've read *Adam Bede*.

The Instituto has been defunct for years, but a private school occupies the building now and it's in good shape, possibly better than it was back then. Not so the Pizzeria El 890, a 30-second walk down 21 de Mayo Street. The restaurant owned by my landlords is boarded up and derelict, its cheerful sign and awnings long gone. Their son Oscar had run the 890, and after he died of AIDS in the '80s it probably did not survive long.

Next door is where I lived for most of my time in Arica, 21 de Mayo 880. The wooden wall and door still look solid, not tumbledown. I put an eye to the crack between the wood and the adjacent brick building, and see a narrow slice of courtyard and some of one wall of my room. The place isn't a wreck, but seems deserted. To investigate I could clamber over the wall the way I did more than once after forgetting my key, but those occasions were always at night, and if the cops showed up, I had the significant advantage of actually living there.

Christine takes my picture. This will be a day of posing in front of the past, a tourist in my own life.

"So," she says, "did you ever bring any women back to this love nest?"

"Well, you know me," I growl in as macho a tone as I can muster.

She pats my shoulder sympathetically. "I didn't think so, dear."

We walk down 21 de Mayo, Arica's main commercial street. Almost nothing I remember is still here. The lower blocks are especially transformed, closed to vehicle traffic now, a welcome change made after a 1987 earthquake battered the city. We join the flocks of pedestrians, then stop at a sidewalk café for a *chop*, a draft beer. Maybe a hundred feet farther down is where I stood the day Pinochet drove by in a chauffeured limousine, giving an occasional brief wave to the people lined along the route. The crowd wasn't sullen, exactly, just far from enthusiastic. All four

TOM HAZUKA

members of the military *junta* were in Arica for a centennial ceremony of the taking of the Morro in 1880. I remember thinking how anyone with a gun could easily have shot the bastard.

There are gray bricks where the asphalt used to be. No limousine could drive here now. We finish our beers and keep walking down the gradual slope, toward the sea. Three beggars used to put in long hours almost every day here. A blind woman sat on a folding chair near a bank, rattling a few nearly worthless *centavos* in a white tin cup. Whenever she collected some pesos, she'd fish them out and put them in her coat pocket. A man with stumps for arms wore a light green suit, a Panama hat, and a canvas bag around his neck for contributions. He would stretch his stumps toward you in supplication, but never say a word. Another man with withered legs, but a massive upper body traveled on short crutches, thick, filthy pads on his knees, his twisted shanks and feet dragging behind. He wore a cardboard shoe box as a hat, which he'd take off and place on the ground whenever he stopped, hoping to catch a few coins. I gave to them often, but never enough to not feel guilty those times that I didn't.

I hesitate about mentioning them to Christine. She's no sissy, but what's to be gained by bringing them up? There are no beggars here now. They're surely not good for business, and evidently Arica's cleaned-up city center won't tolerate them. We can walk these blocks guilt-free, but also without the chance to feel a cheap thrill of charity.

"You're awfully quiet all of a sudden," she says. "Is something on your mind?"

"The usual. Stuff that's not here anymore." I tell her about the beggars, because sharing my past with her is part of what this return to Chile is about. And I tell her because she asked.

I have several friends who are oral historians. They interview people—"witnesses" seems to be the right word, though maybe

67

it's freighted with too much crime baggage—to discover and record their perspectives on the past. Obviously, this means talking to people while they're still alive, a finite window. The more time has passed since the time in question, the more likely that someone's memory has faded or been affected by subsequent events. Even when time is not a factor, any cop knows that if six people witness an event, there will be six different versions of what happened. The differences might be slight, might be extreme, but they'll exist. At the very least, each story depends on where the witness was, and who the witness is.

For example, when I think about my camera being stolen in Peru, I jump back in my mind to that Arequipa hotel. I'm washing socks at that sink on the roof in the chilly sunshine, a small voice in my head worrying that I'd left my stuff alone with a stranger. I return to the room and find my own Master lock on the door. Should I run downstairs, assuming the worst and hoping to find the guy? But I don't even know if he did anything. Should I open the lock and look? Heart thumping, I pick option two and find my camera gone. You know the rest of that story.

At least you know my version of it. What if an oral historian located the thief and got him to recount his version? Did he not steal the pouch with my passport and travelers checks because he didn't think to check under my pillow? (Yes, incredibly, that's where I'd left them. Better than out in plain sight like my camera.) Did he not know how to fence that stuff? Was he decent enough not to clean me out completely? Or did he just snatch the camera and bolt, heart hammering even harder than mine after I'd discovered the theft? If so, he took the time to snap my lock on the latch.

There's so much we humans don't know, even about what affects us the most. Here's my journal again (Thursday, August 9, 1979): "Screw it, at least I'm seeing things that most people

68

never have (such as how South American police work—maybe something literary will result from this mess), and now I must start clean." I'll flatter myself by assuming that yes, something literary is finally resulting from that mess. The more interesting comment, though, is the one about starting clean.

Who hasn't wanted to start over, at one point or another? A clean slate is an attractive concept, and like most attractive things in this world, not easy to attain. After years of teaching, I know that erasing a blackboard does not leave it clean. Plenty of chalk residue remains, including on your clothes if you forget and lean against the board during class. The new whiteboards with colored pens are worse—not for marking your clothes, but for being tough to clean. You need to press down on the eraser fairly hard, and even then, the board is soon a palimpsest of ghostly symbols lurking in limbo beneath what's written on top of them.

The future is always affected, and sometimes infected, by the past. At Machu Picchu a week later, and countless other times during that Peru trip, I framed photos in my mind and cursed that pudgy, snake-smiling lowlife who ripped off my camera. People talk of letting something go, of achieving "closure." This does seem quite obviously to be the healthiest emotional and psychological course of action. If only it weren't so hard to do. Life doesn't hand out mulligans like your friends do in a hackers' round of golf. Good luck creating a witness protection program for yourself.

Sometimes, out of nowhere I see the kid batting in front of me swing at a pitch over his head for strike three, causing me to end my Little League career in the on-deck circle. I admit I pounded my bat (still wood in those days) once on the ground. I hadn't expected that from him; he was one of our best players, batting third in the lineup. The Shoreline All Stars were down 6-0, I was the losing pitcher, and I was burning to get one more chance to swing. I *knew* I was going to get a hit, probably a home run. The count had been three balls and two strikes; if the kid had taken that pitch for ball four as he should have, I'd have been up with at least one duck on the pond.

Many decades later, the memory slips onto the screen behind my eyes, playing in color with sharp resolution. I see the batter (I wish I could remember his name), eyes down and lip quivering as he walks past me. "Sorry, Tom," he says, barely above a whisper, and I tell him it's OK, because...what else can you say? Is it worse to blow your chance, or to never get that chance? To swing at strike three over your head, or end frustrated in the on-deck circle? An oral historian would need to interview him, to get his story. Does that memory still ambush him at times?

The year before, our Little League all-star squad had won a tournament game, 1-0, on a throwing error by the other team's second baseman in extra innings. We mobbed Jimmy Verry when he crossed the plate with the winning run. It didn't occur to me to look for the kid who blew it, probably sobbing in their dugout. Only now do I wonder what his teammates said to him, or what his ride home from the game was like, or whether he slept that night. Only now do I wonder if out of nowhere he sometimes still bobbles that grounder, still grabs that ball and feels the seams crooked under his fingers, still hurries the throw and bounces it past the first baseman. And for the first time I wonder what it felt like out on the field watching Jimmy score that run, watching us erupt from our dugout to pound him on the back. I'm sure that boy has "moved on," has "let it go." But "closure"? Never. Even if our conscious mind manages to leave something behind, who knows what remains bubbling beneath the surface.

I cried once during my two and a half years in Chile. There should have been no reason for tears that day, May 25, 1980,

70

two months before I left Arica for good. It was a typical Sunday morning doubleheader with *intermedia* players, thirteen to fifteen years old. The second game, though, had some bragging rights involved. The Yankees and Villa Empart had the lion's share of the kids who would be on Arica's team to compete for the national championship in July. Although by now I had trained adults to coach, umpire and keep score, because soon they would have to do it on their own without my help, both teams asked me to ump this game to ensure impartiality. No problem, I said.

I had a leisurely breakfast of tea made on the hot plate in my room, with some whole wheat rolls from the nearby bakery, then took a *colectivo* to the Villa Empart at ten. That might sound like a home game for the Villa Empart, but any advantage was minimal—mainly that the Villa Empart players could just stroll on over. It was the only field in the city of 95,000 people dedicated solely to baseball. A year or so earlier we had played on an empty lot on the north side of town near Chinchorro Beach and the Olympic swimming pool, but it wasn't close to most players' homes and not well-served by public transportation. Many of the kids' families did not own cars, so just getting to the field was problematic. The Villa Empart field was convenient for almost everyone. Besides, it didn't have *jerjeles*, the vicious biting flies that lived down by the pool.

Even now, long after my Peace Corps days, when I fly into an American city, I notice the baseball fields below. There are usually quite a few. It's a reaction brought on by thirty months in Chile trying to find places to play baseball. Far more often than not, that place was a soccer field. That means (if you can get permission from the soccer folks) extending the line of the penalty area to both sidelines, or at least to the sideline to the left of one of the goals. Why to the left? So you can use that sideline as a left field foul line, with home plate at the point where the two lines intersect. This creates an unbalanced outfield, with the left fielder patrolling a huge expanse all the way to the opposite goal line, while the right fielder is hemmed in by the opposite sideline and whatever lies beyond (usually a wall on our Arica fields). Notwithstanding the skewed aesthetics, it wasn't a big problem for us. Few of our young players had enough power to take advantage of the short porch in right, especially since virtually all of them batted right-handed. I have no idea why, but *zurdos*—lefthanders—were rare in Chile.

The Villa Empart baseball field was a temporary arrangement, with new houses and apartment buildings growing up around it, and we knew that before long it would be paved over and/or built upon as well. But for the time being it was ours. It even had the incredible luxury of a backstop: four six-meter metal poles sunk in rings of aboveground concrete, draped with fishing nets. It was an ingenious contraption and worked fine, though just as in the States, there were always younger brothers or other neighborhood kids to race after any foul balls.

Like all but two or three irrigated grass soccer fields in Arica, this one was brown desert dirt. Most of the biggest rocks had been tossed aside, at least in the infield, so bad hops weren't a major factor. *"Juego!"* I yelled, put on a mask, and hunkered down behind the catcher. We had a big old inflatable chest protector that made you feel invulnerable. It weighed almost nothing, so was comfortable to use; you could snuggle it right up to your chin and hide practically your whole body. Every time I see an umpire today get nailed by a foul tip, I wonder why they stopped using them.

Since neighborhood pride was at stake, the crowd was bigger than usual, fifty people or more. Although I'd been blind to it when I first came to Arica, I knew by now that neighborhood pride had social and economic components. By and large, the Villa

Empart was a working-class neighborhood, while the Yankees were from a tonier part of town. Most of the Villa Empart players had to borrow a glove from our communal collection to play, while many of the Yankees owned a glove (hard to find in Chile and therefore quite expensive) and a few even had their own bat. You could see it even in the quality and age of the clothes, both of the players and of the adults watching from the sidelines. It was like seeing kids in their school uniforms. Every boy had to wear dark blue pants and a light blue shirt, but there was an obvious difference between a new pair of pants with a shiny belt, and ragged, dirty ones held at the waist with a safety pin. The Villa Empart vs. Yankees rivalry wasn't class warfare, but money *was* part of the equation—and money, or the lack of it, can influence people.

The game featured the usual plentiful errors, but also good hitting and few walks, which made for a fine spectator's game. In the bottom of the last inning the Yankees led 22-18, but the Villa Empart had the bases loaded with two outs. Yerko Luza strayed off third base and catcher Cristian Cerpa tried to pick him off. We usually had an umpire for the bases as well, but fear of biased decisions had caused both teams to prefer leaving everything in my hands. Now I had to make a snap judgment on a play sixty-five feet away. I called it as I saw it.

"Out!" I shouted from behind the plate, thumb jabbing toward the sun.

Holy hell broke loose. According to my journal, "The *rotos* from Empart exploded." *Roto* is a charged and complicated word in Chile. Today it refers mainly to a low-rent, trashy person (which can be a woman: *una rota*), though historically *los rotos chilenos* were the ferocious soldiers such as those who wrested El Morro from the Peruvians in 1880. Source of patriotic pride, or classless bozo? Plenty of ambivalence to go around.

My journal wasn't ambivalent. I said *rotos* because I was hurt and disappointed by the behavior of some of those characters. Jeers rained from the crowd.

"*Arbitro vendido!*" [Umpire on the take!]

"*Bigoteo!*" [Inside job!]

When Manuel Molina, a fifty-something member of the old guard of Arican baseball, insinuated to my face that I had favored the Yankees, I lost my cool and called him a meddling asshole. I walked away a few steps to calm down. Suddenly there was Yerko, the kid I'd called out at third, offering me his hand. I took it gratefully.

I had to ask. "*Fuiste* out, *Yerko?*" [Were you out?]

He spoke softly. "*No, pero no importa. Manuel es así.*" [No, but it doesn't matter. Manuel is like that.]

That did me in. The combination of seeing the difference between one of "my" classy kids and the pathetic example set by the *béisbol antiguo* losers like Molina, plus the possibility that I'd blown the call, overwhelmed me. I walked behind a building to try to hide what was happening, but I was sobbing well before I got there. My friend Chancho San Martín came over to comfort me, and before long I was OK, though I was glad I was wearing sunglasses. I was even better a few minutes later when four friends and colleagues who'd been standing near third said I made the right call. Maybe they were just trying to make me feel better (these men were the diametrical opposites of *rotos*), but I doubt it.

Chancho invited me to his place for a delicious chicken lunch, then I went to my room to write my weekly (unpaid) column for *La Estrella* about the games. I stuck to baseball, leaving out the post-game travails of the gringo umpire. I broke out my cheap little cassette player and recorded two new songs I'd written. At sunset I wandered through a *barrio* at the base of the Morro, an area that somehow I had never explored during eighteen months in Arica. "A fresh point of view," my journal says. "I felt content watching the darkness settle in as the electric specks ignited to do their heroic best to illuminate what we don't see in the sunlight anyway."

The next day was eventful too. At two o'clock I was playing tennis when an earthquake hit. The epicenter was in Mollendo, Peru; the temblor registered 6 on the Richter scale in Iquique. The wild part, though, was how my partner, lawyer Ronnie Ferreira, froze just as he was about to serve.

"*Qué pasa?*" I asked.

He held up his hand. I took a step toward him and suddenly was surfing on the swaying red clay of the court. It lasted maybe twenty seconds, easily the strongest quake I'd experienced. I felt like running, though we were in probably the safest spot in the whole city.

When the earth calmed down, we met at the net. My heart was beating faster than it had been while we were playing. "How'd you know that was about to happen?" I asked.

Ronnie shrugged. "Long years of living in earthquake country."

I had a good practice at 3:30 with the *preseleccionados*, the group from which we'd pick the teams (for kids aged 10-12 and 13-15) who would represent Arica at the national championship in July. I ran two sessions every day, at 9:30 and 3:30, because some players went to school in the morning, some in the afternoon. After practice I checked at the Instituto Chileno-Norteamericano and found two welcome pieces of mail: a telegram from Gene de la Torre extending my Peace Corps time till August 15, and a letter from Agnès Philippon in St. Étienne, France.

I had met Agnès in Cuzco, Peru, a few days after my camera was stolen in Arequipa. It was a classic backpacker travel connection. In Puno on Lake Titicaca (altitude 12,500 feet) a Canadian told me about the Hotel Bolivar in Cuzco; on the train from Puno to Cuzco I met a Mexican named Miguel Barriga; walking from the station to the Bolivar, Miguel offered me coca leaves that a woman had given him on the train; after sharing the leaves we decided to share a room (no, I wasn't worried he was a thief; besides, my camera was already gone); the room turned out to be a triple, and minutes later Agnès walked in and took the third bed. We were free, we were travelers, and no one thought twice about the arrangement (except perhaps about the possibilities). To save money, backpackers often shared rooms with people they'd never seen before and were unlikely to ever see again.

Agnès was twenty-one and had been vagabonding for months in South America. Her camera had been ripped off in Peru; we had that in common, and a lot more. We spent plenty of time together over the next week, speaking mostly French, but sometimes Spanish, reveling in being young and on the road with no responsibilities outside of making the most of every minute. My journal entry for August 19, 1979 ends:

> Agnès came for me in the [hotel] office and...we hit George's for a nightcap. She got some milk, egg and pisco concoction, I sipped an herb tea as we listened to early Dylan till midnight. Our parting at her door was lingering, tender and heartfelt. Even as I began to walk away our hands remained clasped, and touched until the last possible instant. I feel very deeply for her, somehow. At George's I promised to write her a song and send it to her, and I intend to keep my word. Paraphrasing Fowles in *The French Lieutenant's Woman*: instead of a Victorian melancholy for what you are "losing," be thankful for having gained it in the first place.

The next morning, I left for Bolivia, thinking about Agnès as the train rattled through the Andes, remembering that last touch of her fingers on mine. I spent the next eight days with Eyal from Israel, Inga from Germany and her French boyfriend, Pascal, who was traveling with his intensely blond five-year-old son, Alain.[9] The local Quechua ladies in their bright, billowing skirts and bowler hats went crazy for Alain, constantly wanting to touch his hair and give him presents. I won't forget those people. They're my friends for life. The fact that I've never seen any of them again doesn't change that a bit.

A few weeks after I took the night train from La Paz home to Arica, I wrote to Agnès in St. Étienne, figuring she was in France by then or soon would be. She wrote back in a tone making it plain that (as my journal says) "she hasn't forgotten." Eventually I wrote a song for her called "Ancient Trail," copied out the lyrics in longhand and sent them to her with a letter. On May 26 an envelope with French stamps on it arrived at the Instituto. Agnès asked for a tape of her song, wondered when I'd be making my promised journey to France—and recalled our last sweet night in Cuzco. She probably spoke some English, but if not, I'm sure she found someone to translate. The chorus ends:

> We met upon an ancient trail whose power still shone through
> I may never see your smile again, but I'll never forget you

I never sent Agnès a cassette of the song. I fully expected to travel to France soon, deliver a tape to her in person, and be ready for whatever adventures came next. Little did I know as I held that onionskin letter in my fingers, reading her loopy,

---

9 Not their real names.

tough-for-an-American-to-decipher European handwriting, that I would not return to France for over five years, and it would be with my graduate school girlfriend, Diane Hargrove. We didn't go to St. Étienne. I've still never been there, and I haven't seen Agnès's smile since that magic week in Cuzco. But the last line of that chorus is as true today as it was when I wrote it in 1979.

Reading Agnès's letter heightened the bittersweet contentment I'd felt all day. A window was closing. The reality of my imminent departure from Arica, and Chile, was beginning to sink in, along with the realization I would be leaving behind some excellent friends. The feeling was reinforced that night during our Asociación de Béisbol de Arica meeting at the Canal Escolar office. To my surprise, association president Enrique González immediately raised the issue of yesterday's postgame nastiness. I'll let my journal do the talking:

> The Villa Empart incident was aired and Manuel Molina duly censured. Enrique handled the tacky affair masterfully. I had to force back the tears when Luis Sakurada related that Reinaldo Saavedra's [a Yankees player] mother told him that Reinaldo returned to his house crying after the game, even though the Yankees had won, because he was crushed at the treatment I'd received. *"Los niños lo tienen a Tom como un ídolo,"* Luis said. ["The boys idolize Tom."] Hell, if I were a kid I'd feel the same way, and it hurts to see your idols trampled in the mud. It pained me just to watch Mickey Mantle's final mediocre years, and to see his lifetime average slip below .300.

For the record, Manuel Molina only semi-apologized, though his son Chavy and other Villa Empart folks more than made up for it. Sum total? Zero hard feelings, and I have photos to prove it: all of us laughing together at the farewell barbecue the baseball people threw for me two months later. I didn't expect an apology, would never have asked for one—but sure appreciated it when it came.

At the end of October 2006, Augusto Pinochet was placed under house arrest in Santiago. The former *Su Excelencia* was indicted for the torture and abuses committed at the Villa Grimaldi detention center after the *golpe*. Torture and killings were rife during that era, and Pinochet was indicted numerous times for similar crimes, though never brought to trial. But this case held particular interest. Among the torture victims at Villa Grimaldi were Michelle Bachelet, Chile's president from 2006-2010, and her mother.

There was no apology from Pinochet or the Chilean military to President Bachelet. As far as I know she never asked for, nor expected one. Has she "let it go?" Has she found "closure?" Once, as my father and I watched a History Channel program on World War II, he quietly said, "Sometimes when I see these shows, it brings it all back." That's as close as he ever came to telling me about the war. Well, and one time when I was looking through his war photos. They were mostly small black and white shots, maybe two by three inches. He never brought them out unless someone asked, and even then, only reluctantly. In one photo from England in 1942, Dad stood grinning with a handsome, Tyrone Power-type soldier. I asked about him.

"That's Joe," Dad said. He stared at the picture in his palm. "He had this habit of kicking at anything he found in his path. One day in Italy he kicked a mine. That was the end of him."

Dad's voice didn't waver but he fell silent. I wanted to ask for details but didn't feel I had the right. Oral historians must face this dilemma all the time, a battle between seeking answers and respecting privacy. My father gently placed the photo back in the box with the others. I wondered if he had ever killed anyone. Probably not. He was in the 809th Engineering Battalion, building airstrips and roads, not an infantryman on the front lines. Still, he was in North Africa for over a year, before advancing from Sicily the whole length of Italy in 1944. You don't do that without seeing—and maybe doing—things you can never get closure on, things you can never let go. Things you never want your sons to have to experience, or probably even to know about. Things that put you in a V.A. hospital for eight months with a "nervous breakdown" after you come home.

Christine and I went to an anti-war rally a few weeks before George W. Bush invaded Iraq in 2003. It was a brutally cold February day in New Britain, Connecticut. Two dozen people had gathered downtown in front of a beautiful brownstone church, a stone's throw from a monument honoring the Civil War dead. Cars passed, most drivers ignoring us. Some honked and gave a thumbs-up. Others flipped us the finger, rolled down their windows and swore at us, or called us traitors.

There was a tinny little sound system, and all were invited to speak. A tall, silver-haired man took the microphone. He said he was a retired minister and had fought at the Battle of the Bulge in 1944, in cold similar to this. As he spoke on that frigid day the emotion in his voice was from experience. "You don't go to war on rumors," he told us. "War is far too horrible to be used as anything but a last resort."

We disbanded after half an hour before frostbite could set in. I tried to stay hopeful, but couldn't shake a sick, sinking feeling that we and millions of other people at rallies around the world that day were wasting our time. It felt like a window was closing, and much more than glass was about to be broken.

CHAPTER SEVEN

The Snows of Yesteryear

"Où sont les neiges d'antan?"

—François Villon
"Ballade (des Dames de Temps Jadis)"
[Ballad (of Women from Bygone Days)]

Villon's fifteenth-century poem is about women (both real and imaginary) from the past, but is best known for its refrain about the snows of yesteryear. Where are the snows of bygone winters, their beauty and danger now relegated to memory, or less? Five and a half centuries of snows have fallen, melted, and seeped into the soil of Villon's grave, wherever it might be. No one knows, just as no one knows much about his life, or when he died. Villon is as real—and as imaginary—as the women in his poem.

81

Snow's powerful, but evanescent presence is a perfect metaphor for the past—and for memory, our personal versions of the past. Snow can be a lovely, evocative blanket, or a cold, treacherous cover-up. It can fade away, disappear, then return in a blizzard—or an avalanche—and bury everything. And sometimes, after it's gone, it can be hard to imagine it was ever there at all.

When I was a kid in Connecticut, snowdrifts would sometimes reach the windows of our house. At Fairfield University, we'd steal cafeteria trays to slide down the snowy slope behind Bellarmine Hall. In Switzerland, during my junior year abroad we rented a chalet for a month, skied Alpine powder and mixed drinks on the deck in the sunshine. In Salt Lake City, we'd play University of Utah softball games in perfect spring weather, with a backdrop of the snow-capped Wasatch Range. In Santiago, winter rain would clear the smog and leave a glorious view of fresh snow on the nearby *cordillera*. In Arica from atop the Morro, I recall seeing snow on the distant peaks of the Andes, but I don't know if that's possible. I mistrust that memory. It feels vague and dreamlike, as if half-lost five seconds after waking.

My memories are sharp, though, of snow in the altiplano and excursions that took me there. An amazing feature of Arica is that you can leave the sea-level city, drive east and climb to 14,000 feet in under four hours—well under four hours now that the road is paved all the way to Bolivia and beyond. When I was in the Peace Corps, the asphalt turned to gravel halfway up, which meant two things: slow down if you care anything for your spine, and eat dust if you get stuck behind another vehicle, especially a truck—and especially an ancient open-backed Bolivian truck loaded with haphazard sacks and boxes, and half a dozen impassive Indian passengers perched on them. Your options were to risk death passing on a mountain curve, wait for an infrequent straightaway, or fall back and let the dirt settle before you drove through it. Of course, in the rearview mirror you saw the cloud your own tires were kicking up.

My first trip to the altiplano was the craziest one, full of gringo enthusiasm and naiveté with a hefty splash of luck thrown in. PCV Mike Welsh was visiting from Constitución,[10] a small city on Chile's central coast, and on March 29, 1979 we rented a red VW Beetle. We used the car to ferry stuff from my grim old room to my new one at 21 de Mayo 880 (what luxury to have hot water after five months of cold showers), tossed my tent and a pair of sleeping bags in the back seat, and headed for the mountains after lunch. The late start didn't matter, because we weren't coming back that day. There'd be plenty of time to find a great spot before dark and set up camp in the high country.

We drove ten kilometers north on the Panamericana, then east into the Lluta[11] Valley. The valley floor was fertile and green from the Lluta River, which flows year-round from the Andes. Small farms clustered along the ribbon of water. Since it virtually never rains in the Atacama Desert, the vegetation stopped dead above the floodplain of the river, a stark line beyond which there was nothing but sand and rock. Far away to our right we saw petroglyphs high on a hill. People had been living there for thousands of years, and traces of a few of them remain.

There were more traces a bit up the road, in the hamlet of Poconchile, site of a colonial-era church and a police *control*. Behind the church were hundreds of wooden crosses, acres of crosses stabbed into the desolate dirt. Desert cemeteries remove the illusion of permanence. The plots and crooked crosses look

---

10 Much of Constitución was destroyed by an earthquake and tsunami in February 2010. Hundreds of people were killed.

11 Pronounced YOO-tah or JOO-tah, just as in Spanish "llama" is YAH-mah or JAH-mah.

so small in the vastness of the desert, so ready to crumble and return to the earth. The aridity actually preserves objects, including bodies, but it doesn't seem that way. Things in the desert are always on the verge of being swallowed by the sand, of being buried and forgotten even if a desiccated version remains intact underground, waiting for archaeologists yet unborn to start digging.

I have a photo of our red VW in the foreground, both doors flung open as if we don't plan to stay in this resting place for long. The field of tilted, weathered crosses stretches haphazardly into the distance, toward the empty hills. No living human is in the picture. The photo of that car, surely long since junked, is a powerful trace for me. That fragile paper rectangle, so easily destroyed, has managed to survive, and its lifeless, fading surface returns me to a lost world.

No one could get through the checkpoint without a *salvoconducto*, a safe-conduct pass. Mike and I were familiar with Chilean bureaucracy by now, so had put in our time at the *Investigaciones* office in Arica and possessed the necessary form, replete with stamps and illegible scrawls. The catch was that Mike had no driver's license with him, and my Connecticut license had expired over a year ago. I flashed it at the *paco* and bluffed our way through. He was clueless about the English, maybe even intimidated by it. As the gate moved aside and we rolled toward parts unknown, it felt like we were getting away with something. The trip was cool enough before, but a touch of outlaw bravado added an edge.

So did the bottle of wine. I wouldn't recommend that approach now, because I'm middle-aged and responsible. At the time, though, we were young and ramblin' like Woody Guthrie (though I'd left my guitar in Arica). Buzzed on the adventure, swigging cheap red *vino* straight from the bottle, munching cheese

84

sandwiches and green apples as we climbed—rarely have I felt more free. Or before long, more stupid.

We took our time, for a variety of reasons, not the least of which was that the Bug's engine seemed designed for a sewing machine and was a dog on the hills—and when you're going from sea level to 14,000 feet, it's mostly hills. But we were in no hurry. Time was sweet and there was so much to see, beginning with the desert's gradual transformation. Precipitation increases there at higher elevations, so at a certain point cactus and scrub vegetation started to show up; the land was less Sahara and more New Mexico.

We stopped at Pukará de Copaquilla, the ruins of an Inca outpost. The Inca constructed hundreds of these forts to protect and connect their empire, places for couriers to stop as they carried goods and news to and from the capital of Cuzco, in Peru. This pukará overlooked an undulating valley far below, with some vegetation around a river slowly cutting its way deeper into the rock. Mike yelled out over the valley and got a righteous echo in return. We took turns shouting, our voices skipping off the hills like flat stones on a pond: four, five, six, seven. I've never heard more impressive echoes anywhere.

Mike took a turn at the wheel. The wine soothed our throats, raspy from conjuring echoes. We marveled at the miracle: two young Americans riding German technology, in a car probably built in Mexico or Brazil, on a lonely Chilean road through country once ruled by the Inca. We felt small, two specks rolling through this dusty corner of Everything, yet full to bursting at the crazy mysteries of life. Somehow, a kid from Queens and one from Connecticut had made it to this place. Somehow, we were actually doing this. People tend to feel more alive while traveling; senses alert in a surge of fresh stimuli. But facing, and even embracing, the unfamiliar is only a partial explanation.

Just as important is that while traveling we're *prepared* to feel. We expect new things, new people, so are ready to notice them, unlike quotidian life where we often shuffle in our ruts, unaware of the potentially strange, the potentially wonderful.

An hour later we reached Putre (pronounced POO-treh), an isolated village with cobblestone streets, backed by two incredibly picturesque mountains, snow-covered from shoulder to peak. Mike damn near slid the car into a stone wall on the descent into town, swerving to avoid a sudden (to us, anyway) flock of sheep. We bought another bottle of Concha y Toro wine, got back on the highway and kept climbing. The altiplano was waiting.

Altiplano means "high plain." We knew that. But knowing what words mean, and what they *mean*, can be two different animals. Our romantic vision had been to camp in God's country, to build a blazing fire from wind-gnarled deadwood and sleep like nomads beneath the infinite stars. As we reached the highest plateaus and the road leveled off, we saw snow-capped volcanos, scrub brush and miles of wild, primal emptiness—but not a single stick of firewood. In our (mostly my) ignorance, we had failed to realize that the altiplano lies far above the tree line—if there *were* a tree line, because trees don't generally grow in a desert. Somehow these basic bits of reality had escaped me, and so had appropriate footwear. I'd forgotten to bring boots so had only my sandals from sunny Arica, fortunately reinforced by two pairs of socks from my pack. When we reached the Chucuyo *control* darkness had set in, bringing body-numbing temperatures. Camping was out of the question. A desert always cools off at night; a desert 14,000 feet above sea level gets seriously cold. Dangerously cold, if you're an idiot not prepared for it.

At Chucuyo, in the middle of Chile's Lauca National Park, the police hut was toasty warm from a potbelly stove. My driver's license passed inspection again and we were free to move on, but hoped we wouldn't have to. We explained our situation, freely admitted to screwing up, rubbed our hands briskly at the stove. We asked about a hotel in the area and they just laughed. Come on, we thought, have a heart and offer to let us stay here. Put us in a cell for all we care; cells have beds, right? But the *pacos* took neither hint nor pity. The closest they came to helping us was to suggest we try Parinacota.

"Parinacota?"

"It's up the road," one said with a vague wave toward the east. "Take a left."

"How far?"

"*No sé.* Just up the road."

"*Gracias,*" I said, silently cursing the bastards. What was easier, offering hospitality now or searching for two frozen bodies tomorrow? We traded the gravel parking lot for the gravel road and poked along through the darkness, fearful of missing the sign to Parinacota—if there even *was* a sign. Our high beams were a meager glimmer in the endless altiplano night.

The sign for Parinacota was weathered, small, crooked, and extremely welcome. We turned and bounced north on the narrow, twisting dirt road. The second bottle of wine sat corked tight in the back seat, untouched for at least an hour. Slow kilometers dragged by: two, three. Despite the sign, we began to worry. Where was this place? Mike braked, hard. A puddle ten feet wide covered a low section of the road. I got out to see if we could drive around. No chance—ditch to the left, rocks to the right. No stick to check the depth of the water.

"What do you think?" I asked, rubbing my hands against the chill.

"What the hell. Those cops will come rescue us, right?"

I walked to the other side of the water, shivering in the wind. Mike gunned the engine and splashed right through. Sometimes anticlimax can be a very good thing.

We crawled along, dodging some holes and rocks, thumping over others. It was more a trail than a road. Suddenly Mike braked again. A dozen or more llamas blocked the way. They were obviously domesticated, with colored yarn tied at their ears, either a form of branding or some sort of fashion statement. They didn't scatter at the sight of us. We tried to nudge through them and they grudgingly cooperated. Then two herders appeared in the headlights, squat indigenous men wearing sandals with no socks. I couldn't believe it. I'd have had frostbite within an hour.

"Excuse me, *señores*. Is this the road to Parinacota?"

"*Sí.*"

"Is it far?"

"No."

"How far?" I asked. "*Un kilometro? Dos?*"

Their broad faces were barely visible in the night. They kept a good ten feet between them and the car.

"*Dos kilometros*," one said, his voice like a shrug. They followed their animals.

We drove two slow kilometers, then three, four. The town was a sudden surprise in the high beams. BIENVENIDOS A PARINACOTA was painted in large white letters on a cinder block wall. We followed the trail around a few white stucco buildings with tin roofs, and stopped in a dirt plaza. Not a single light shone in the tiny village. The last thing we saw before turning off our lights was a white wall surrounding an old church with a thatch roof.

People began to materialize from the darkness. None of them spoke; a silent, spooky semicircle formed around the car. I wasn't exactly scared, just intensely aware of being an outsider, an intruder in someone else's world. Mike and I shared a glance, then rolled down our windows.

"*Buenas noches,*" I said. "*Hay un hotel aquí?*"

There wasn't. Parinacota was a town of maybe fifty souls, far off the beaten path, whose path itself was beat. Our only hope was that an altruist or entrepreneur would take us in for the night, an impromptu altiplano B & B.

"You can stay with me," a slight young man said. "I have another guest so cannot offer you a bed, but if the floor is acceptable, you're welcome." Two freezing gringo beggars were in no position to be choosy. We got our sleeping bags and packs, then despite qualms of being perceived as Ugly Americans, did the smart thing and locked the car.

The man carried a lantern. "*Cortaron la luz,*" he said. ["The electricity's out."] He told us he was the village schoolteacher. I asked if he was from Parinacota and he shook his head sadly; at least it seemed sad to me. Maybe he drew some sort of hazardous duty pay for this hinterland assignment.

It was a half-minute walk to his house, which consisted of one fairly large rectangular room. Feeble light from the lantern barely reached the corners. Two metal-frame twin beds jutted out from the wall opposite the door. On the closer bed sat a man around sixty-five years old, wearing a black coat and round, gold-rim glasses. He stood up as we entered, though he didn't smile. The teacher introduced us, saying his guest was originally from Germany, and we shook hands. I don't remember the man's name, but for convenience will call him Schaffner, the name I gave the character in my short story "Altiplano," a fictionalized account of this trip.

"So," Mike asked in Spanish, "how long have you been in Chile?"

The man stared at him an instant. "Over thirty years," he said.

A strange little pause ensued. I'm not sure that it was awkward, but it was definitely strange. The year was 1979. It didn't take a genius to calculate that Schaffner had come to Chile shortly after World War II—along with numerous other Germans, many of them Nazis. The four of us talked before extinguishing the lantern. Schaffner spoke excellent Spanish, though with a heavy German accent. The conversation turned to politics, as conversations often did in Chile at that time. Mike and I danced around the topic: prudent behavior under a military dictatorship, especially when you're in some lost corner of the world, halfway disappeared already. We didn't know these people, or if we could trust them. Before long, Schaffner spoke glowingly of Pinochet, then talked of "Adolfo" Hitler, how he had made mistakes, sure, but the people respected him and the trains ran on time, not like here in goddamn South America.

Even today, remembering that man makes my stomach squirm.

We crawled into our sleeping bags fully clothed. The wooden floor was grimy and hard, and something unexpected came as a side effect of the altitude. Earth's atmosphere is thin at 14,000 feet. Time and again I would nearly drift off, breathing getting shallow, slowing as I slipped toward sleep...then suddenly I'd have to gulp for air, fighting for oxygen like a bass in the bottom of a boat. It was frustrating, even scary. I eventually dropped off to spotty sleep, but it was a restless, uncomfortable night.

Mike and I woke early, sore and weary. The teacher put a kettle on the stove. Warm liquid would have been wonderful, but despite the usual incredible Chilean hospitality, he didn't invite us to share bread and coffee with him and the Nazi. We said thanks and goodbye and stowed our sleeping bags, smeared with dirt from that foul floor, in the back seat. Time to ball the jack to fabled Lago Chungará, the highest lake on earth, with its primeval volcanos and famous pink flamingos. I turned the key, ready for adventure. What I got instead was the groan of a car in pain.

The Bug had been spoiled by easy duty at sea level in the eternal spring of Arica. Its puny engine was no match for the cold and the altitude, and had done the mechanical equivalent of curling into the fetal position. Mike pushed while I popped the clutch, but that was as hopeless as using the key. The only choice was to wait for the sun.

We raised the hood to expose the motor, located in the back where the trunk usually is. A few locals had paid minimal attention during our jump-start attempts, but now kids began to gather around us. One or two, then four, five, half a dozen. In a village this small and remote, a pair of tousled gringos and a wounded VW were decent entertainment on a Friday morning. Two boys huddled near the engine, pointing to parts and pretending they knew what they were talking about.

To my surprise, these indigenous kids all wore store-bought clothes: corduroy pants or blue jeans, machine-made sweaters and hats, the girls in skirts over trousers or tights. I'd expected to see handmade stuff that tourists (including me) buy, alpaca hats and sweaters and such. Maybe those items didn't last as long as store-bought ones, or fetched good prices in Arica's markets so made more sense to sell than to wear, or were only used on special occasions. Maybe the old ways of self-sufficiency were simply gone, like almost everywhere else, and no one in Parinacota knew how to make clothes anymore—outside of a few old women wearing ancient-patterned sweaters they had knitted, who shook their heads, chewed their coca leaves and wondered aloud what this world was coming to. Though for all I knew, those women were already dead, or sick of knitting and ready to welcome the fruits of mass production as a godsend.

One boy was rolling a wheel with a stick over the uneven ground. Didn't American kids used to do that, back in the 1890s or the presidency of Teddy Roosevelt? I remembered reading about it in Booth Tarkington's novel *Penrod*, or maybe it was just the drawing on the cover of the paperback. When I asked if I could give it a shot the boy smiled and handed over the implements. Soon the whole group was laughing, no one harder than Mike, as I botched try after try. That damn wheel kept wanting to flop sideways and become one with the earth. I'd need a lot of practice to learn this useless skill.

"Come on, Slick," I said to Mike in English. "Show us your game. You probably grew up doing this on the mean streets of Queens."

"First things first." He turned the key and the engine blessedly coughed to life. "I'd like to school you, chump, but the flamingos are waiting. Don't violate any of them or I'll alert the *pacos*."

I grinned and closed the hood. We waved to the kids and bounced back toward the main road. Inside half an hour we were at sky-blue Lake Chungará, where hundreds of pink flamingos dotted the water, and I photographed the perfect cone of Parinacota Volcano and its reflection in the placid lake.

We wished we could stay for a few hours, but had to return the car or get charged an extra day. We made good time on the mostly downhill run, coasting for miles with the engine off to save fuel. Running out of gas up there would have been a severe bummer.

Mike decided to get a flat tire instead. An hour outside of Poconchile he started swerving, and we heard the thumping rim. We tried to put on the spare, but of course the jack didn't work. There was nothing to do but wait. Eventually, three soldiers in a camouflage truck pulled over, and with the help of their strong backs we changed the tire. It made me remember that despite my disdain for Pinochet and the dictatorship, most low-ranking soldiers were just ordinary guys putting in their mandatory two years of military service. And even if those three men were pro-Pinochet to the core, at that moment I felt nothing toward them but gratitude.

During my Peace Corps years, I made two other trips up to what Aricans call *el interior*, under varying circumstances yet with one common element: I was young. The next time I went, twenty-four years had melted away. Somehow, I had become forty-seven, a college professor, a middle-class American with a mortgage, credit cards—and most important, a wife, a stepdaughter and a granddaughter. Despite being decades removed from the Peace Corps, though, I still felt like that kid who had spent nearly three years in South America, questing for adventure to postpone the rest of his life, the expected part, the acquiescence to comfortable, pleasant middle-class America. The problem, of course, or at least the distinction, is that no matter how connected I feel to him, I'm *not* that kid anymore.

I return to the altiplano, not in a VW Beetle with an expired license and a bottle of wine, but in a tour bus with Christine, Panchy, Juan Marcos and twenty-one other travelers, only a handful of them Chilean. There are no misguided plans to rough it in the wilderness. This is strictly a day trip, with a driver and a pleasant guide named Jorge, a structured itinerary and no decisions to make except what food to order or which souvenirs to buy.

I'm not usually a fan of tours, because of the us/them dichotomy they can create. A herd of Americans, or Japanese, or Germans, or whoever, steps from a bus, swarms a place and overwhelms it for a few minutes or an hour, sticking with their own kind, speaking their own language (which of course the tour guide does as well), only dealing with local people, if they deal with them at all, as sources of cheap souvenirs. I almost added "and cheap food," but these tourists likely avoid the native fare out of squeamishness and fear of the unknown. Better to wait for a good old reliable burger or T-bone back at the Hilton.

In contrast, the twenty-five passengers on our altiplano bus are from Chile, the U.S. (just Christine and me), Germany, South Korea, Australia, Peru, France, Japan and Ecuador. None of us knew we'd have such an international group, but no one is surprised or scandalized, either. Everyone enjoys the exotic mix. This is a collection of people traveling solo or in pairs, after all, not as part of a package tour collective. The sort of person for whom meeting foreigners different from yourself is fascinating, not threatening. Rather than isolating us among "our own kind," this tour shows that our own kind is human beings, regardless of facial features, skin color, language or birthplace.

Jorge speaks Spanish and a little English, and the passengers help each other with translations. We retrace the route Mike and I took twenty-four years ago up the Lluta Valley. The police checkpoint in Poconchile is gone, maybe a sign of decreased military control over the people now that the dictatorship is history. Or possibly a sign of globalization and increased traffic between Chile and Bolivia, especially with the highway paved all the way to La Paz. The Arica-La Paz railroad, which I rode in 1979 and which used to be the primary link between the two cities, after more than a century of service no longer carries passengers—a victim of the good road and consequent cheap bus service.

Poconchile's colonial church is in ruins, hammered by the 1987 earthquake that severely damaged Arica. The building is little more than a shell: roof gone, west wall collapsed. Nearby, thousands of adobe bricks are stacked three and four high, waiting for reconstruction to begin. Four bricks high might not sound like much, but instead of typical bricks these are nearly two by three-foot slabs, six to eight inches thick. I see no sign of rebar or other reinforcing elements, so I fear that someday a temblor will drop the new church as well. I can only hope I'm wrong.

The desert cemetery behind the church is still there, and life being what it is, of course it has stretched its boundaries. There's a bit more color than in 1979: plastic flowers here and there, more crosses painted white instead of just bare brown, weathered wood. Unlike epitaphs carved in stone, which memorialize people long after memory of them is gone, inscriptions on wooden crosses are erased within a few seasons, the dearly departed rendered anonymous, no one and everyone.

The bus climbs the Quebrada de Cardones, quickly leaving sea level behind and entering the mountain world. Jorge points out sights and passes along information. For example, "candelabra cactus" is the name of the branching cacti Mike and I had seen, and they exist nowhere else on the planet (I'm not sure I believe Jorge on that claim). Somewhere along the route we stop at the bottom of a gradual incline. The driver puts the bus in neutral, kills the engine, and slowly, eerily, we begin to roll in reverse back up the hill—a weird sensation. I don't pretend to understand it, and God knows how anyone ever figured it out, but a strong magnetic field in that spot somehow causes the phenomenon. If I had only known to pull that one on Mike, complete with tales of Inca legends, bloodthirsty *brujos* and the curse of the *conquistadores*. Sometimes a guide does come in handy.

We pull into the gravel parking lot of Restaurant Zapahuira, on the site of an Inca food depot 3200 meters above sea level.[12] Breakfast is cheese sandwiches with coffee, tea or *mate de coca*, coca leaf tea. Christine and I drink *mate*, not just because it is by far the most interesting choice and feels vaguely dangerous and illegal (though it's neither), but because it's reputed to ward off *puna* or *soroche*, the interchangeable Chilean words for altitude sickness. *La puna* is unpredictable. It might hit you and it might not, but if it does, prepare for headaches and lethargy instead of fun. The last time I'd been at anywhere near this altitude was years before in Colorado's Rocky Mountain National Park, when to my surprise and chagrin I was too *apunado* to handle walking five minutes to a lookout point. How the mighty had fallen; Mr. Altiplano had to stick with the car, a pathetic lightweight. I certainly want to avoid that today.

The bus rolls on to the Pukará de Copaquilla. The parking lot has been enlarged; the view is still spectacular. Somehow there's a small farm far below, a patch of green in the desert, and even a man-made pond. It has to be an oasis. Jorge informs the group about the echo, and soon a laughing babel of languages and international nonsense syllables is bouncing off the canyon walls.

The first sure sign of increased altiplano tourism comes outside Putre. At a curve in the road that provides a superb overlook of the town, where I took a gorgeous photo in 1979, there's now a parking lot. An Indian woman has set up shop under two beach

---

12 For a souvenir, at the restaurant I bought a bottle of El Inca Bi-Cervecina beer from Bolivia. The colorful, tacky label was too wonderful to pass up: two images of Inca warriors, one epicene but probably female holding a spear, the other, definitely a woman, brandishing a bow. Fine print at the bottom says, in Spanish: "Iron-rich tonic beer, recommended by the most renowned doctors for anemic, weak or convalescing people." When I opened the bottle on a nostalgic whim several months later, I found the thick dark beer to be syrupy-sweet and undrinkable. But the glory of the label remains.

umbrellas, peddling typical Andean tourist wares: blankets, hats, ponchos (called *mantas* in Chile), sweaters, bags. The stuff probably all came from Bolivia, where labor costs are unconscionably low. The bus parks next to her and we have our first chance to buy.

Instead, I snap shots of Putre. The town hasn't grown much; population 542 then, around 600 now. The countryside looks scrubby after the long dry season. Hillside terraces probably built by the Incas seem gray and uncultivated, though I can't be sure from this distance. The snowy mountains of 1979 today are bald and obscured by mist, a sign that the *invierno boliviano* is starting. It's called "Bolivian winter" though it happens in the South American summer, because it's the rainy season that brings snow to the mountains. Mike and I had come through in March, after wet "winter" was over, leaving clear days and land as green as that rugged land gets, the higher elevations a glorious white.

The biggest changes between 1979 and 2003 come next. The police station at Chucuyo is still there, though like at Poconchile the checkpoint gate is gone. But capitalism has arrived, in the form of a few shacks selling the same goods as the woman near Putre, as well as soft drinks and snacks. There are even restrooms, halfway clean ones at that. The main attraction, though, is an altiplano version of the Catskill Game Farm. Half a dozen llamas and alpacas of various colors wander about, casually communing with the tourists, posing for photos and cadging handouts of cookies and crackers. No one can resist stroking their amazingly thick, soft wool. Grinning like a kid at a petting zoo is an absurdly far cry from arriving here after dark, shivering, worried how we would make it till morning.

Instead of driving hesitantly into the night to find an unknown potential haven, this time I just ride the bus. Parinacota is on the itinerary. Both the town and the church have been declared Chilean National Monuments. The road to the village is still dirt, though somewhat wider and better maintained. My mind is a blizzard of the snows of yesteryear. Nearly a quarter-century ago, a drive into the dark, toward the unknown. Today, a comfortable jaunt in daylight, a guided tour down memory lane. Suddenly it's overwhelming, far more emotional an experience than I'd expected. I have to remind myself to breathe. Feelings this strong for an adventure with a friend, a symbol of our youth and all that it meant and still means.... I can only begin to imagine those feelings overlain with the pain of losing not just youth, but friends as well: soldiers returning years later to Normandy, to Vietnam, and inevitably, someday, to Iraq and Afghanistan.

Parinacota, as isolated as it remains, has become a small part of the tourist infrastructure. Near where Mike and I parked the VW across from the church, four wooden huts now stand—shops for tourists. I doubt they stay open long hours. More likely they just cater to the couple of buses that arrive daily, and maybe kick back a percentage to the tour companies that provide the customers.

Christine falls in love at one of the shops, with the two-year-old daughter of the owner. At Christine's request, I ask the woman if we can take the child for a walk. Without hesitation (and undoubtedly sensing a sale) she agrees. Christine carries the girl to the church, talking to her in English and limited Spanish, kissing her on the head. It is her version of the snows of yesteryear: she misses our four-year-old granddaughter Olivia, and wishes she and our daughter Maggie were with us the way they'd been the previous Christmas in Brazil. Besides, the tiny girl is incredibly cute, in her miniature gray alpaca *manta* with fringe and white trim.

Parinacota's church is a bizarre history lesson, a clash of cultures brought to an uneasy truce but never a resolution. Spanish *conquistadores* reached this area in the sixteenth century, and missionaries built the original church in the 1600s. It was reconstructed in its present form in 1789. There's a bell tower in one corner of the wall surrounding the church. I wish I could have gone up to see the bell and the date, and maybe place, of its casting.[13] The thatch-roofed church is small, with a crooked cross on the roof. Inside, there are wood ceilings and exposed, rough-hewn beams. To the left as you walk in is a dark alcove with a skull and other relics; I never manage to discover what that's about. On the opposite wall is a seventeenth-century fresco of the Last Judgment with a mixture of native people, Spaniards, and demons worthy of Hieronymus Bosch. A blue monster with bulging eyes, shark-like teeth and gaping, fire-breathing mouth is devouring several figures, either sinners damned to hell or devils going home. The once bright colors have faded and chunks of plaster have chipped away, but the effect is still arresting. And unsettling.

Jorge tells us that many Spaniards considered Indians to be sub-humans without souls, which begs a pretty obvious question: Why spend so much time and effort, not to mention violence in the name of God, to convert soulless sub-humans? Jorge says the natives would give their gods the names of Catholic saints, then name churches after them so the pagan gods would be higher than the Catholic ones, even if they had to do it incognito. It reminds me of U.S. slaves singing double-entendre blues and gospel songs to keep their masters ignorant of what the supposedly inferior creatures were up to. This also explains the wild popularity of the Virgin Mary in Central and South American Catholicism, sometimes to the point of cult status. Mary was easily adapted to

---

13 In East Haddam, Connecticut, the bell in granite St. Stephen's Episcopal church was cast in Spain in 815. Yes, 815. The year is plainly visible on the green-tinged black metal. Next to the church is a colonial-era cemetery; it's a short stroll up the hill to Nathan Hale's one-room schoolhouse. From there the hill slopes down to the broad Connecticut River, which has carried millennia of the snows of yesteryear to the sea.

ubiquitous indigenous Earth Mother deities, and easily adopted by people predisposed to worship any power that might bring bountiful harvests.

We walk the little girl back, Christine gently holding her hand. We take pictures of us with the mother and daughter, and of course buy some stuff at the shop. Not until I began writing this book, though, and compared photos from different eras, did I wonder something that now seems so obvious. Had that mother been one of the kids hanging around our frozen Volkswagen in 1979? It felt like a loopy historical version of *l'esprit d'escalier*, when the perfect comment comes to you, but too late. Odds are excellent that she appears in two different unnamed incarnations in photos shot twenty-four years apart. She might not remember, of course, but there's only one way to find out. Yet I didn't think to ask her, the moment is gone, and I doubt that I'll ever return to Parinacota.

Jorge says we have to go. Gripping my hand, Christine turns several times to wave to the little girl as we walk to the bus. She fights not to cry as we drive off. She has to wipe her eyes a few times on the jouncing ride back to the highway. She tries to smile and I'm reminded for the millionth time why I love her.

There's a special intensity to human encounters while traveling, precisely because most meetings are as fleeting as they are random. Orson Welles illustrated this beautifully in *Citizen Kane*, when Mr. Bernstein wistfully recalls glimpsing a woman wearing a white dress on a ferry as his ferry sails away from her. She only touched his life for a moment, and never even saw him, but "I'll bet a month hasn't gone by since that I haven't thought of that girl." Whether consciously or subconsciously, encounters on the road are heightened by the knowledge that you'll likely never see that person again. If you ever do make it back, the reunion might be joyous and heartfelt—at least partially because of a sense that you beat the odds—or supremely empty if the people are gone and that piece of your past can never be recovered. It's worse, of course, if the place is also transformed, maybe unrecognizably so: debased by strip malls; bulldozed under a housing development cynically named for the place destroyed in its construction; locked behind a gate with KEEP OUT signs announcing that you and your memories don't count anymore.

It's a short ride to Lake Chungará, formed by a volcanic eruption 8,000 years ago. There are no condos on its shores, no Golden Arches framing the snowy twin volcanos Parinacota and Pomerape, no luxury hotel or casino—not yet, anyway. The absolute wild nothing of 1979, though, has been somewhat tamed by modest tourist amenities: a paved parking lot, toilets, the inevitable crafts and souvenirs shop.

The lake is steel gray, not the deep blue of my earlier visits—because of the weather, fortunately, not pollution. This is my first trip to the altiplano in the rainy season. My 1979 photo of Volcán Parinacota reflected upside-down in the lake isn't an option today. The water is too dull and wind-rippled for decent reflection; mist and clouds scud across the two volcanos, obscuring the view. Branches of lightning flash in the distance, but my shutter finger is slow, or unlucky. Our photos of the lake are filled with primeval elements—and floating flocks of pink flamingos unconcerned with it all—but not one of them manages to capture that violent spark.

The sky is spitting cold rain as we leave. Everyone looks tired, from a combination of getting up early and the unforgiving altitude. Life feels different at 14,000 feet. A *puna* headache begins drilling my temples. I know the throb will ease as we descend toward sea level, but it's still pounding when we reach Putre at five o'clock for lunch. With a bit of a pang, but nowhere near enough to overcome my curiosity (and my desire to be able to say I did it), I order the Kuchu-Marka restaurant's *especialidad de casa*: alpaca. Several of us eat on the back patio in temporary sun. I mention my headache; Anna, a young Australian woman with close-cropped blonde hair, says to give her my hand. She squeezes the webbing and meat between my thumb and forefinger, so hard I cry out. Within seconds the headache ebbs. Not gone, but greatly diminished. I thank her, she smiles, and I realize once again how little I know and how much there is to learn.

Not far outside of Putre, we hit thick fog. Two-lane roads are always treacherous, and this one involves sharp curves and drops of hundreds of feet. Not that we can see the cliffs through this soup; it's tough enough to follow the white lines on the highway. Fortunately, our driver is cautious, not macho or impatient, and we make slow, sane progress. On a straightaway we come upon a small, smashed car and the truck that crumpled it. A police car's light reflects crazily off the twisted metal. No one says a word in any language as we crawl past.[14]

We don't get to Arica till 9:30. Earlier, Jorge told me he needed to leave his house by 6:30 A.M. That's a long day. It must be even more grueling for the driver. I ask Jorge if the job gets boring. "No," he said, "because every group is different and the trip is new to them." I suppose it's similar to me assigning a story or book I've taught numerous times before. It's new to the students, so each class is a somewhat fresh experience. But class is only an hour or two, not an exhausting, all-day marathon. And I don't teach the same book day after day after day.

Back at the house, we pop a bottle of champagne to celebrate Hugo's birthday. Though Chilean *vino* is justly famous, sparkling wine is its weak link, generally sweet and mediocre at best. But

---

14 I read in *La Estrella* the next day that five members of a Bolivian family had been injured, though none fatally.

it's the bubbly thought that counts. We toast with the *champaña* then switch to beer. Hugo collects American coins, so along with various state quarters I'd been culling from my change, I give him a 1976 U.S. Mint proof set.

"*Muchisimas gracias*, Gringo," Hugo says. He switches to English. "The Bicentennial, man. That's great."

I had missed America's two-hundredth birthday, at least the whiz-bang part. I was in Europe for my junior year in college, and by the time I returned to the U.S. on July 31, 1976 the fireworks were over, though patriotic commercialism was still in full swing. On the Fourth of July, a number of us Americans had gone to the Café des Chemins de Fer, our favorite bar in Fribourg, Switzerland. A Swiss guy played a record of Jimi Hendrix wailing the "Star Spangled Banner," and people of various nations stood and raised their glasses in grinning salute. Someone put on the Beatles' "Birthday." I felt like part of something worthwhile, part of a wide, wonderful world that just might find a way to fix itself.

In September of 1985 I went back to Europe and spent a day in Fribourg with my then-girlfriend Diane Hargrove. I tried to take her to the Chemins de Fer, psyched for *une canette*, a half-liter mug of local Cardinal beer. But I couldn't find the place. We searched a few blocks around, in case my memory was dim after nine years. Finally, I asked a pedestrian. Oh yes, he said, the Chemins de Fer was right here. They tore it down a few weeks ago.[15]

There had been snow during our winter in Europe, despite a drought. At the Innsbruck Olympics, Greg Abell and I stood in snow to watch Rosie Mittermaier win the women's downhill, and climbed into snowy woods to the ski jump ramp to see (and hear—they rumble down the slope, then actually whistle when

---

15 I found out years later that a bank was built on the site.

they rocket into the air) the jumpers launch themselves. "*Ooh, des cailloux!*" cried a woman at Switzerland's Lac Noir, as she skied over pebbles on a bare patch in the snow. The day Teddy (Theodosia) Price[16] and I hitchhiked to join our friends in a Swiss chalet for Christmas, fresh snow and ice shimmered like jewels on naked tree branches in the mist, so beautiful we could hardly stand it.

Outside my Connecticut window as I write this, eight inches of snow dazzle in the sunshine, fighting a hopeless battle to the death. Tomorrow is the first day of spring. After all my nostalgic musings about the snows of yesteryear, right now I just want the snow of today to lose the fight and disappear.

---

16 The only person I've ever known from Normal, Illinois.

CHAPTER EIGHT

The Broken House

"The past is gone but something might be found
to take its place..."

—Gin Blossoms, "Hey Jealousy"

On our fourth day in Arica, Hugo and Any's son Hugo Tomás finally arrives from Santiago. He'd been busy studying for exams, delayed getting his bus ticket, and wound up stuck with a 30-hour trip and two long nights on the road. With his arm around his weary son in the living room Hugo laughingly says, "Hugo Tom is at the top of his dental school class, but he can't make a decent bus reservation!"

Hugo Tomás was born three years after I left Arica. This is the first time I've met him, so I feel no shock like when I saw adult

Panchy; my memory has no picture to compare to the present. He's a good-looking kid, much taller than his parents, and like his sister speaks American-accented English from a year in a U.S. high school. Soon he heads to his room to sleep.

Hugo and I take Chato Rojas to run some errands. Downtown to the Banco del Estado, then a detour up to Yungay Street and Hugo's old house, still collapsed from the 1987 earthquake. Fortunately, they had moved a few years earlier. When the toddler Hugo Tomás saw the damage he called the place *la casa rota*, "the broken house," the name the family uses for it to this day. I hand Hugo my camera and cross the street to pose by the broken house where I spent so many evenings.

We drive to the Líder (pronounced "leader," which is what it means), a new, big-box supermarket near what was once the edge of town that has since been swallowed by the expanding city. Hugo pulls into the sprawling parking lot and prowls for a space. The Líder dwarfs any store that was around when I lived here. Even the few self-styled *supermercados* were the size of a 7-11 today. Most people shopped at tiny neighborhood grocery stores, and went there on foot. Plenty of those *almacenes* still exist, but far more folks have cars these days and are willing to join the crowds saving money from faceless economies of scale. I'm making an observation, not a value judgment. Hugo and I soon add to the shopping cart traffic jam, after all, and it's hard to argue with the prices, selection (including an impressive wine aisle) and convenience of being able to use my credit card. Yes, after a struggle Hugo finally allows me to pay for something.

We leave with an array of white plastic bags stuffed with groceries, which we load in the trunk. What a contrast to the old way of walking to the corner shop with your reusable wire mesh bag. Hardly any stores supplied plastic bags then, so you rarely saw discarded *sacos* littering the sidewalks, or trapped and flapping in a fence. Everyone used those sturdy mesh bags that lasted for years. It's weird to realize most Chilean kids have probably never even seen one of those bags, just as they've never paid a deposit on virtually every beverage. During my years in Chile that meant bottles, the kind that are washed and re-used, the most efficient form of recycling; cans were uncommon and usually imported. Now plastic bottles and aluminum cans are ubiquitous, almost all *no retornable* (as are most glass bottles) and therefore destined for landfills or worse, because there's no recycling program in Arica. Seductive convenience has become the new, passively accepted Way It Is.

I'll be adding to the trash a five-liter plastic jug of water from the Líder. I've been buying liters of water from the liquor store a thirty-second walk from Hugo's house; this big bottle will save me some trips and pesos as well. I never buy bottled water in the States, but when Christine and I arrived Hugo recommended that we not drink tap water. "Just in case," he added in English. Though Arica's water is perfectly potable, why not lessen the odds of spending any of our short time here being sick? Especially for Christine; her system isn't used to South America. Still, it seems wimpy to avoid the water I'd ingested without a thought for the better part of two years. The simple, intelligent precaution makes me feel like a soft American who doesn't live here anymore.

On the drive home I notice two billboards advertising new private schools, next to buildings still under construction. I've seen several such signs in the past few days, in various parts of the city, advertising both elementary and high schools. A handful of private schools existed during my time in Arica, mostly for kids from wealthier families. But Arica's economy is in the toilet. How can so many parents afford private school? This building boom doesn't make sense.

107

"Hugo, what's with all these new private schools? Has education become a good business?"

I'm surprised at both the answer, and the venom in my friend's voice. "It's not a *good* business, Gringo. It's the best business in Chile."

"How? If Arica's economy sucks, who can afford tuition?"

Hugo's bitter tone escalates as he gives me the details. Sometime during the 1980s, with Pinochet espousing the free-market economics of Milton Friedman and the "Chicago Boys," a system of educational subvention was put in place. The government pays a certain amount for each student, and parents are free to spend that money wherever they like. It's essentially the school choice voucher system some people want to establish in the U.S. Entrepreneurs open schools and compete for students and their government subsidies. The theory is that competition creates improvement and everyone wins, especially kids from underperforming public schools who now have other educational options.

In reality, though, there are many losers, and this system has gutted Chilean public education. Private school tuition is higher, often far higher, than the government subsidy, so poor families don't have the resources to send their kids to the new schools. In most cases the subvention merely cuts costs for middle- and upper-class parents who would send their children to private schools anyway. The result is severely underfunded public schools, populated almost exclusively by disadvantaged students.

Through selective admissions and the ability to expel students who don't measure up, private schools pick and choose their clientele, whereas public schools must try to accommodate virtually anyone. This puts public schools at a huge competitive disadvantage. Hugo desperately wants to retire because students whose families can possibly afford it have fled to private schools, leaving public classrooms full of disadvantaged children with little interest in learning, myriad problems in their home lives, and precious little respect for much of anything, especially teachers. Discipline problems have multiplied exponentially in recent years.

"Have you thought about moving to a private school?" I ask.

Hugo shakes his head. "I've spent my career working for crap wages, but at least I get a pension when I retire. Not much, but a pension. Most private school teachers get no benefits, no retirement plan. If they don't like it, too bad. Complain and the school just fires you and hires someone younger and cheaper. Capitalism at its best."

The drive turns quiet. We pass the Arequipeña beer billboard without comment. I'm thinking about privatization efforts in the U.S.: education, prisons, Social Security. Proponents tout competition and accountability, but ignore human nature. Public policy based on the profit motive is an invitation for greed to sooner or later pervert that policy. And people who can least afford the consequences are inevitably the ones who pay.

In a personal manifestation of human nature, I soon drop the serious thoughts. Morning clouds have dispersed, the midday sun is shining through, and we're going on a *paseo* this afternoon. Back at the house we join the others and pack beach gear and beer, while Betty the Peruvian housekeeper washes a mountain of dishes. Evidently, she comes once a week to help out. Any is reading *La Tercera* newspaper at the dining room table.

"You're not going?" Christine asks.

Any closes the paper. "Not today. I think I'll just relax here."

Hugo catches my eye and nods almost imperceptibly. I follow him into the hallway that leads to the bedrooms.

"Any has to stay and watch Betty," he whispers.

"She's not honest?"

"Yes, but it's better to avoid temptation. *La ocasión hace el ladrón. Entiendes?*"

"*Claro.*" Opportunity makes the thief.

We pile into Chato Rojas, me in the front with Hugo, Christine in back with Panchy and Juan Marcos. Not a minute down the road Panchy says in English, "They're playing baseball!"

"Can we stop?" I ask.

"Why not?" Hugo says with fake snideness. "I *love* baseball. It's so much better than the beach." He continues a few hundred feet to a traffic circle, winds around and drives back. We park and start down the dusty slope to the field. Juan Marcos and Panchy stay with the car, probably to make out, argue, or both. Each possibility is equally plausible.

I hand Christine my camera, the same one I had when I left Arica. "Take a bunch, OK?" I'm almost as nervous as when our plane landed in Arica. Will I know any of these people? The boys have left the field and are sitting in the bleachers, listening to their coach. They're around twelve, like most of my players were—my kids who are in their mid-thirties now.

We reach level ground and draw near. Could that coach be Enrique Vivanco? Despite the thick waistline and sunglasses, he sure looks like one of my former all stars. He notices the kids seeing us approach—we're obviously an unusual sight—and glances over.

"Enrique?"

There's a flutter of uncertainty in his face, and I wonder if I'm wrong. Suddenly a wide grin erases the doubt.

"*No lo puedo creer. Tom!*"

Seconds later we're hugging in front of the bleachers. The players smile at the sight of their coach embracing some gringo who appeared out of nowhere. Enrique introduces them as the *selección infantil*, Little League-age all stars who will represent Arica in this year's national championships. I listen with an overfull heart as he gives the team a short history lesson of when he was their age, and I was his coach.

To my surprise, they listen intently and actually seem to care. Practice is over, but only a couple of kids leave. The rest of them want to see me play. The equipment is packed in the familiar dusty canvas bag, but laughing boys dump out *bates, bolas, guantes*.

This I have not foreseen. Two years ago, I ruptured a disk in my back, and outside of an occasional softball toss on campus between classes I haven't played since. I certainly haven't swung a bat, with all the stress that puts on your back. But it shouldn't be a problem if I'm careful. After all, I still play tennis—though with a frayed rotator cuff I don't serve anymore.

"I'm going to hit a few," I tell Christine.

Worry furrows her forehead. She remembers how ruined I was in when my back seized up, so incapacitated I couldn't walk. "Please don't be a hero. Better yet, don't be stupid."

"Have you ever known me to be either one?"

"I've known you to be stupid," Hugo says. "Plenty of times."

Christine holds up my camera. "OK, Babe Ruth, this is going on record."

The shutter clicks as I gingerly swing a pair of bats to warm up. I take my stance near the backstop instead of at home plate, so there's no need of a catcher. I'm wearing shorts and sandals and no helmet.

"*Suavecito, ya?*" I tell the pitcher. "*Hace mucho tiempo que no juego.*" Nice and easy, ok? I haven't played in a long time.

The kids in the outfield are absurdly deep. It would be idiotic to try, but I can't help wanting to let loose and really crank a few out there. It's the temptation major leaguers feel at the all-star home run derby to bash towering drives to impress the crowd, though guys who do that nearly always burn out and lose in the last round to someone who popped just enough fly balls into the second row.

Maybe it's common sense, maybe a heightened sense of mortality, but I don't take a single big cut. I don't try to show off. I swing with my wrists and arms, slapping mostly ground balls and not following through. The boys in deep left field move closer. After fifteen or so pitches I quit before I can do something I'll regret. Another round of hugs and we start the climb back to the car.

Hugo claps me on the shoulder. "Well, that was lucky. For you, not for us."

"Did you get some good shots?" I ask Christine.

"I *took* a lot, but with that rusty swing I don't know how *good* they are."

"Fine, bring on the abuse. Story of my life."

We all laugh. What a treat this was, especially since it was totally unexpected. From Hugo and Any's comments I figured baseball in Arica had died, that everything I did here professionally was in the past tense. But now there's a link, however tenuous, and it surprises the hell out of me how emotional I feel because of it.

I'm still on a high as Chato Rojas chugs toward the beach. Then a jagged thought burrows into me. What if Hugo and I had been in slower lines at the supermarket, or had tarried longer in the wine section? What if we had spent more time talking before leaving the house? Just a couple minutes later and practice would have been over, the players gone, the field empty as we drove by. This wonderful moment in my life would not only never have happened, I wouldn't even know it *could* have happened. It's crazy to realize how big a role chance plays in our lives, and how often we can't even know that it does. Every road we take means we didn't take all the others.

112

We stop at a stand for *salteñas*, the Bolivian version of the Chilean *empanada*—a pastry shell containing spicy ground meat, peas and potatoes. The bag of *salteñas* smells delicious as we drive the coast road to Playa Las Machas on the north end of the city. Hugo parks at a long stretch of nearly unpopulated beach, and we unload the car.

"What does *macha* mean?" I ask as we trudge on fine gray sand toward the water. "Sounds like me, *muy macho.*"

Panchy giggles. "So, you're a girl macho, Tom?"

"Exactly," Hugo says. "Your secret is out, Gringo."

Christine squeezes my biceps. "Don't worry, dear, you fake it quite well."

"La macha es un tipo de almeja," Juan Marcos tells me. Macha is a type of clam.

"This beach used to be full of machas," Hugo says. "We'd collect them all the time when I was young. But people are idiots and overdid it. Some *conchasumadres* even used machines to dig them up by the thousands to sell, and now they're all gone."

"Unbelievable," I say.

Hugo shakes his head. "Not unbelievable. Just Chile."

We pick a spot and shove two beach umbrellas into the sand. The sun feels like the blazing star that it is; without the shade I'd burn in no time. I think of my brown face in photos taken after a few months in Arica. It was the darkest tan of my life, by far, and I naively thought it was healthy. Now I can only hope I don't pay a price for it someday.

There's a tremendous view of El Morro from here. Arica lies right where South America bends like the crook of an elbow. The coastline on this side of town veers northwest toward Peru instead of north/south like the rest of Chile, so back across the water we have an unobstructed vista of the city. The massive Morro jutting above the Pacific is sublime, if something sublime can simultaneously be a perfect subject for postcards sold at tourist kiosks. As far as I'm concerned, it's sublime, especially when we clink our glasses of beer and take our first bite into the golden crust of the *salteñas*.

After a while Hugo and I slip off our shirts and stroll to the water. The sun immediately heats my skin and I know I have to be careful. Speaking of careful, Hugo tells me dead seriously not to go in above my knees.

"My *knees?*"

"I mean it. The currents here are treacherous." Even Hugo, one of the strongest swimmers I know, only wades to his lower thighs then takes a quick dip, diving parallel to the shore to avoid going any farther out. When I see that sort of caution I figure calf-high water is good enough for Gringo Tom. Soon I feel my shoulders burning and retreat to the umbrellas. Even Christine, who loves the sun and generally feels invulnerable to it, has moved to the shade.

Juan Marcos is pouring the second bottle of Arequipeña when we notice two men on horseback coming slowly toward us, ambling south on the packed sand near the waterline. Hugo hisses for us to hide the beer. As the men draw closer, I see they're *carabineros*, paramilitary cops in gray-green uniforms. Hugo sits stiffly, staring off to the north behind his sunglasses, ignoring the mounted *pacos* as they pass a hundred feet away. Instantly the uneasiness, mistrust and dislike that I'd learned in Chile for armed men in uniform comes flooding back. I remember stone-faced soldiers guarding government buildings, cradling machine guns like giant wasps.

With hardly a glance in our direction, but an unmistakable aura of arrogant authority, the riders continue down the beach toward town. When the horses' asses are safely distant, Juan Marcos resumes pouring. It was a non-issue, I tell myself. Chile is a democracy now. That sort of worry is a thing of the past. The only *desaparecidos* would be the pesos to pay the fine for drinking on the beach.

But when something is a big part of your life it never truly goes away. Hugo, and I to a much lesser degree, lived under Pinochet's dictatorship, and those experiences molded us. Panchy and Juan Marcos were children during those years, so are essentially unaffected by them. Like Christine, most of what they know about Pinochet comes from stories they've heard, stories they often find less than fascinating. That was a different world, and they're busy living in the one that exists now.

"*Un brindis,*" I say. "*A la casa rota!*"

Hugo and Panchy smile as we touch glasses. Juan Marcos seems puzzled but joins in.

"The something house?" Christine asks.

"The broken house."

"What's that?"

I swallow more cool, foamy beer. "Just the pieces of a place where we used to live."

"Can we go there?"

"Sure. I'm warning you, though, there's not much left."

"That's OK, I like archaeology. And you can tell me stories—I like mythology, too."

I look into my wife's laughing eyes and am reminded yet again why I love her.

CHAPTER NINE

Pilgrimage to Pisagua

"Believing is seeing."

—Ian McEwan, *Enduring Love*

Hugo finds it strange that I want to see Pisagua. He's lived in Arica his whole life without visiting the little fishing town, and doesn't feel the lack. During my Peace Corps days, I'd traveled far and wide without making any effort to go there. But that was before I heard about the hotel.

Pisagua is infamous as the site of one of Pinochet's detention and torture centers. It wasn't a secret prison; people knew about the place. In 1973 and 1974, the Iquique newspaper published notices of political prisoners executed by firing squad, summarily condemned by "military trial in wartime" *("juicio militar en tiempo de guerra").* Others were shot when they supposedly tried to escape. The bodies of the murdered were not returned to their families, although military authorities assured that they were given "Christian burial." By the late seventies, I'd hear the word "Pisagua" mentioned occasionally in Arica, in either hushed tones or grafted to sardonic laughter. It certainly was no tourist destination. There was definitely no hotel then.

How could a building where prisoners were tortured and killed be converted into a hotel? To even consider such an action seems to smudge some surreal boundary, like moving into the Clutter farmhouse after the murders described in Capote's *In Cold Blood*.[17] What would staying in the moment involve, if at the moment you're staying in a well-appointed former cell? How could you not feel the ghosts of political prisoners held without charge, without recourse? I've been to Dachau, the Nazi concentration camp outside Munich. The idea of sleeping there, well fed, in a comfortable bed, seems wrong on every conceivable level. It would be like Abu Ghraib transformed into a bed and breakfast, or Guantánamo bought by Hilton or Marriott. Torture Tourism, with free continental breakfast and a brightly wrapped mint on your pillow.

I want to experience Pisagua and the hotel. The trip will either provide answers, or raise new questions I've been too naive—or sheltered, or scared—to imagine. I rent a car and head south on the Pan-American Highway with Christine and Panchy. It's the only chance left to make the trip, at least with Christine, because she's flying home the day after tomorrow. I want her to see the town and the prison/hotel, to push beyond her intellectual knowledge of the *desaparecidos* to visceral knowledge of Pinochet's

---

17 Lizzie Borden's house in Fall River, Massachusetts, where she likely hacked her parents to death with a hatchet, is now a B&B.

atrocities. That visceral knowledge will mean she knows me better as well. And yes, I want her with me when I go there.

Juan Marcos has a queasy stomach so doesn't come with us; bathrooms will be in short supply on this trip. Hugo stays home as well. He has to teach private English classes this evening and knows we won't be back in time. Still, he could postpone the classes if he really wanted to go. I didn't push him, but can't help wondering if Pisagua has a more personal meaning for him that he'd rather try to leave in the past.

It's some two hundred kilometers to the turn-off west to Pisagua, then forty more to the sea. A hundred and fifty miles one way. (To convert kilometers to miles, divide by eight, then multiply by five.) I fill the tank on our way out of town; actually, an attendant does, which feels odd after years of self-service. I'm a little worried about running dry in the desert, but figure there must be at least one gas station between Arica and Pisagua. I figure wrong. The few meager outposts along that desolate stretch have no pumps, at least not public ones. Even the *control* at Cuya, a police station at the bottom of a ravine between two massive hills, has only a pair of small restaurants *cum* convenience stores. Every driver has to stop in Cuya and show documents to the *carabineros*, but if you need gas, keep going and good luck.

The *cuestas*, those huge, bald, gray-brown hills, are even more intimidating than I remember. There are three between Arica and the Pisagua turn-off. The highway clings to their flanks, vertiginous switchbacks up and down. In the valley far below, thin, sinuous strips of green trace arroyos that are sometimes rivers, sometimes dry washes. The view is amazing, but outside of quick glances my eyes stay on the road, because I'm not thrilled about tumbling to oblivion. Though negotiating the *cuestas* is nerve-racking, it's better than having our fate in the hands of a bus driver harboring an evident death wish, careening around those curves as if he can't wait to get to the bottom, even if that means plunging a thousand feet. I rode those buses often during Peace Corps days. As my friend Lucho Varas said with a grin before my first trip to Iquique, "When there's an accident, there are no survivors."

Outside of a few sections in and around major cities, the Panamericana is a two-lane highway. Two-lane roads with steep grades lead to impatient drivers stuck behind trucks crawling uphill, and heavy trucks either riding their brakes or barreling downhill. There are no breakdown lanes. Some places have guardrails; most places don't. This is earthquake country, so it's common to come upon rocks in the road—pebbles, football-sized, and on occasion, boulders big enough to crush your car.

On one of the *cuestas,* we run into (almost literally) the most reckless driving I have ever seen. Until then, the topper had been an idiot in Portugal who was passing a car in front of us on a blind, uphill curve of a two-lane road. Suddenly a car came from the other direction. The putz didn't even brake, just straddled the centerline as the other two drivers swerved just wide enough for all three cars to squeeze by.

This jackass is even worse. We're behind a semi going downhill when a tandem truck barrels by us both toward a curve—around which a small car appears. I can only imagine the terror that driver feels. We're horrified, sure that hideous carnage will ensue before our eyes. The truck in front of us slows, we slow, and the car stops—which allows the tandem driver to brake and barely swing back into our lane before a head-on collision. I'm so disgusted I wouldn't care if he crashed through the rails and plunged to kingdom come, especially since he immediately starts speeding again, rear trailer swaying wildly in the wind.

I'm not saying it's suicidal to drive the Panamericana, just that being extra cautious makes sense. Two hours later we take the turn-off toward Pisagua, and soon pass the crumpled, burned wreckage of a car beneath a highway sign erected by the Pisagua *carabineros*:

!ACCIDENTE!
PUDO EVITARSE
QUEREMOS QUE
UD. VIVA.

(Accident! This could have been avoided. We want you to live.)

A few kilometers later we see two dozen tilted wooden crosses near the road, a desolate little cemetery on the outskirts of nowhere. I have no idea why it's there. Maybe the dead were connected with the nitrate mining of Pisagua's heyday, a century or more before. Some utility cables hang high above the graves, strung between a series of poles snaking through the desert, presumably bringing electricity and telephone service to isolated Pisagua. One pole rises at the edge of the cemetery, the tallest cross among the graves.

The unreliable gas gauge needle is bobbing consistently below half a tank. I kill the engine when gravity is on our side, and we coast for fifteen of the forty kilometers, through a moonscape that suddenly opens up into a hallucinatingly beautiful view. The horizon is an illusion, lost in limitless blue. Where does the cloudless sky end and the boundless sea begin?

The switchbacks down to Pisagua are some of the steepest I've ever seen, and I ride the brakes mercilessly. The beat-up road is slippery on the curves from wind-blown sand. Suddenly my heart starts thumping as I take the tight, steep curves, my hands sweaty on the wheel. The nervousness isn't from the hairy drive, though, but from a source I hadn't anticipated.

I keep imagining what it was like for prisoners on this descent in 1973 or '74.

Had they seen the grim patch of wooden crosses? Maybe they were blindfolded; maybe it was night. The road was probably unpaved then, just washboard gravel—as parts of it still are. Did the brakes screech on the army buses and vans? Did the *chofer* drive as if none of their lives mattered, including his own? How many of them knew anything about Pisagua? Were they shackled? Allowed to speak? Did the guards mock them for their supposed communism? Taunt them with stories of torture? Did they wonder if they'd ever leave—at least alive? Out here on the edge of the world they were as helpless as kittens in a sack, driven to a lake to be drowned.

I park the car on a stark brown bluff overlooking the town. I'm sure no prison vehicle paused here for photographs and admiration of the view: dozens of fishing boats in the ocean, deep blue water now easily distinguished from paler sky. Low, drab buildings scattered along the lazy curve of a bay. White strands of surf dancing and breaking on the shore. If I were a prisoner with this vista, would it even register as beautiful, or simply as cut off from the rest of the world, a place practically *desaparecido* on its own? I once heard Pisagua described as *una cárcel natural,* "a natural prison." A place where anything could happen to you, and no one would know.

I coast down the last long incline, motor off, brutalizing the brakes. Pisagua is more colorful than it looked from high above. Most of the paint isn't fresh, but it's there. I notice a pastel blue-gray, three-story box in the center of town. The building is ugly but it's not the paint's fault. Next to it is an official-looking structure, a spiffy rose color with dark red trim.

That must be it. What else could it be?

I don't care if it's not so long a drop now—keep your eyes on the road.

We drive the length of the village in two minutes, then turn around and park facing south on Arturo Prat, the main street, one of only two paved roads. Finding a spot is easy; cars are scarce in minuscule Pisagua. My slim hope of seeing an Esso or Shell station here fizzles to zero. I think of the steep switchbacks, and the fuel we'll burn just climbing back to the Panamericana. Somehow, we need to find gas.

To the right of our car is a small but surprisingly well-maintained waterfront plaza, with shade trees, a curving concrete esplanade and several nineteenth-century cannons aimed at the ocean. To our left are, from north to south: a hotel that used to be a concentration camp; a fenced-in playground with basketball hoops, as well as miniature soccer goals for *baby fútbol*; and a row of small, hardscrabble houses, one displaying a 5' by 4' bright yellow SpongeBob SquarePants doll on its flat roof.

These juxtapositions are not easy to reconcile, or even to process. We postpone trying and stroll to the plaza, feel the sun on our faces, watch the waves break on the rocks. Christine and Panchy pose on a cannon and I take their picture. We're the only people here. Was this park built for tourists, a pleasant promenade a few feet from the hotel? Presumably the ocean view rooms were more expensive. Did any rooms have a view to the north, to the grim cube right behind with its barred windows? Just bars—no glass to muffle the screams inside.

We cross the street. My goal on this pilgrimage is to see the prison hotel, and we do—but only from the outside, and not even looking in. The front door is locked, the windows shuttered and black. My questions about the interior, about the lobby and the rooms and the ghosts, will remain unanswered. The gringo as outsider, unable to penetrate the past. Sure, I lived in Chile for two and a half years under Pinochet. I knew people who had been imprisoned or tortured. But I can never truly know what the *golpe* had been like, any more than I can know what it was like to fight in Vietnam, my generation's war, or in World War II, the war that transformed my father. The truth, of course, is that I don't want to know, not really, not completely. There's a sad slice of voyeurism in my self-righteous investigation.

Meanwhile, SpongeBob SquarePants is grinning over the playground at three tourists locked out of a dressed-up death camp.

We walk around the three sides of the complex that are accessible. A wall ten feet high extends from the back corners of the hotel and encloses the prison. The east wall is white stucco, on a dirt street parallel to Arturo Prat. The west wall along Prat is bare cinder block. I expected to find the whole place renovated. Instead, the contrast between the attractive hotel and the dire rest of the prison is so stark no one could fail to notice. Even a visitor ignorant of Pisagua's history would wonder about the ugly building next door, if only to speculate why they didn't tear it down to improve the view, or to upgrade the tourist infrastructure.

The town scarcely seems alive. Even the main street is practically deserted, so it takes a while to find someone to ask. A man with a deeply lined, sunbaked face tells us the hotel has been closed for months, maybe a year or more. He can't remember for sure. We thank him and he shuffles down Prat in the slim strip of shade next to the buildings. The hotel had tried to survive, but independent of its miserable karma, the reality is that few visitors come to Pisagua. In this fishing village we had planned to have a memorable seafood lunch, but there's no restaurant. There's no bus service. Of the trains that had hauled tons of nitrate in the mining days, nothing remains but a few sad scraps of rail on the north end of town, and a derelict station partially scavenged for its wood.

The exception occurs in a bizarre confluence every spring. In 1990, a mass grave was discovered on the outskirts of Pisagua: nineteen bullet-riddled bodies in burlap bags, hands tied behind their backs, blindfolds still hiding their eyes. On the last Sunday of October, surviving prisoners, friends, family and others gather at the gravesite to commemorate the murdered prisoners. A few days later, on November 2, there's a military celebration of Chile's 1879 taking of Pisagua from Peru during the War of the Pacific. I doubt that either event ever brought much business to the hotel. Who in the first group could stand to sleep in a building that had housed torturers and killers? For November 2, most of the soldiers presumably bunk in the local *carabinero* barracks. That's if anyone stays in Pisagua at all, rather than heading a few hours south to Iquique after the ceremonies. Even if the hotel did manage to fill during these days, what about the rest of the year?

On Prat at the north end of town, only a five-minute walk from the prison, we find a small red building with signs that read Museum and Tourist Office. The door is locked. Panchy tries the old rotary dial phone outside that supposedly alerts the owner at home. No one answers. We press our faces to the window but can see next to nothing inside.

Then we turn around and see the mural.

It's painted on the side wall of a nondescript one-story building, nestled in the wide V created by Pisagua's only other paved street, angling north off Prat and parallel to the ocean until petering into dirt after a few hundred feet. From Prat you could easily miss the mural, but from this spot it's unmistakable, a blue-gray rectangle a shade darker than the prison, stretching thirty feet to the back corner of the building, where it meets the lighter blue backdrop of the Pacific. It's painted in six sections, alternating words and images:

"What hurts most is not defeat, nor the shameless hegemony of the ever-powerful, or even the pardon of the executioners to their victims, the most painful thing is to forget, to make a deal with the past on the altar of an authoritarian and optimistic democratic present."[18]

A red hammer and sickle

"The memory of suffering obliges us to always struggle to keep democracy democratic, true democracy and not just a decorative mask on a system in which property rights subjugate all other rights, and which grants freedom of expression only to those who can pay for it..."[19]

An executed, blindfolded prisoner

"25 YEARS PISAGUA
NOTHING IS FORGOTTEN!!"[20]

---

18 *Lo que más duele no es la derrota, tampoco la hegemonía descaradada de los poderosos de siempre en el proceso, ni siquiera el perdón de los verdugos a sus víctimas, lo mas doloroso es siempre el olvido, el tener que pactar el pasado, en aras de un presente autoritario y optimista democrático...*

19 *La memoria del dolor nos ha obligado siempre a luchar para que la democracia sea democracia, democracia de verdad en vez de ser apenas la decorativa careta de un sistema en que el derecho de propiedad sacrifica los demás derechos y que solo otorga libertad de expresión a quienes puedan pagarla...*

20 *NADA ESTA OLVIDADO!!*

A prisoner seen from behind with his hands on his head, as if being marched to his death.

"25 Years" means the mural must have been painted in 1998 or 1999. It's still in good shape, except for a few vandalized patches on the hammer and sickle. A communist symbol won't sit well with everyone no matter where you go, and it's especially inflammatory in Chile.

To me, though, the amazing thing is that the mural is there at all. Nothing like it could have existed when I lived in this country, five years after the Pisagua atrocities. I'd see an occasional bit of anti-Pinochet graffiti, hastily spray painted or scrawled on a wall, but nothing like this mural, carefully created with no fear of retribution, despite the *carabineros* barracks just up the street. The *carabineros* had been part of Pinochet's government, along with the army, navy and air force; the commanders of each branch formed the four-man military junta. Anyone caught painting such a mural in the late 70s would almost certainly be charged with sedition and severely punished. At minimum a prison term, at worst killed and *desaparecido*. For a famous person, if the government hoped to avoid negative international publicity, possibly exile from Chile.

Panchy wanders off while Christine and I look at the mural. Soon we hear her calling to us. Outside the nearby Teatro Municipal she has met a man who offers to give us a tour of the locked theater. The 1892 building is run down, but not wretchedly so. It had been built during the nitrate boom, when ships arrived from all over the world, the English were making huge profits, and as many as 6,000 people lived here. (Now there are fewer than 200.) In the balcony, several dusty mannequins dressed in Victorian costumes wait for the next performance. Our guide, a pleasant, fleshy guy around thirty, says the theater is occasionally still used. He doesn't mention that the theater was where women prisoners were detained in 1973 and 1974. Were these creepy mannequins there at that time, stiff in their wooden chairs, staring dead-eyed from the balcony at the women herded below?

He takes us next door to another substantial building, obviously designed to house more than the tiny library there now. I'm impressed that a library exists in Pisagua at all. The back part of the structure bumps up against the Pacific. It had been a warehouse in the town's glory days, with large, barn-like doors in the rear wall for loading and unloading. Antiquated machinery and other artifacts lie strewn about the concrete floor. Sunlight streams through holes in the wooden doors as our guide gives us a history lesson. His stories are interesting, but I keep getting distracted by a doll.

Two adjacent buildings, two examples of inanimate humanity past its prime. Here, instead of mannequins in outdated finery stands a naked doll the size of a five-year-old child, propped against the side brick wall. Although it has the usual sexless crotch of a doll, it seems to be a boy. Its arms are gone, sheared off at the shoulder. Two thoughts grab me and won't let go. One is of a marble angel I saw at the ruined Abbaye de Jumièges in France in 1985. The angel was the same size as the doll and still had its arms, but had been decapitated, its neck worn smooth by time. The other is of Iraqi children being maimed at that moment in a hideous war.

I try to pay attention to our guide, for his sake and for mine. Before long, we thank him and leave the doll behind. We walk north along the beach, keep going past any signs of civilization, climb up and over a rocky outcropping and find a secluded cove. I take a photo of Christine and Panchy in bathing suits, arms around each other, screaming as a frigid wave breaks against their backs. I love seeing their smiles.

But I keep thinking about that doll. How did it lose its arms? How did it end up in that forlorn place? How would it feel to be five years old in a war zone, and have both arms blown off? Or to be a soldier fighting a war in which you get both arms blown off?

I watch the women toweling off on the sand, two pairs of healthy arms at work. Suddenly Panchy shrieks. *"Me picó un tábano! Ai, otra vez!"* Bitten twice by a horsefly. The Chilean variety is big and slow, but if one nails you, it really stings.

Enough of the beach; it's time to go. The questions of the doll recede, replaced by a more immediate one: Where can we find gasoline? I've worried off and on all day about filling the tank. But then I'd think of the prisoners in that grim blue stucco box and tell myself: At least you can leave. Even if you don't make it all the way back, at least you can get out of here.

That line of reasoning is coming up short now. Though vastly preferable to torture, I definitely do not want to be stranded in the desert after dark. Panchy has her cell phone, but who knows if it will work out in the vast, empty *pampa*. This trip was my idea and my responsibility. If anything goes wrong, it's my fault. How could I not have had sense enough to plan ahead and bring a can of fuel, just in case?

These are a few of my thoughts as we head back to town. Another is more prosaic: I need a bathroom. We make for the public *baño* on Prat, which turns out to be so fetid that even my young Peace Corps self would have been revolted (though I've seen, and used, worse). But what matters is not that vile visit. What matters is a blue, long-bed pickup truck with someone tinkering under the hood. It's on the far side of the empty dirt lot buffering the restroom, across the street from the weathered

CLUB DPTVO. PISAGUA building. I don't know what activities the Pisagua Sports [*Deportivo*] Club sanctions, or how long it has been since its doors last opened. But I know that trucks need gasoline.

José the mechanic turns out to be a good guy. He owns the truck and makes a living hauling goods between Pisagua and Iquique. Unfortunately for us, that means he always fills up in Iquique, and doesn't need to carry gas. But José has a suggestion.

"*Pregunte arriba a Don Julio.*" He gestures up the hill with an oily wrench. "*Puede ser que el tenga bencina.*"

"*Un millón de gracias.*"

"*Nada. Buena suerte.*"

We get the car, turn around and negotiate rutted dirt roads to the only street on higher ground parallel to Prat and the ocean—another rutted dirt road. José's directions are simple, and Don Julio's ramshackle compound is hard to miss. I'm not sure where his property begins and ends, but it appears to comprise at least three buildings, and two small fenced-in yards stuffed with a daunting array of potentially useful junk.

"Don Julio!" I call, and Panchy joins in. "Don Julio! Don Julio!" We move to different spots outside the compound and keep shouting. Minutes pass. Hope fades.

A teenage boy walks around the corner, licking a melting red popsicle.

"*Sabe si Don Julio está?*" I ask.

He shrugs. "*Grite más fuerte. El está medio sordo.*" ("Yell louder. He's half deaf.") He joins in our "Don Julio" chorus. Suddenly a door opens, near the back fence. A wizened, walnut-brown face peers out from under a battered canvas hat.

"*Allí está,*" the boy says, and continues on his way.

Panchy explains our plight as Don Julio slowly picks a path through the junk. He wears a long sleeve gray shirt with just the middle two buttons fastened above his paunch. He puts a hand to his ear and we realize he has heard nothing. When he reaches the gate she repeats our story, and asks if we can buy gas. He hesitates just long enough for me to worry.

"I could do that." His wrinkled face creases further with a smile. "650 *pesos el litro.*"

"*Bueno.*" Gas costs 490 a liter in Arica, but I'm obviously ready to pay whatever Don Julio asks. He unlatches the gate, comes out and removes the padlock from the doors of a semitrailer in his yard that opens onto the street. I see oil drums inside and a memory hits me: Don Roberto, a.k.a. the Chilean Flem Snopes. Just before Christmas, 1979, PCVs Mike Welsh, Jocko Vertin and I had encountered Don Roberto in Ralún, a southern Chile hamlet of six houses on the Río Petrohue. He ran the rope-drawn ferry there, which as far as we could see was the only reason for the town's existence. He looked like a runty Sean Penn who'd smoked two packs a day for sixty years. Don Roberto shamelessly overcharged us for everything from food to boat rental, then had the gall to steal the mess kits we left outside our tent. (We had no proof that he did it, but also no doubt.)

Fortunately, Don Julio doesn't seem sleazy at all. He fills two wicker-covered, five-liter wine *chuicas* from the drum. He's 82, he tells us, a lifelong Pisaguan. I wonder how far his longest trip has been. I wonder if he has ever left the desert.

Don Julio has two funnels. I try both, but they're too big to fit in the tank. We finally find gas and can't get it in the car? Don Julio rummages in his truck and finds a four-foot orange hose on the filthy floor. He offers it to me. "*Sifón,*" he says. "*No hay problema.*"

The last time I siphoned gas, in the distant days of my youth, I nearly puked, then tasted gas for a week.

131

"Be a man," Panchy says. "Come on." She's not joking, and I don't like her a whole lot right now.

Don Julio sees my hesitation and rescues me. I gratefully cede any macho honor to his expertise. He sucks a bit, spits once, and soon the fuel is flowing. I hold the jug high and let gravity do its job. We repeat the process for the second bottle, and my fear of being stranded fades like yesterday. I tend to forget how sweet relief is until I need some, like taking good health for granted until the sudden spike of a headache, or the first gassy rumblings in the gut.

We thank our savior and drive off, but within seconds I stop. After the row of buildings that contains Don Julio's compound, to the right the hill steepens and nothing is built there. Fifty yards below are the prison hotel and the baby football field. Bizarre yellow SpongeBob is grinning over on the roof. We get out to take a final few pictures. I'm framing a hotel shot—ocean backdrop, shoreline hills vanishing in the misty horizon—when I realize that Don Julio's house directly overlooks the prison.

I'd been too focused on finding gas to notice the obvious. Don Julio said he'd lived in Pisagua his whole life. What had he seen, and done, in 1973 and 1974, a man then in his early fifties? The door we saw him emerge from is at most a hundred feet from the prison wall. The screams of the tortured had to have been audible from there. Hell, they must have been loud enough to wake a man from a nightmare. Maybe Don Julio wishes he'd been deaf thirty years ago. How amazing it would be to interview him, to sift through his memories. Show up with a few bottles of wine or pisco, drink deep into the darkness, search for *veritas* in the *vino* and the night.

Too late for that now: the chance is gone and won't likely come again. I drive up the switchbacks far faster than I'd crept down, and soon Pisagua is lost in the rearview. Somewhere past

132

Cuya, primeval dusk begins to settle over the *pampa*. Nowhere in the world have I seen skies so full of stars as in the empty Atacama Desert, far away from cities and their lights that push back the night.

But not this time. The longest day of the year was scarcely a week ago. It won't be full dark until late, and the three of us just want to get home.

CHAPTER TEN

The Past on Paper

"Isn't an artist's life honestly lived a kind of slow recuperation, a recovery of lost spirit, a knitting of broken time?"

—Robert Grudin, *Book*

On the wall of Hugo and Any's bedroom are dozens of photographs, arranged under glass. The oldest, faded ones chronicle times a decade or more before I came to Arica. I point out to Christine the faces I can identify. Most of the shots from my era were taken by me, so I'm only in a couple that I did with the timer: pushing the button, rushing to join the group then watching the red light blink until the shutter clicked. I don't recall Hugo taking a single picture in those days. If he had a camera, I never saw it. Photography was a luxury he couldn't afford.

135

Christine smiles at a shot of me with my arm around Hugo's shoulders, both of us beaming. She taps the glass. "I love this one. Where is it?"

"In my room by the pizzeria."

She nods. "I wish we could have gone in there." Her arm slips around my waist. "You're so into documenting everything. Have Hugo and Any taken any pictures since we've been here?"

"Now that you mention it, I don't think so."

Maybe it wasn't just lack of funds that explained why Hugo hadn't been a photographer. He can afford a camera now; hell, there's one in his cell phone. Evidently Hugo and Any just aren't much interested in taking pictures. Yet one way or another they have accumulated, and evidently treasure, these paper memories on the wall.

My Peace Corps memories began on January 4, 1978, when I arrived in Miami after two and a half hours sleep my last night in Connecticut. Following instructions from the Peace Corps (including a reminder to tip drivers and bellhops), I took a van from the airport and checked into the Howard Johnson hotel around noon. My roommate, Terry Stanley from Tucson, was already there. To my surprise he told me he had only joined the Peace Corps to perfect his Spanish, which he already spoke quite well from living near Mexico. We went to two orientation meetings that day, the second at 8 P.M., then headed straight to our room. We were beat.

I decided to do some sit-ups before bed. Within seconds Terry said, "Tom, you'll kill your back that way." I was doing them as I'd been taught, hands behind my head, elbows alternately touching each bent knee. "Just go up far enough to feel your stomach muscles tighten. Hold it there for a few counts—that's where you get the benefit. Go any farther and all you do is stress your back and distend your gut, not flatten it."

136

I gave it a try. Immediately I saw—and felt—that his way was better. How could I have never noticed before?[21] One of my college professors told us of an anthropologist who studied a society where all the older women were painfully hunchbacked. Why should that be? Then he noticed that the brooms they used had very short handles. A lifetime of bent-over sweeping with short-handled brooms had ruined their backs. Evidently it never occurred to anyone to lengthen the handles. Brooms had short handles; that's just the way it was. At the time I wondered how they could be so stupid, or at least so blind, never imagining that I might have my own blind spots.[22] Terry's sit-up demonstration was humbling. How many other things in my life did I do lemming-like, accepting without thinking, simply because that's how I was taught, or the way I'd always done it? It was my first Peace Corps lesson.

I took a photo of Terry with my Canon FTb, practicing with the new flash I'd bought. I asked Terry what kind of camera he had.

"I don't own a camera," he said.

---

21 When I was in school the common wisdom was not to drink water during sports practice, because "it will make you sick." We only felt sick *after* practice, from gulping ridiculous quantities of water into our dehydrated bodies.

22 Soon after arriving in Santiago I went to a cafe and ordered *una hamburguesa y una cerveza*. I squirted ketchup from a plastic bottle and took a bite of the burger. I knew the stereotype about fiery Latin cuisine, but still was surprised at how spicy that mouthful was. My sips of Cristal pilsener turned to gulps to try and put out the fire. I ordered another beer and slathered on more ketchup to mask the heat, but every bite was hotter than the last. I ordered a third beer (two more than I'd planned on drinking), squeezed on lots more ketchup and forced myself to finish, then walked out into the sunshine unexpectedly tipsy and breathing fire, wondering how I could possibly survive this food for two years.

My new Chilean friends burst out laughing when they heard the story. That red stuff I poured on to beat the culinary heat wasn't ketchup, it was ají—hot pepper sauce!

"Are you serious? You don't want photos?"

He smiled and touched a finger to his head. "They're all in here."

"But what if you want to show them to other people?"

He paused, as if somehow that thought had never occurred to him. Terry smiled again, a bit crookedly this time. "You might have a point there," he said.

What neither of us realized in our naive youth was that someday *we* would need to be shown. I haven't seen Terry since 1979, but I guarantee he wouldn't tap his temple today and claim every picture from Chile is still in his head. At least he wouldn't claim he can locate them all. A complete life history might linger in some dusty corner of each brain's attic, but if so, our paths to them is blocked by all manner of detritus we'd gladly jettison if we could. I've talked to many friends about our adventures and misadventures, trying to get every detail right for this book. The one constant I discovered? We're all astonished by how much we've forgotten. Such is the lot of human wanderers in the hazy maze of time.

I could not write this book—not remotely accurately, anyway—without the help of photographs, and especially if I hadn't kept a journal during my Peace Corps days. (I use the singular "my journal" for convenience; I filled nearly six notebooks in South America.) My friends marvel at my supposedly excellent memory, but re-reading my journal I'm amazed at how many people, places, events—and thoughts, oh yes, thoughts—have drifted away down unknown trails. They're gone, even with the journal to remind me that they once existed. In some passages, fortunately covering only hours, not days, it's almost as if I'm reading about someone else. Of course, in a sense that's true: I was a different person at twenty-two than I am today. But that's not what I mean here. I'm talking about absolutely zero recollection of certain pieces of my life, as if I'm learning facts for the first time from a stranger's story.

More often, thankfully, the journal kick-starts my memory. Time and again I've been writing about some piece of my past, then opened my journal for confirmation or catalysis. It has been a useful record of facts, but far more important are the observations and confessions by the person I used to be. Sometimes I'm impressed when I read them; sometimes I cringe. And sometimes, for purposes of this book, I try to be a dispassionate detective.

The first clue is my handwriting, what grade school teachers used to call penmanship. In the Peace Corps, mine was still good. There it is on the lined notebook pages, a fairly graceful cursive that would bring, if not glory, at least no great shame to devotees of the Palmer Method. In those days I took my time, forming my letters carefully. Today, my handwriting has devolved into a printing/cursive hybrid scrawl that reflects my transformation into a more Type A personality. I've got responsibilities; let's get this task done and move on to the next item on the list—and there's always a next item. Patience is a virtue I don't have time for anymore.

That sounds glib and I suppose it is. It's also largely true. Summers don't stretch endlessly before me the way they did when I was a kid. Adults know winter is waiting in the wings, with another summer nudging it from behind, ready to melt the snows of yesteryear and be buried by a blizzard in turn. Time means more to me now. It's more precious and more terrifying.

I still keep a journal. I also have writer's notebooks with dated entries (the first is June 1, 1977), scraps of language that might spark my writing later on. My writer friend Chuck Rosenthal told me years ago he doesn't keep a notebook, that if he doesn't remember something it's a sign it wasn't important. Possibly, but I don't want my fickle memory in charge of deciding what matters. Better to record something before it can slip away. Maybe I'll use it someday, probably not; I'll let the future me figure that out. I can't presume to decide now, and memory is not only tricky, it's treacherous.

Step two of my detective work involves reading letters. Letters are a tangible piece of the past on paper, because the kind of paper, writing implement, handwriting, stamp, postmark and envelope reveal an individual personality. The "same" letter is different if written on lined (college ruled or wide ruled?) or unlined paper; or a sheet ripped from a spiral notebook with ragged paper tags on one side; or fancy stationery; or onionskin paper; or a blue aerogram[23]; or a postcard; or a telegram (a method we used fairly often to communicate quickly in Chile). It's different if typed (manual? electric? laser printed?) or written in pencil or pen (ballpoint? felt tip? fountain?), with blue or black or whatever color ink. It's different if comfortably slipped into a business envelope, awkwardly folded and crammed into a smaller one, or stuffed into a 10 X 13 envelope along with news clippings and photographs. (One of the first things I notice is how thick an envelope is and speculate on what's inside.) I got letters in Chile with words and/or drawings on the envelopes that made me laugh before I even opened them. The time an envelope arrived with "SHORTS MY EAT" on the flap, under a sketch of a gap-toothed cretin, I knew I'd soon be grinning at a gonzo epistle from Jay Clark.

It had been decades since I'd looked at the letters I received in Chile. I'd been using my journal all along to write this book,

---

23 Aerograms are already a thing of the past, so I'd better define the term. It's a single sheet of flimsy paper with gummed flaps, that when folded and licked turns the paper into an extremely light envelope with nothing inside but your words. They were the cheapest way to send an overseas airmail letter.

but not until this chapter did I trudge to the basement for my first box of letters. (A box of more recent letters, also long unread, is in my second-floor office.) The only problem was the addictive nature of the research: dozens upon dozens of letters, full of information and sentiments largely forgotten and therefore as interesting to me as the day I first read them. Possibly *more* interesting, because I perused them with the gift and curse of hindsight. Many hours passed before I wrote another word, unfolding instead piece after piece of the past on paper.

I browsed unsystematically, reading randomly, avoiding a few I feared would be more painful than helpful. The letters brought the past to life and left me wistful, grateful, nostalgic. Elation and sadness intertwined like clematis vines with poison ivy. Take care separating them, or you can kill the flowering plant you want. I'd rather let the weed live than sacrifice beauty to destroy it.

Unfortunately, investigating the letters is a one-way street. I have only those that I received, not the ones I sent. Unlike Hunter S. Thompson, who always used carbon paper in his typewriter (demonstrating an ego matched only by his foresight), I didn't keep copies of letters I wrote. I could ask my friends if they still have any of them, but I'm pretty sure of the answer. Only oddballs like my father and me put such a premium on struggling to retain what's gone—and, sometimes, to pretending that it isn't.

Both of my boxes of letters are overflowing, but I doubt that I'll need a third one. Hardly anyone writes letters anymore. I occasionally get a card with a very welcome written message, but a good old-fashioned letter? It's been years. Just about everyone today uses e-mail, text-messaging or social media to communicate. My stepdaughter Maggie, born in 1974, is from the last American generation that knows what it's like to write and receive letters, before the ease and immediacy of the internet transformed communication. People have been transformed as a result.

Writing and mailing a letter involves commitment, trust and patience (and sometimes, frustration). No one thinks twice about sending a one-sentence, or even a one-word, e-mail or text. When you bother to write a letter, though, you commit to spending some time in its creation. Then you entrust it to the post office, which in some parts of the world is a huge leap of faith, and wait. Days, weeks, even months can elapse before the letter is delivered (*if* it's delivered), then the entire process has to be repeated in the other direction for you to get a response. Therefore, letters happen less often, but mean more when they do.

I'm being neither a Luddite nor holier-than-thou. If I haven't received a real paper letter in years, I've hardly written any, either. Like most of the world, I'm in thrall to the utilitarian efficiency of electronic communication. It's wonderful to connect with someone within seconds. For travelers, especially, a portable address where you can receive messages anywhere in the world there's an internet connection sure beats the old way: haunting American Express offices in hopes that mail arrives before you leave the city. It's great to get e-mail from an internet cafe halfway around the world, but it's even better when a letter or postcard arrives from the same locale, with an exotic stamp and postmark. Holding the artifact in my hand, I feel an almost mystical sense that other hands—unknown hands in unknown places—have cooperated to deliver these words to my door. The whole process feels more human. A letter is a tangible object, touched by the sender and now by me. That means something; that's a connection. I could print out an e-mail, even put it in a box of letters, but the human connection is attenuated: the writer's fingers never touched that piece of paper, never physically placed the words upon it, never stained it with a leaky pen, a drop of wine or a tear. Electrons, not human hands, delivered it to me.[24]

If I had been a Peace Corps Volunteer in Chile more recently, virtually all of my correspondence, both in-country and around the world, would have been via e-mail or texting. Even my parents might have bought a computer under the circumstances, something they never did otherwise. Consequently, I'd have no box of letters now, no cache of the past on paper, or at least a far smaller one.

Advances in communication have surely changed the Peace Corps experience. Except for Volunteers in truly remote areas, keeping in frequent contact with family and friends is as easy as logging on to a computer or turning on a smartphone. Internet cafes are common, especially in places where few people have a computer at home. It seems like ancient history to read an AT&T ad in the November, 1966 *National Geographic* that brags, "Today you can reach 96.8 percent of the phones in the world by Long Distance. You can ask questions, get the answers...quickly and conveniently. And the cost is low. For only $12, plus tax, for the first three minutes, you can call almost anywhere in the world." $12 to talk for three minutes—and that's in 1966 dollars! What would that be today, fifty bucks or more? Obviously, the definitions of "quickly" and "conveniently," not to mention "low cost," have modified over the years.

My two best Chilean friends, Veronica Inostroza in Santiago and Hugo Buitano in Arica, did not have a telephone. Phones were expensive, and there was a waiting list to get one installed. Veronica's neighbor had a phone, and she would occasionally

---

24 I have a 1912 Gibson mandolin. Sometimes I cradle it in my hands and with something akin to reverence ponder the unknowable: what fingers have played it over the years, what places it has been, what secrets it could tell, but never will.

go next door to make or receive a call. Hugo taught English part-time at the Instituto Chileno-Norteamericano and could use their phone if he needed to. But he rarely did. When I lived in Santiago with ex-PCV baseball coach David Osinski and his Chilean wife Nancy, there was a phone in the house, an old black clunker whose heavy receiver had somehow been snapped in the middle and cobbled together with athletic tape like a broken ankle. The phone came in handy, though as often as it saved time or made our lives easier, it wasted time by allowing some bozo to find us who we'd rather avoid. (No answering machine or caller ID in those days.)

I had no phone in Arica. What I sheepishly admit seems to me a virtual necessity now, for the most part we lived quite happily without. Once or twice during my twenty months in Arica I walked downtown to the Compañia de Telefonos to call my parents. Calls were expensive, you had to wait your turn for a phone, and the overseas connections were lousy (in addition to the background hiss that all long-distance calls had before fiber optic cables). Since the room was always crowded, the din of voices all trying to be heard added to the ambience.

Given the ease of staying connected with those left behind, it would be human nature for PCVs today not to disengage as completely from home, not to immerse themselves as completely in their host country society. Making new friends might not feel so urgent if you can talk daily to old ones. Some PCVs might be less homesick as a result of this constant connection, and therefore less likely to bail out before their two years are up. Others might be *more* homesick. The variables are endless, and I'm no psychologist; my point is simply that Peace Corps life, like life everywhere, is different now than in the past. And with every passing day, less of that past is on paper.

That includes the work that writers do. I've seen a fair copy of *The Great Gatsby* in F. Scott Fitzgerald's handwriting—in pencil, if I remember correctly. Hemingway supposedly drafted thirty-six endings for *A Farewell to Arms*. Recently, a previously unknown, handwritten manuscript of *Huckleberry Finn* was discovered, complete with Mark Twain's corrections, cross-outs and revisions. It's fascinating to study these documents that show a writer's mind at work. Increasingly, though, such pieces of history cease to exist. Most writers use computers now, which allow quick, easy—and invisible—changes to be made. No need to cross out words, or scrawl changes in the margins with arrows indicating insertion points. Most revisions happen on the screen, never to be printed in "hard copy." I have made thousands of changes so far in this book, only a small fraction of which ever appeared on paper. When writers created using pen, pencil or typewriter, virtually every word was put on paper. Not all drafts were saved, obviously. But a lot more of the past was on paper. Much more of the past was available to the future.

That also applies to photographs. Until recently, photos were printed on paper. Special photographic paper, to be sure, but paper, which could then be reproduced on the common paper of books, magazines and newspapers. Some people shot slide film, but the vast majority of photos became prints. Today, digital cameras make the paper format optional and increasingly irrelevant for people accustomed to viewing electronic screens. Photo albums are for older people with their older ways, who stick with what they're used to. Why bother to print a photo when you can call it up on your phone or computer screen anytime you want? The picture is waiting obediently for you in the nowhere but everywhere ether of cyberspace.

I'm not passing judgment on either approach, just pointing out the differences. Each method has its advantages and disadvantages. The quality of film photos is supposedly better, but if you run out of film—no more pictures. With a digital camera, if the memory card is full, just delete some photos to free up space and keep shooting. Of course, with a phone, the way most people take photos now, you don't even need a memory card. If not properly backed up, digital photos can be lost through system crashes or computer malfunctions. Printed photos can be lost in a disaster like a fire or flood, but then so can a computer, and a thief is far more likely to snatch a laptop than a photo album. Prints fade and degrade, especially earlier color film and Polaroid instant photos. Photo negatives stay in good shape far longer, but that only matters if you 1) save them, and 2) can find them years later. Do digital pictures remain pristine indefinitely? If so, they're the first human creation able to make that claim.

Photos, like written or recorded words, often outlast the people who created them, or the people they depict. Our memories only survive as long as we do, unless we put them in some communicable form. Experience has taught me to label the people and places in my photos. Even in the unlikely event that my memory never fails me, what about someone looking at the photos after I'm gone? Provide information for the future; create links. I have a photo of my paternal grandparents' wedding, ten people posing outside in the bloom of a youth that looks immediately old-fashioned to me, yet was their "normal," their unquestioned and unexamined "way it is." There are three bare trees in the background but no one seems cold. The wedding party is lined up on a strip of dark cloth, presumably to protect their clothes from mud, so I'm guessing that it's early spring, maybe 1913. Probably most if not all of them are Slovakian immigrants.

Everyone in the photo is a mystery to me except for my grandparents, standing with arms linked in the center, both wearing white gloves. (They're a mystery to me too, but at least

I can identify them, though in incarnations foreign to anything I ever saw.) I removed the back of the frame, hoping for help, but found no labels, no annotations. I have no idea why the man on the far left (with his rakehell mustache) and the woman on the far right (the only female not wearing white, and not carrying flowers) are sitting, while the others stand. I wonder if the two solemn flower girls, five or six years old, are sisters. Possibly I met them when I was a kid, and they were old women with childhood memories of that wedding day.

My brother Don's wife Maria has an old family photo with a man conspicuously cut out, cropped like Trotsky from official Soviet photos. All that remains is his hand on a woman's shoulder. Someone wanted to rip him from history, to transform him into a non-person—and it worked. No one in Maria's family knows who he was, though her mother Mary Ann theorizes that he was removed to keep him anonymous, in an attempt to protect him from raiding Cossacks. Despite retaining their faces, the anonymous people at my grandparents' wedding are also essentially non-persons. Their names and personalities are gone. *They're* gone; probably no one alive remembers them. Any thoughts or judgments I make are pure speculation deriving from this elusive surface, a posed, artificial instant frozen in black and white—all that remains of their lives. Who got drunk that day? Who made love? Who saw something he or she never forgot? Who wandered outside that night, peered up at the stars and thought for a long time, alone, then shivered a little and walked back through the damp grass to rejoin a patch of light filled with laughter?

Sometimes the past is on paper where you least expect it. I have a 5 x 7, black and white photo of my father sitting across from two friends at a restaurant booth. They're all wearing suits and smiling, the two men at the camera, my dad at his friends. He looks trim and handsome, almost dapper, like F. Scott Fitzgerald. On the broadly striped tablecloth are two packs of cigarettes, though Dad and one other man are holding cigars. They're drinking a bottle of Imperator champagne, with ice cubes in their glasses. Above the photo, on the thick paper frame, is "Sept. 1945" in black ink from what looks like a cartridge pen: Dad's handwriting. He has been home from the war since June, after three years with the 809th Engineering Battalion in Europe and North Africa. He is thirty years old.

According to its fold-over cover, the photo is a "Souvenir of GUSTL'S Rendezvous," which offered "Dancing — Entertainment Nitely" in Elizabeth, New Jersey. Under a drawing of four nattily dressed couples are the words "HARRY VOSBURGH, Mgr." The back of the frame says "SOUVENIR PHOTO-GRAPH $1.00." So, I know more about the nightclub than I do about the two men with my father.

I was adjusting the photo in its frame, trying to read a poster hanging behind them on the wood-paneled wall, when I noticed a small, pale half-moon next to one man's left ear. Careful not to tear it, I lifted the frame on the right side and uncovered a woman's face peering curiously over her shoulder at the camera. She's not smiling. I have no idea whether she expects to be in the picture. Her chin is hidden behind two men's shoulders; neither of her ears is visible. From halfway through her left eye that side of her face disappears off the edge of the photo. It was a shock to see her, to find her right there yet out of sight. Weirder still was realizing that my father might not be smiling at his friends, but rather at that woman in the next booth, turning toward the flash bulb. Did he know her? That will remain a mystery, but I'd guess that he didn't. I think she just happened to notice the photographer, happened to look back at the right instant and became a peripheral part of the frozen moment, then returned to her life and left theirs. Maybe somewhere in a musty box or a dusty attic there's a photo of the group at her table, taken just before or just after my father's—another $1.00 Souvenir of Gustl's Rendezvous, bought when a buck was still a buck, when that dollar could have put four gallons of gas in your Studebaker, which an attendant would pump for you, as well as wash your windows without asking and check the oil.

She's no more of a stranger to me than my dad's two friends are, because outside of the date, he didn't label the photo. He assumed he'd never forget their names, but that's no help to me. Almost surely, they're army buddies from the 809th Battalion; presumably they're among the soldiers mentioned in my dad's World War II diary.

I wonder how often my father looked at this picture over the years. Rarely, if he was like me with my photos—but he knew it was there, and that was enough. Did he remember the woman, hidden just out of sight? Possibly he never checked below the frame and didn't know she *was* there. If so, maybe he forgot she ever existed—that is, if he even noticed her in the first place.

When my maternal grandfather died, I inherited his pocket watch. Walt Lindner had been one of the best athletes in Connecticut. Everyone said he would have been a major league pitcher if only he had a little more size and a little more luck: he hurt his arm on a pickoff throw to first base while playing professionally in New Haven and was never the same. At 5' 7" and 145 pounds he dominated high school batters and was a star in the minor leagues and for the Deep River town team from the 1920s to the 1940s. (Later in life he was an avid duckpin bowler, and for a time held the world record for high triple; i.e., three-game score.) In those days most towns fielded a baseball team, and their games were a big deal. My dad told me that Sunday afternoon games when he was a young man were practically like the circus coming to town. Some folks had cars but more people didn't, and there'd be a festive parade of vehicles and pedestrians streaming toward the ballpark. Blue laws reigned in Connecticut then, so stores were closed on Sunday; there was no television or the myriad other distractions available to us today. This event was literally the biggest game in town, and a lot was riding on it: local pride, a sense of community—and plenty of dollars.

Somehow the monetary angle had never occurred to me. If anyone was betting on my high school baseball games, I sure didn't know about it. But a big leaguer set me straight about the way things used to be. Paul Hopkins, born in Chester, Connecticut in 1904, pitched part of two seasons for the Washington Senators. He was locally famous for giving up—on the big stage, in Yankee Stadium—Babe Ruth's 59th home run in 1927, the year Ruth set the record of 60 that stood till Roger Maris hit 61 in 1961. One day out of the blue I called Mr. Hopkins, and he graciously invited some guy he'd never met to come visit him. I drove to his apartment in Deep River—a second floor walk-up for a man over ninety years old—and spent a fascinating few hours asking questions and listening to his stories.

He'd appeared on the Johnny Carson show and in Ken Burns' *Baseball* documentary, but the story that matters here involves a less glorious incident when he pitched poorly in a town league game, and Chester lost. As he left the park an old woman screamed at him, reamed him out in language you'd never knew people used back then if your only source was Hollywood movies. She had lost money betting on Chester and wasn't shy about informing Paul that it was his fault. He told me people bet all the time on those games; I didn't ask, but it's safe to assume some players were among those with greenbacks on the line.

What does this have to do with my grandfather's watch? Nothing that I'd expected, or was ready for. I hadn't looked at the watch in twenty years or more when I found it in a drawer, sharing a small box with wheat sheaf pennies, superannuated New York subway tokens, Brazilian cruzeiros worth fractions of a cent, a metal coach's whistle from God knows where, a card that supposedly measures your stress level when you press it with your thumb, a plastic dreidel, photos of my wife from elementary school.... To be honest, I'd forgotten the watch entirely.

The crystal was yellowed with age and marred by three ancient brown strips of what once might have been scotch tape. Engraved on the silver back were my grandfather's initials, WFL, cursive and heavily stylized to fit in a circle, as hard to read as the psychedelic letters on a Fillmore West concert poster. Thrilled at finding the watch—and guilty that I'd neglected it—I took it to a watchmaker to see about restoration. He told me he could fix the mechanism, make it good as new, but the watch face would be forever corroded by the acrylic crystal that people at the time thought was a wonderful new material, less likely than glass to scratch or shatter.[25]

"No big deal," he said. "The scars give it character." He pried at the watch and the back swung open, revealing a compartment I had no idea was there. Inside the door was a round piece of paper cut to fit, a black and white photograph of my grandparents, smiling cheek to cheek in the sunshine. Engraved on the inside silver surface of the watch were these words in lovely, flowing script:

---

[25] I'm reminded of restorers with good intentions who messed up paintings while attempting to save them, and da Vinci's "The Last Supper," painted on the dining hall wall of the Santa Maria delle Grazie monastery. To avoid the rush the fresco technique required, Leonardo invented a new process that he thought would let him work slowly and carefully, with time to revise. The result was a masterpiece that didn't stick. The painting soon began to degrade, and Leonardo watched his artistry flake away before his eyes.

To Walt Lindner
from the fans of
Deep River
Sept. 8th 1929

Thanks from the people of Deep River, many of whom had surely collected on bets because of Walt Lindner's skill at pitching a baseball. My grandfather must have been an amazing player to earn such adulation, not to mention such an expensive gift. I remembered throwing to him in his small front yard when I was a kid, burning it in as hard as I could, Grampy crouching to give me a target and catching the ball barehanded. My mother and grandmother warned him to be careful. I was only five or six, but big for my age with a good arm, and I couldn't have been more than twenty feet away. He waved away their concern, grinning with the joy of playing catch with his grandson. Not for a second did I worry about him. Whether that was from confidence in my grandfather or a selfish desire to keep throwing, I don't know. Probably both. He handled all my pitches with ease, then lit another Marlboro from the pack in his shirt pocket.

The photo slipped out and fluttered face down on the counter. A date stared back at us, written in black ink, or possibly blue ink darkened with time: Oct. 15, 1929. Five weeks after Walt Lindner received the watch. Two weeks before the stock market crash that delivered the coup de grâce to the Roaring Twenties and began the slide into the Great Depression. The writer had miscalculated and begun too close to the center of the circle; the final 9 in 1929 is cramped at the edge of the paper, though its stem extends well below the other numbers, like a tadpole's tail.

Whose handwriting is it?

I hadn't found the watch yet when I began writing about the past on paper. To my surprise, though, it became a perfect metaphor for this chapter, combining the elements of writing, photography and time. But this perfection makes me feel a bit cheap, as if I'm exploiting it for my purposes. I don't really believe that; if I did, I'd stop writing. Yet there's a nagging whisper in the rusty bucket of my brain that I'm a fraud, a poseur, a grabber of what's gone like a creep who steals rocks from a historic stone wall to build a barbecue pit.

The watch and the photograph rest on a notebook next to my computer. At intervals I reach for them, study them, literally holding the past while trying to hold on to it. My grandparents look impossibly young, two kids in love preserved on a fragile paper disk scarcely over an inch in diameter, edges slightly curled, traces of mildew staining the circumference.

Oct. 15, 1929. Two weeks before the Crash. Fifty-one weeks before the birth of my mother.

Whose handwriting is it?

CHAPTER ELEVEN

On Time

"Ah, time is a riddling thing, and hard it is to expound its essence!"

—Thomas Mann, *The Magic Mountain*

New Year's Eve starts with pisco sours in the back yard, Juan Marcos tending the blender. Slowly we progress to champagne, then red wine, with turkey cutlets for our usual late dinner. At midnight, shouts and explosions interrupt the meal, and we fan out in the street to watch fireworks bursting over both El Morro and Chinchorro Beach.

Half an hour later Hugo, Any, Panchy, Juan Marcos, Christine and I squeeze into Chato Rojas and drive to the Casa Degli Italiani, an Italian social club in the Azapa Valley. New Year's Eve is technically already over, but in typical South American style the party has hardly started. We dance to mostly dreadful music, much of it a truly misguided techno-salsa hybrid. The fiesta is still hopping when we leave, passing families with coolers and small children who are just arriving—at 4:30 in the morning.

"When we were young," Hugo says, "on New Year's we'd party here until dawn, sleep on the beach, then dig up a bunch of machas for breakfast."

"Why don't we do that tonight?" I ask.

"Three reasons. The music is too crappy to stay any longer, the machas are gone, and you're too big a pussy to sleep on the beach."

"You can't argue with that logic," Christine says.

"No, and I don't intend to."

"Macha, macha man," Panchy sings.

"Hey, you're young," I tell her. "Why don't *you* go sleep on the beach?"

"Because young people today aren't stupid."

We crash early, at 5:00 A.M. instead of at sunrise, and in beds instead of on sand. How the mighty have fallen. Christine and I get up at 11:30, and I help her with last-minute packing. She's leaving today. Her Christmas break is shorter than mine, and school starts the day after tomorrow.

"I'm totally jealous that you're staying," she says jokingly, but there's no doubt she means it.

"I don't blame you. I would be too." We were originally scheduled to travel together, but a few days ago I paid American Airlines an extortionate fee to postpone my return flight and depart from Santiago instead of Arica. Christine not only supported the idea, she encouraged me to do it, but that doesn't make returning to work and to winter any more inviting.

"You'd better have a lot of fun or I won't forgive you." She takes two steps toward me; I open my arms and we hug. Her fingernails dig briefly into my back. "And don't let those skimpy bathing suits at the beach give you any ideas."

"Come on, dear, you know I don't need bathing suits to get ideas."

"Dog." She gives me a quick bite on the earlobe. Our eyes lock for two seconds, five seconds, seven…until we can't help grinning, and hand in hand head to breakfast.

Hugo and Any drive us to the airport at 1:30. We take photos in the bright sunshine, then inside the small terminal as takeoff time draws near.

"These eight days have flown by," I say.

Christine puts her head on my shoulder. "Pretty corny verb for an airport."

Everyone tries to keep things light, but the farewells turn emotional, the hugs lingering. I'll see my wife in ten days, but who knows how long it will be until she and her new friends are together again.

My return to Chile has had a corollary I never expected: somehow during this week I've come to love Christine more than ever. I take one last photo of her smiling over her shoulder at us from the gate, before she disappears around the corner.

Her plane leaves right on time.

It's a quiet ride back to town. Finally, Hugo speaks.

"OK, Gringo, the party's over. Christine's gone and we want our bed back."

"Hugo! *Pesado!*" Any swats him from the back seat, and the somber mood is broken.

It takes me two minutes to move my things across the hall to Panchy's room. She and Juan Marcos will share Hugo Tomás's twin bed for a few nights, then have the run of the place when Hugo, Any and I go to Santiago. Hugo Tomás already left for

Santiago yesterday, worried about staying away from his dental studies too long.

I transfer three stuffed animals from Panchy's pillow to a bookshelf. Behind the head of the bed are windows that give onto the laundry room, with its clotheslines and *califont*, the gas heater you need to light with a match when you want hot water. I flash back to the first time I saw one of those devices, in France in 1975. I was living with the Bessat family in Clermont-Ferrand for three weeks before spending the academic year in Switzerland, and the first few times I lit the heater to take a shower I worried I'd screw up and blow the house halfway to Paris.

That was over two years before I came to Chile. How can it simultaneously feel like last week, yet so long ago? It's a paradox, but a paradigm of human life as well. After all, we live each day knowing that sooner or later we won't have a next one.

I never saw my French family again. Soon, though, I'll be returning to Santiago, a mini-triumph over time. Sitting on Panchy's sagging bed, listening to Any preparing lunch, I recall how time weighed heavily on me during my first weeks in Chile. Not often, because I was busy learning Spanish and acclimating myself to a new place—and having fun—but occasionally I'd lie in bed, stare at the ceiling and wonder what I was doing there. I was twenty-one years old. Two years stretched dauntingly far into the fog of the future. At one point or another, probably every person in our group had doubts about making it through. But only a few of us left early. Everyone else stuck it out, sharing eventual amazement at how quickly those two endless years disappeared.

One of the first concepts our Peace Corps group learned about in Santiago was *hora chilena*, Chilean time. *Hora chilena* is fluid and imprecise, but never, ever means early. Two o'clock *hora chilena* means "sometime after two o'clock"—possibly long after. The words *"hora chilena"* are rarely expressed, however. The

158

casual attitude toward time is simply taken for granted. On occasions when promptness is necessary or desired, people will add *"hora inglesa"*—English time—to the invitation or information. *Hora inglesa* means an event will (supposedly) truly start at the designated hour, so you should be on time, that quirky English phrase that sounds as if we're standing atop time, or riding it. Or maybe are addicted to it, like being on heroin, though you might also be on the wagon.

At lunch I ask if globalization and standardization, exemplified by the arrival in Chile of worldwide brands like Home Depot, have affected the *hora chilena* attitude.

"Pucha," Any says, "nothing has changed. When I went to England last year with some Chilean schoolteachers, the local organizers got upset with us for always being late." She shakes her head. "That's just the way we are. Eat, Gringo, eat. There's more turkey, more rice."

I've heard claims that chronic lateness is a passive-aggressive way of saying that your time is more important than someone else's. In gringo countries, that might make sense. In Latin countries, so far as I can tell, it's essentially a non-issue. If there's hardly such a thing as "lateness," it's hard to *be* late. Hugo was, however, irked at Hugo Tomás for procrastinating about buying his ticket from Santiago, and therefore getting such a lousy schedule that he not only didn't reach Arica till after Christmas, but had to spend two miserable nights on the bus during the 30-hour trip.

The stereotype would pit American go-getting vs. the Latino *"mañana"* approach. Given the expanding Latino population in the U.S., and the human propensity to stereotype, conflicts about time are likely to intensify. (Here's hoping that a lovely synthesis results, where things get done efficiently but not stressfully, and life is lived, not rushed through like a sprint to a finish line.) As usual, there's a grain of truth to the stereotype, along with a host of exceptions giving it the lie. But it's more a worldview than a question of ambition. What's more important, putting in extra hours at work, or enjoying life with your friends and family?

Conventional wisdom holds that at death's door no one sighs wistfully and says, "Damn, I wish I'd spent more time at the office." There's also the story of a man who slaves his whole life to finally escape the rat race, retire to a seacoast village, live the simple life and fish—which the local people have done all their lives, without stress-filled decades in corporate America to be able to afford it. Yes, there's some ironic truth in the situation. But that guy also has the financial resources to leave anytime he wants, to only fish when he feels like it, to buy a nice house and to receive the best medical care. Thoreau enjoins us to "Simplify, simplify," which sounds like sage advice and usually is. But sometimes more *is* simpler. It's simpler to have more money, and not have to spend most of each day foraging for enough food to fend off starvation. It's simpler to have more living space than to cram fifteen people in a room, and to have more of a retirement plan than hoping that your children take you in.

Often, time only becomes an issue when you have responsibilities, and even then, only when you act on those responsibilities. Personally, I'm lazy, which I suspect places me in the largest category among human beings. But there's lazy, and then there's irresponsible. Irresponsible I'm not, at least not often. In the Peace Corps I'd occasionally get frustrated with some of my colleagues. One returns baseball equipment an hour late, so kids at practice can't even play catch. (Remember, only a few of the richest boys owned gloves.) Another promises to help drive a team to Iquique, four hours away, then never shows up. The line between casual and irresponsible can be blurry, but occasionally I had no doubt that it was crossed. Maybe I was being an uptight gringo, but I think I was just being responsible, like most of the people I worked with.

The American mania for multitasking, for putting every moment to use, can be as irresponsible as it is stressful. I once saw a woman driving while holding a cell phone to her ear and applying makeup with her other hand. Maybe it's a remnant of our Puritan heritage, this compulsion not to "waste" time. But judging by the content of most cell phone conversations I hear (and it's often tough not to hear them), that time would be far better spent listening to birds sing, or watching leaves skitter over a sidewalk, or noticing a sunset cloud shaped like a dachshund wearing a baseball cap.

So much depends on your definition of "waste." If it's a variant of the maxim "time is money," that we should adapt our lives to the principles of Scientific Management and the assembly line, it makes a sad sort of sense to try to make hay while the sun shines and apportion your eggs among several baskets, all while keeping your nose firmly pegged to the grindstone. Some people thought I was wasting my time in the Peace Corps, making barely any money, getting a late start on my "career" (not that I had a clue what that would be). Maybe they'd be more supportive today, since Spanish is useful in business.

I mentioned earlier how we gringos had bristled when a party at the Peace Corps training center shut down at midnight so all could get home before 2:00 A.M. curfew. Let's at least stay till one, we said. That still leaves plenty of time. We resented the dictatorship and its petty rules but were too naive yet to be afraid. The Chileans, on the other hand, had lived through *desaparecidos* and death in the streets. They knew defying the *toque de queda* was idiotic bravado serving no useful purpose. Besides, the training center teachers and our host families were responsible for our safety, so were extra cautious. Not until later, when I really came to understand Chileans, did I realize how much most of them had also wanted to stay at that party. Not only did the curfew undercut the general Latin American penchant for eating dinner late and partying even later, it set an onerous daily deadline—get caught on the street even one minute late and you risked arrest. The curfew was more than the imposition and restriction we gringos felt, more than just a dictator's strong-arm thuggery. It was the ultimate example of *hora inglesa*. It chafed against the national character, the relaxed *hora chilena* attitude toward life.

The curfew was generally less enforced in the provinces than in Santiago, and was lifted sooner. It was gone by the time I moved to Arica in October of 1978. *Hora chilena* reigned, with all that it entailed for good or ill. I had been in Arica for only three weeks when I took a Norte Pullman bus to Iquique to see how well (or even if) the school baseball program was functioning there. Turned out they had more interested kids than Arica did, but none of the teachers who had taken a coaching course were working with a team. Problem. On Saturday I umpired a city championship game for Little League-age boys. The coach of the winning team, Beto Gomez, decided to take his players to the desert oasis of Pica the next day and invited me along. Sounds like fun, I thought, and gratefully accepted. My journal will provide the details:

Sun. Nov. 12 [1978]—Got up at 6.7 A.M. *hora inglesa* [Beto] told me. Bus didn't show till 7:40, it's now 8:15, the bus is parked, motor turned off, and we haven't left Iquique. Sometimes tolerance goes by the board. The amusing "quaintness" of local customs has long since faded and now, realistically speaking, these people can really be pathetic, so friggin' lazy it'd be laughable if it weren't so pitiful. No wonder the country doesn't get anywhere. Now they're searching practically door to door for kids, why I don't know unless it's to pay for the bus. I got up at 6 to arrive at 7 sharp—*and there wasn't one person.* We were supposed to leave then. How sad that they're not even responsible enough to show up for an outing that an unselfish person, who works without pay coaching them because all the other adults are too goddamn lazy to help their kids out themselves, arranges for them.

8:25 now, still parked. Lazy, irresponsible, always quick to heap the blame on the other guy, thinking throwing your hand in the air is the answer to their problems—is it any wonder this country's in the state it's in? 8:28—movin'! Passing Plaza Prat, 2 blocks from my hotel. Could have risen at 7:30, eaten breakfast (I'm hungry) and leisurely waited in the plaza.

9:07. Been parked here at the checkpoint, a few miles outside Iquique, better than 15 minutes. These assholes defy belief. A group of kids on the way to a picnic in Pica, 100 km distant, and the absurd *pacos* make a bloody production out of it. One more manifestation of how fucked up this country is. Do you think Americans would stand for this garbage, even at state borders?[26] They'll probably turn us back, after all this crap. Should be in Pica by now, and instead we're begging to be allowed to pass.

Yep, we've been turned back. Have to advise them by 5 P.M. Friday of weekend *"excursiones especiales."* For whatever reason under the sun is beyond me. Screaming assholes. Get rid of these checkpoints and half the *pacos* and *milicos* [soldiers] and use the cash to

---

26 Maybe, if they get cowed enough by fearmongers and anti-immigration xenophobes.

feed the undernourished people, not harass them. I've never seen anything so ludicrous. Never. And they talk of *subdesarrollado*[underdevelopment].

10:32. The absurdity rolls on unabated. Parked in Iquique, still waiting for Beto and the driver to return from the Transportation Dept., totally unsure of whether they'll come sporting glum faces, or the asinine piece of paper dictating that yes, these dozen kids and their trip to Pica do not pose a grave threat to national security. The *paco/milico* "mind" does not deserve the name.

Forty-five minutes later the coveted piece of paper had been obtained, covered with official stamps and seals and unreadable signatures. We eventually got to Pica, and the kids enjoyed swimming in the tepid spring. After a quick dip in the shallow water, I walked out alone into the desert, high above the town. Pica was a patch of dark green surrounded by eerie moonscape stretching to the horizon. I felt the primal power of desolation. Broiling sun, utter silence but for the haunting whoosh of wind that swirled up cyclones of sand, some tiny, a few almost alarmingly large. Time is measured in centuries out there, if not eons. But I'm a human; I don't have eons. Drained by the sun and the hike, I was ready to roll back to Iquique by 6:30, though we ended up staying till 9:00. I sat on a concrete dam and wrote poetry until it was too dark to see the page.

Four months later I was with some friends outside a drive-in restaurant in Arica, down by the ocean. It was Saturday night. I'd lived in Arica for a while by then and had met quite a few people my age, many of them at the beach. I had signed up for the Peace Corps expecting and perfectly willing to live in a mud hut, but if circumstances conspired to place me instead in *La Ciudad de la Eterna Primavera* ("The City of Eternal Spring"), well, I was going to run with it. Many of my new friends were upper middle class kids, with cars, leisure time and spending money.

A girl was throwing a party that night out in Azapa, which sounded interesting (not to mention I was interested in her). When I suggested we head over to the *fiesta* Fernando Brito looked at me like I was *loco*.

"Way too early," he said. "It's barely midnight."

I thought of the Peace Corps training center party the year before, which had shut down at the same time the party in Arica was just starting. I reached no conclusions, just was amazed to realize how much things can change, including my circumstances. Unlike in Santiago, I had a responsibility: a ballgame to umpire at nine the next morning. Falling into bed at 4:00 A.M. would exact a miserable toll. I knew the game wouldn't start at nine sharp, because this was Chile, but still. Being twenty-three years old, I of course, went to the party anyway, got to sleep at some ungodly hour, woke scant minutes before nine, took a taxi across town to the field near Chinchorro Beach and the Olympic swimming pool, gutted it out through six hot, blurry innings behind the plate, then kept score for the second game. Later I went home for a nap before spending a few hours at the beach, bouncing in the waves at the Playa Brava, flirting with girls in their tiny bikinis, watching the endless blue ocean until the sun sank low on another day.

Sometimes I'd walk from my room on 21 de Mayo away from *el centro* and the Pacific, and end up sitting on a wall above the city. It wasn't far, ten minutes or so. I almost always went there in the early evening, partly because that's when I had the time, but also because the lengthening shadows and the first lights blinking on invited reflection in a way the midday sun never did. It was a perfect place for thinking: about time, and the world, and how the quotidian reality in Arica that I often took for granted was actually pretty astonishing. Somehow, I was here, really here, in this place so far from Westbrook, Connecticut and so different.

My thoughts would inevitably drift from space and place to time, especially as the end of my days in Arica drew near. Two years that seemed to stretch ahead forever in January of 1978 were gone like smoke in the wind. By April of 1980 the rest of my Peace Corps training group had left Chile. I was still there because of an extension granted so I could stay through the national baseball championship in Arica in June. My request for a full-year extension had been denied. I never got a straight answer why, but presumably it was to save money (PCVs extending for a third year get a free ticket for a month's paid vacation in the States), and because baseball programs were quite possibly the lowest priority in the entire Peace Corps operation. "Basic human needs" had become the organization's new mantra, and Peace Corps director Carolyn Payton had been dismissed in late 1978 for running afoul of this mission. The February 10, 1979 *The New Republic* quotes a staffer that, "[Carolyn] was all for going into any countries that asked, and doing whatever they asked us to do. If Chile wanted a baseball coach, Carolyn would send them a baseball coach." Evidently my job had become something of a punch line back in Washington. Since my work was considered a joke, I suppose I was lucky to be allowed any extension at all.

Sometime in the 1980s 21 de Mayo was extended, out along the arid hills and past the Carlos Dittborn soccer stadium to the Villa Empart, the barrio[27] where Hugo and Any now live. After our late lunch on New Year's Day, we take siestas, but before long I wake up and am too restless to sleep. I'm already missing

27 In Spanish, *barrio* simply means neighborhood, with neither a positive nor a negative connotation.

Christine. On a whim I decide to walk to the wall where I used to sit overlooking the city. The sun is low in the sky. Summer heat has vanished into the sand, and in Arica there's never any humidity to speak of. I feel comfortable, roaming in the gloaming, until I start thinking about time.

It begins when I can't find the wall. It's gone, probably a casualty of *la prolongación* of 21 de Mayo. I stand on the new sidewalk, new to me, anyway—it's at least fifteen years old, maybe twenty—gazing out over this city that isn't mine anymore. From this spot Arica looks pretty much the same. The differences are mostly in me. I need to sit down and there's nowhere to do it, so I start walking back up the road that didn't used to be here, away from the place where I used to live.

Suddenly I feel every year that I've been gone. The years aren't heavy; they're just there. Or more accurately, they *aren't* there. It's their absence I feel, a hollowness, an emptiness impossible to bridge. It's not sadness, exactly, but more as if I'm carrying a huge hole on my shoulders. I'm weighed down by something not even there, oppressed by nothing. Not the *nada* of Hemingway's "A Clean, Well-Lighted Place," spiritual malaise and existential dread that nothing matters. I feel that way sometimes—who doesn't?—but not right now. I'm just hyper aware of all the chasms around us that can never be crossed. With some of them you can't even see the other side, and certainly not the bottom.

It's time to go "home"—that is, to Hugo's. Not that I'm on a schedule, or that they expect me at a certain time. "*Estás en tu casa,*" they've told me, and they mean it. It's only time to get back because I've had enough of my thoughts for a while, enough of being by myself with infinity all around. I pick up my pace. I want to drink a cold beer with my friends, and then another. I want to hold the sweating glass, and toast, and laugh, and later on fire up the charcoal and grill the big fish Juan Marcos bought

167

at the docks today, and eat outside at midnight at a plastic picnic table in the glow from the picture window, drinking cool white wine, maybe smoking a cigar, having a wonderful time in our fragile little universe, in a tiny, high-walled back yard that shuts out everything but the sky.

CHAPTER TWELVE

Barriers: Broken Glass, Ropes and Dotted Lines

"Something there is that doesn't love a wall/That wants it down."

—Robert Frost, "Mending Wall"

During my return walk to Hugo's house, a brick wall painted light blue catches my eye. Hundreds of shards of glass are stuck in concrete on the top, jutting up like a phalanx of spear-wielding warriors. A low-tech, but effective deterrent that could, according to Carolyn Forché's prose poem/flash fiction "The Colonel," "scoop the kneecaps from a man's legs or cut his hands to lace." I've seen similar home-security systems sparkle in the sun, but not now. The sea has swallowed the sun, and the glass just looks dull and dangerous. Half a dozen ragged, rusty strands of barbed wire hang above the wall. All this protection for a typical one-story

169

Arica house with a shallow-pitched roof. What sorts of riches are hidden within? Or what sorts of fear?

The first time I noticed broken glass on a wall was in Santiago during Peace Corps training. It was more of a shock than I would have expected—if I had expected it—and I needed a few seconds to register what I was seeing. The sharp points were so basic, as primal and indiscriminate as shark's teeth. Their obvious purpose was protection, to keep people out, and I had no doubt that they did the job. I imagined trying to climb over that wall, felt the slice, saw my blood running crimson down the stucco. I wondered if cats would be small enough and smart enough to pick their way unscathed through the blades. Every neighborhood has cats, right?

I imagined building those walls. Layer of brick, layer of mortar until reaching the required height, then a final layer of wet cement. The pieces of broken glass are ready. Presumably someone has smashed bottles to create the stationary shivs, which are now set in the last stratum of cement. How much care does one take in their placement? It's a permanent cap to your wall, after all. Do you take time to choose appropriate colors of glass and arrange them just so? The mortar doesn't harden right away, so you could come down from the ladder, step back and survey your handiwork, then make adjustments. Or someone with an eye for color and design could supervise from below, from the angles at which the glass would later be seen by people of the house living their lives, and by their guests.

"No, try a green piece there."

"Do you have something taller for the corner?"

"Definitely clear glass by the palm tree. It picks up the muted brown of the bark."

"I changed my mind—the corner's too tall now."

170

If I sound flippant, I don't mean to. Surrounding your yard with sharp glass requires a series of decisions, beginning with deciding to do it in the first place. Most people don't, after all. Walls topped with broken glass are fairly rare. My point is that there are barriers, and there are barriers. The glass might be uncommon, but the walls are not.

I was semi-oblivious to this until a nineteen-year-old girl brought it to my attention. In 1991-92, Maria Elisa Cabral from Brazil lived with us in Salt Lake City. She was studying for the year at the University of Utah, where I was teaching. One day as we were driving home from campus, she mentioned how strange it was to her that the front yards of the houses all ran together. In Brazil, virtually everyone who has a yard completely fences it in. I thought back to Chile: same thing.

Maria Elisa smiled. "Americans must trust each other more."

"Possibly," I said, though I had my doubts. In Salt Lake City, like many places in the U.S., generally the back yards *are* fenced in. But not in much of Connecticut, at least in the smaller towns. From the window of my second-story office I can see a dozen houses but only one backyard fence. Is this lack of property-line barriers a vestige of English settlers, rather than Spanish and Portuguese? Maybe it's just that the smaller the yard, the more likely you want to keep it to yourself, like your personal space in an elevator. Still, broken glass and barred windows demonstrate a significantly different worldview. Fences for privacy and fences for protection are two very different animals.

Whatever the reasons for them, and whether or not we're even aware of it, where we place our barriers—and which side of them we're on—profoundly affects our lives. Often, it's easy to recognize barriers erected by others. If you're on the outside looking in (or if the wall is high enough, *not* looking in), you know it. You know if you're on the wrong side of the velvet rope, or standing in line at Studio 54 while others deemed more worthy than you are allowed through, or watching your Enron retirement account nose-dive while insiders sold their stock just before it tanked. You know it, and despite any rationalization like Aesop's fox about sour grapes, chances are you're resentful.

Sometimes, though, the barriers are less obvious. The first time I crossed a state line as a kid I was excited, certain that I would feel some sort of transformation. Instead, I was surprised and disappointed that Massachusetts didn't seem any different than Connecticut. But even if crossing the border is a big deal (remember your first passport stamp?), the fact that the border is there at all is taken as a given, just part of reality. Rarely do we consider that such divisions are artificial human constructs. Maps have dotted lines to show territorial divisions; the world doesn't. In pre-1884 maps, Chile was still skinny, but much shorter. After the War of the Pacific Chile annexed almost 600 miles of land, including massive nitrate deposits in the Atacama Desert, and Bolivia's entire seacoast. Landlocked Bolivia has been kvetching about the invisible dotted lines ever since.

People shed real blood for imaginary lines; people die so the next map will have lines in different places. When I was in the Peace Corps, Chile and Argentina sparred over who owned the Beagle Canal in Patagonia, invoking both national pride and—surprise!—the potential oil reserves in the region. Rumors of war occasionally surfaced over the dispute, which I attributed to saber-rattling by two dictatorships (probably in cahoots) trying to distract their people from real issues: whip up patriotic fervor to defend the honor of the beloved country that denies your civil and political rights. In 1982, though, to my amazement Argentina did actually attack the Falkland Islands (Islas Malvinas in Spanish) to reclaim them from England, and the ensuing defeat toppled the military junta. Pandering to nationalist pride led to the exact opposite of the intended result, when that pride was trampled by the English rout.

My two favorite artistic examples of the dotted-line insanity come from Jean Renoir's film *Grand Illusion* and Tim O'Brien's short story "On the Rainy River." At the end of *Grand Illusion*, two World War I French soldiers who escaped from a German prison of war camp have nearly reached neutral Switzerland. A German patrol arrives and prepares to gun them down. Suddenly, the German officer tells his men to lower their rifles: "They're in Switzerland." The film's gloriously ironic final image is a distant shot of two men trudging down a beautiful mountain slope, safe on the other side of an invisible line in the virgin snow.[28]

In "On the Rainy River," a fictional character named Tim O'Brien is drafted to fight in Vietnam. He drives to northern Minnesota, intending to dodge the draft in Canada, but remains conflicted and stays for a while at a lodge on the Rainy River, which forms part of the U.S.-Canada border. One day, old Elroy Bardahl, owner of the lodge, takes O'Brien fishing on the river. Elroy guns the boat north. At some point they cross an invisible line and enter Canadian waters, water flowing in the same river, but here, a few ironic yards farther north, through a country not at war. Bardahl anchors near shore, giving Tim every chance to escape. O'Brien wants to run from an unjust war he despises, but can't force himself to act. He can't overcome his fears about what folks in his hometown will think of him if he does what he's convinced is the right thing and goes to Canada. In the end, O'Brien the narrator tells us, "I was a coward. I went to war."

These two examples both involve war, and that's no accident. Boundaries frequently lead to conflict. Whether it's a dispute over a fence six inches into a neighbor's property, siblings bickering

---

28 In a final irony, the men plan to rejoin their units in France and return to the war.

about sharing a bedroom, a couple arguing about snooping through e-mail, Nazi tanks rolling east to conquer Russia, or Russian tanks rolling west supposedly to save Ukraine from Nazis, borders matter to people.

After moving back to Connecticut and buying a house, one of the first things I did was take down the chain link fence separating my small front yard from next door. My neighbor Lou helped me do it; removing the barrier would make mowing easier and we wouldn't have to trim the grass along the fence. Lou said the previous owner of my house had erected the fence without a word of explanation or warning. Was he motivated by paranoia? Misanthropy? Isolationism? Maybe all three, though it's not as if the fence offered privacy or security. You could easily see through and over it. Besides, it stopped at the sidewalk and the whole rest of the front yard was open, so it was easier to outflank than the Maginot Line and nowhere near as well armed. Essentially, the fence was the human equivalent of an animal spraying to mark its territory.

The epigraph that starts this chapter is not the best-known quote from Robert Frost's poem "Mending Wall." That honor goes to, "Good fences make good neighbors." Too often, though, it's forgotten that Frost completely disagrees with this sentiment. The neighbor of the poem's narrator is the one who says it, then is so proud of himself for mouthing the cliché that he later repeats it to end the poem. The narrator, meanwhile, wants to ask him *why* fences make good neighbors. He yearns for the neighbor to go beyond received wisdom and actually think for himself, but no such luck: "He moves in darkness as it seems to me,/Not of woods only and the shade of trees." The man is metaphorically in the dark and perfectly content to stay there, living an unexamined life behind walls of his own making.

These can be the saddest barriers—the ones we build around ourselves, when we hunker down behind our own invisible dotted lines, excluding certain people and possibilities. I remember being disappointed at some of my middle-class Chilean friends' dismissive attitudes toward the street artisans in Arica. I often stopped to talk with the *artesanos* on the downtown sidewalks as they made bracelets and such, and sometimes bought their wares. (I still have a hand-tooled leather belt and leather sandals with rubber soles cut from tires, now extremely worse for the wear.) I didn't support my friends' snobby comments, but I didn't speak up against them, either. The closest I came to courage was continuing to associate with whomever I wanted. Since the groups rarely overlapped, though, socially or in any other way, I was never strongly tested by having to choose one or the other.

My nearly three years in South America were my only extended experience as an "other." This barrier was generally not a hardship (I've already discussed the Gringo Advantage), largely because I lived in cities, first Santiago, then Arica. For Peace Corps Volunteers in small towns, though, it was a different story. They were not only "other," they were constantly on display: the so-called fishbowl existence. Only at home did they have a measure of privacy, like a guppy hiding in the rocks. But even then, people noticed when they went in, and out, and with whom, and if they stayed in too long it would cause worry—or suspicion.

The fishbowl existence was especially limiting for women. The barriers of gender expectations and gender prejudices were considerable and inescapable. To my surprise, female PCVs told me that other women were often the staunchest members of the gender police. Or maybe it's not so surprising. Maybe it's human nature that if you're confined in a narrow box of a life, you'd be jealous of someone else's freedom. The upshot is that if a PCV of either gender had a lover spend the night, local tongues would wag. The difference is that a man would likely be forgiven, probably even (wink, wink) congratulated by some, while a woman's reputation would suffer, maybe to the point that it damaged her ability to do her job.

This meant that to enjoy any degree of sexual freedom, female PCVs living in small towns had to get away to escape from prying eyes, to distance themselves from restrictive social barriers. Given the bonds that PCVs felt for each other, this led to R & R rendezvous in bigger cities, either with Volunteers who lived in those cities, Volunteers from elsewhere who had agreed to meet there, or both. It could be just a chance to have some drinks, vent about work and speak English for a while. It could also be a chance to release some sexual tension: "friends with benefits" before any of us had heard that phrase. And yes, the Peace Corps provided free condoms to Volunteers.

Living in Santiago and Arica I got frequent visitors, both male and female. Sometimes, small-town elements arose in the city as well. Once in Santiago, after a female PCV had spent the night at my place, the maid[29] came the next morning and grinned malevolently when she saw my blushing friend. It turned out that Señora Julia also worked for the host family where the PCV had lived during language training, so this juicy scuttlebutt was going to spread in a hurry. Another time in Arica, my landlady hassled me when a female PCV stayed in my room for two days en route to Peru. I told her the girl was sick so I had to give her my bed. That was semi-true, but I didn't think it politic to mention that I slept in the bed too. "This isn't the *Estados Unidos*," my landlady said with a frown. "We do things differently here."

---

29 Yes, having a maid went against my democratic grain. But she was already coming to the house twice a week when I moved in. Maids are extremely common in South America. Should I have appeased my conscience by firing her so she lost the income?

I wonder if she would have thrown me out if I were a woman. I doubt it. The rental income would probably trump morality. In a small town she might have felt obliged to evict or face social stigma for renting to a *puta* who let a man share her bed. But in Arica, no one was likely to know unless she decided to gossip.

Over time, my sense of otherness in Chile diminished to the point of vanishing. After several years, I practically considered myself a native, and people who knew me felt the same way. But to strangers, one look betrayed my origin and branded me a probable outsider. Fair-haired Chileans exist but are quite rare. And my Spanish, while excellent, held a hint of an accent (especially that bloody trilled "rr").

I wonder what people in Arica thought when they kept seeing me walking on their streets. As Chile's most northerly city, the gateway to and from Peru and Bolivia, Arica is constantly visited by gringo tourists, especially backpackers. But travelers move on within a few days. For some reason, this brown-haired, pale-skinned guy with a green daypack slung over his shoulder didn't go away: weeks, months, a year. His skin grew dark from the sun. What's he doing here?

Not long after I moved to Arica, the local television station interviewed me at a baseball practice. Curious to see it, that night I wandered around downtown searching for a TV tuned to that channel. Most bars and restaurants had on a national channel instead. Eventually I found a small *fuente de soda* with an equally small black and white *televisor* on top of the refrigerator (color TV was just arriving in Chile). Despite the name, soda fountains often serve beer, so I sat at the counter and ordered a Cristal while watching the lame local news till my face came on the screen. That certainly didn't make the program any less lame, but my answers to the reporter's questions seemed OK, and it was good publicity for our baseball program. The funny part, though, was a man two stools away who kept looking at the screen, then at me, then the TV, then back at me, but didn't say anything. I finished my beer and left before he did. I didn't say anything either, out of shyness that could easily have been misinterpreted as haughtiness.

I went to China in August of 2007, in the heat and humidity and the height of the tourist season. Visitors from all over the world crowded the Great Wall. Never have I heard so many languages in one place; I counted a minimum of fifteen, and surely there were more. This amazing rampart, built to keep invaders out of China, has been transformed into a magnet drawing outsiders (and their money) into the country. The Great Wall is a literal monument to duality, to ambiguity and ambivalence, to change—but to some extent, so is every wall.

There are so many different kinds of barriers, from stone walls crisscrossing New England, to pleasant white pickets bordered with flowers, to penitentiary walls topped with razor wire. Every barrier creates at least two sides, and potential conflicts over which side you're on. Some barriers are designed to keep people out, such as the walls being built between Israel and the West Bank, and the U.S. and Mexico, or around a gated community. Others are intended to keep people in, like the Berlin Wall, the North Korean border, or prisons from Auschwitz to the local lock-up.

The walls that people build around themselves, whether tangible or invisible, do both things at once. They keep the world at bay, and their builders protected. But at a price. Bricks, mortar and barbed wire cost money. Psychic, intellectual and emotional barriers cost us freedom and awareness. They deprive us of a spirit of generosity, openness and curiosity, leaving us afraid to venture away from the familiar. The unknown comes to be seen not as an exciting opportunity or adventure, but as a threat. The "other" becomes not a person to potentially connect with and learn from, but an inhuman, fearsome bogeyman. We lose our ability to empathize, choosing instead to be "safe" inside the armor of our prejudices and received wisdom, unable or unwilling to imagine other perspectives.

George Bernard Shaw's quip that "Patriotism is the belief that one country is better than all others because you were born there," contains a dishearteningly large grain of truth. When I was a kid during the Vietnam War, I saw photos of burly men with "America Love It Or Leave It" stickers on their yellow hardhats. I've seen "My country, right or wrong" bumper stickers on Country Squire station wagons in 1968, and "These colors don't run" flag decals on SUVs now. These quotes are all about erecting barriers, about imposing a simplistic Us vs. Them dynamic on a complicated world. Jefferson said in the Declaration of Independence that backing your country and its leaders if they do wrong is not patriotic, it's immoral and cowardly. It's easy to see that fault in others, such as Germans under Hitler, but immeasurably more difficult to see in ourselves, when we're the ones who are afraid and searching for scapegoats. When "These colors don't run" could just as aptly describe the actions of Crips and Bloods street gangs as it does U.S. foreign policy, it's time to tear down some barriers and consider building a few bridges instead.

I once took a bus from La Paz, Bolivia, to Arica, possibly the most picturesque nine hours of my life. The scenery was like a series of spectacular national parks, from badlands to altiplano to mountains to snow-covered volcanoes. At Bolivian customs at Tambo Quemado, high in the Andes, word spread through the queue that there was a charge of seventy *bolivianos* per person, more than nine dollars. I had only twenty-seven *bolivianos* left in my pocket, but wasn't worried. There were black market moneychangers outside (the authorities didn't hassle them so I guess they got their cut), and an American ten-dollar bill would probably also do the trick. Still, it was weird and annoying. I'd never heard of such a *tarifa* before.

Neither had the tall, balding guy standing next to me in line. His bus seat was across the aisle and one row up from mine, and he had slept through much of the scenery. He said with no little irritation that he had crossed many borders all over the world, and never been charged for the privilege of *leaving*. His accent was obviously Spanish, not South American, with a lot of theta sounds. I told him it was a first for me too. When we reached the window, without a word the dour official stamped the Spaniard's passport, then mine, and pushed them back to us. No eye contact, but also no charge. We shared quick, amazed glances and left before he could change his mind.

We laughed about it outside, in the bright, cool sun and thin air at 14,000 feet. Turns out that for bizarre political reasons only Chileans and Bolivians had to pay: seventy *bolivianos* for Chileans, ten for Bolivians. Undoubtedly, Chile charged similar fees in the opposite direction.

The Spaniard was around my age. It occurred to me that he must have grown up under General Franco's military dictatorship. I was doing a junior year abroad in Switzerland when Franco died on November 20, 1975, thirty-six years after seizing power. No European head of state attended Franco's funeral except Prince Rainier of Monaco. But fellow military dictators Augusto Pinochet of Chile and Hugo Banzer of Bolivia made the trip, paying last respects to one of their own.

Our college friend Joe Scarano, who was studying in Madrid that year, visited us in Fribourg on November 22. A huge event in Spanish history, and Joe was traveling and missed it. We must have talked about Franco but my journal doesn't mention a word. I was nineteen; military dictators hardly registered in my world. Little did I know how that would change, barely two years later.

The following spring, on a train to Madrid from Barcelona, a man with three days' worth of white whiskers on his wrinkled face offered me a cigarette. I put up a hand and shook my head, politely, I hope. He said something that sounded like a question, though I didn't understand a word. "*No hablo,*" I said, pretty much exhausting my Spanish vocabulary, and smiled apologetically. He nodded and smiled back.

It was March 20, 1976. This *caballero* had been a young man during the Spanish Civil War, from 1936-39. Did he support the Loyalists or Franco's Nationalists? Did he fight or stay out of the war? At the time, I had neither the Spanish nor the knowledge to ask these questions.

The old man lit an unfiltered cigarette. The smoke was rank but I didn't mind. We stared out the window at the sere Castilian countryside.

"*Bonito,*" he said. I smiled and nodded. I wasn't positive what the word meant, but it had to be good.

Despite our laugh together, I never spoke to the Spaniard again once we returned to the bus. If we had been in a second-class Spanish train compartment, facing each other next to the window, we'd probably have talked for hours, maybe even hit it off and exchanged addresses. Maybe we'd still be in touch. But instead, we were on a bus sitting in different rows, on opposite sides of the aisle. We didn't even make eye contact before going our separate ways at the Arica bus station.

CHAPTER THIRTEEN

Santiago Mon Amour

"In Chile, a river of glass bubbled, cooled,
hardened, and rose in sheets, only to crash and rise again.
One day, years later, the soldiers wheeled around
to find themselves in a city of glass.
Their rifles turned to carnival glass;
bullets dissolved, glittering, in their hands.

—Martín Espada, "City of Glass"

I rode a lot of buses in the Peace Corps. City buses large and small, long-distance buses, school buses, international buses. They were usually the cheapest, and sometimes the only way to get places. Trains to far northern Chile from Santiago carried cargo, not passengers, and were reportedly deadly slow to boot.

183

2,050 kilometers (1,280 miles) separate Arica and Santiago, most of it desert. Occasionally I flew, especially if it was official business and the Peace Corps paid the fare. But most of the time I rode the bus.

Never, though, did I do it in a straight shot, a twenty-eight to thirty-hour marathon (more if the bus broke down, a far from uncommon occurrence). I always had friends to see and people to look up along the way, so normally my longest leg was between Santiago and Antofagasta, maybe eighteen hours. I'd stop in Antofagasta to see fellow PCV baseball coaches Mike and Sylvia Gonzales and Bob Maurer, then a few days later head six hours north to Iquique to visit Neil McFadden before the final four-hour hop to Arica.

I haven't taken the bus south since July 29, 1980—the day I left Arica, knowing the odds were long that I'd ever see it again. I despair of describing those events now better than I did at the time, so here's my journal again:

Delightful weather for my final day in Arica. Hugo came at 6:10 [P.M.] to accompany us to the terminal. Big *abrazo* [hug] and Don Oscar [my landlord] was history. Hugo and I drank a final beer.

"*Tu has sido un buen amigo,*" I told him before entering the bus. ["You've been a good friend."]

"*Más bien hemos sido como hermanos,*" he responded. ["We've been like brothers, is more like it."]

It was my most emotional farewell moment, with my best friend in Arica. At 6:45 I waved goodbye, gave him the clenched fist as the bus rolled away, and left 1 1/2 years of my life behind me. I was reminded of the day I left Veronica at the station [in Santiago] and set off toward

Arica. Thoughts of her occupied me the whole trip as I watched the changing landscape of Chile through the bus window. Tonight it was the moon, a bright, full, huge low moon that belonged there, hovering over the desert.

No matter how long away something seems, it soon comes. The future is much longer than the past...

It took me six days to reach Santiago in 1980, breaking up the trip with visits to Chilean and Peace Corps friends in Iquique, Antofagasta and La Serena. This time, Hugo and I will ride one bus all the way to Santiago, arriving tomorrow unless mishaps intervene. Instead of a choked-up departure from Hugo at the station, I sit next to him in a Tur Bus window seat. As the bus pulls out at 11 A.M., my feelings couldn't be more different than they were all those years ago. Although I'm leaving Arica it doesn't seem like goodbye. Instead, I'm off to visit my old friend Santiago, with whom I had a conflicted, convoluted, but ultimately important and memorable relationship. We've fallen out of touch over the years; I'm eager, and a little scared, to renew old ties. Obviously, we both have changed, so who knows how this reunion will go.

When we bought our tickets yesterday, I suggested we take Flota Barrios, which in my day had gleaming double-decker buses with seats like first class in an airplane, wine, good meals and smiling stewardesses. (Yes, we still said "stewardess" in those days; it's *azafata* in Spanish). Flota Barrios used to cost maybe 40% more than a regular bus and was worth every peso. I told Hugo I'd pay but he said I was living in the past, and Flota Barrios is not the elite ride it once was. *Semi-cama* (semi-bed) is the best option these days, he assured me. When a Flota Barrios rep told me the *azafatas* were long gone—too many trysts with the drivers, among other more economic reasons—I was convinced.

I discover that *semi-cama* means a sleeve opens in the seat in front of you so your legs can stretch out, though not in a position high enough to be truly comfortable. Better than a cramped coach airline seat, but a far cry from first class. I doze off and on in the heat of the day, despite the television sets hanging throughout the bus. First, they show *Legally Blonde II*, then *Mission Impossible II*, both dubbed in Spanish and inescapable because unlike on a plane, no earphones are involved. The soundtrack simply blares from the small TVs, and unless you have great earplugs, great concentration, or both, Reese Witherspoon and Tom Cruise speaking crisply enunciated Spanish in voices nothing like their own are tough to ignore.

I tend to think a lot on long-haul buses and trains. This is less true on planes, possibly because in the back of my mind—and in the front of it if we're bouncing through a thunderstorm—is a gnawing suspicion that humans don't really belong six miles above the earth in a winged metal tube far heavier than air with a tank full (I hope it's full!) of flammable liquid.

I'd love to report that 29 hours on a bus transform my life, that a sublime revelation descends upon me somewhere deep in the desert, gloriously reconciling the past and present via a burst of Kerouacian insight. If this were a novel, I'd probably make sure that occurred, or at least arrange some nice ironic reasons why not, but with this book I'm stuck inside the tight box of what really happened. So, I'll toss in the towel and just quote my journal: "What can you say about an all-day bus ride through the Atacama Desert?"

I talk to Hugo. I take notes. I read. I sleep halfway decently, aided by two allergy pills (taken not for allergies, but because a kindly pharmacist once told me they have the same active ingredient as over-the-counter sleeping pills at a fraction of the cost.) I try to be Zen and live in the moment, but unfortunately most of the moments are humdrum. On this sort of trip, it's hard not to just want to get through it, hard to focus on the journey rather than the destination, especially if your thinking is mostly *about* your destination. And especially when the next morning the bus company has the gall to subject you to the same two movies they showed the day before.

The main thing I hoped for during the trip—desert stars—never happens. I get a taste through the window of the moving bus, but our night stops are in cities like Antofagasta, with their inevitable light pollution. I realize that my long-ago rides had been similar. Memories of a dazzling night sky occurred only because one time our bus broke down in the middle of nowhere, in the middle of the night. We passengers groaned at our misfortune, sure we'd be delayed for hours—and we were. But the bad luck turned good when I stepped outside to stretch my legs and wandered off a bit into the desert emptiness. No hint of human habitation. Not a glimmer of electric light. Just the distant outline of hills and a sky as black as a bottomless well, ablaze with uncountable stars from horizon to horizon. I watched in awe for as long as I could stand it, shivering from cold and more than cold, then climbed back in the dark bus. Through the window I saw our driver pacing slowly back and forth, and the glowing tip of his cigarette.

Riding a bus for nearly thirty hours is not something I'm eager to do again, but I'm glad I *did* do it. I'm reminded of the line that most writers don't so much like to write, they like to have written. Call it my wimpy version of skydiving, mountain climbing, or eating that Japanese puffer fish that kills you if it's not prepared correctly—none of which I've done or have the slightest desire to ever do.

187

Anyway, the bus gets us to Santiago. Rolling past farms and suburbs and new commercial sprawl as we approach the city, I feel as beat and excited as I was on the bus with my Peace Corps group driving in from the airport. I don't feel nostalgic—not yet—but I certainly feel curious. In 1978 my questions all faced the future; now I'm peering back over my shoulder, trying to catch up to what's behind me while not stumbling on the path ahead. In 1978 I was coming to live in Chile for several years; now my return flight leaves in a week. In 1978 I had to learn Spanish, meet loads of new people and prepare to do a job; now my only responsibility is the self-imposed task of comparing "is" with "was."

From the bus terminal Hugo and I catch the Metro to the Salvador station, then continue on foot to his apartment at the base of Cerro San Cristóbal (St. Christopher Hill). He bought the apartment for his kids to use while they're in college. It's small but comfortable, two bedrooms and a combination living room/dining room. Any will be coming tomorrow, by plane because she has education bureaucracy business in Santiago so the government is springing for her airfare. We walk fifteen minutes to a Líder Express, a compact, downtown city version of the large Líder supermarket in Arica. Instead of paying cash, like everyone used to do in Chile, I swipe a credit card through the same little machines that U.S. stores have, and we lug home our beer and food in plastic sacks.

Santiago is the heart of Chile, its literal and figurative center. Throughout Chilean history people have abandoned the provinces and their limited economic opportunities to search for a better life in the capital. Hugo's children are typical of the process—the high-end, success story part of the process. They came to Santiago to attend college, and Panchy the lawyer and Hugo Tomás the dentist will likely stay here. Even if they prefer living in Arica, jobs are scarce. Of course, uneducated people with few skills also migrate to Santiago, often just trading rural poverty for an urban one.

My first day at Hugo's apartment I connect with three old friends from Arica, all now living in Santiago. Their stories illustrate different facets of the exodus to the capital. I phone Carlos Correa and arrange to have dinner the next day. Carlos had been a great ally in Arica's education bureaucracy, helping out me and the kids time and again. He's a native *ariqueño* and hates the bustle and stress of Santiago, but has lived here for over twenty years because the government sent him. He had two choices: go or be out of a job.

Hugo phones Tito "Cara de Loco" Soriano for me. In Arica, "Crazy Face" had worked at the DIN, an electronics store. In Santiago he owns a *cafe con piernas* called La Selva (The Jungle). I hadn't heard the term before but discover that a "cafe with legs" means the servers are women wearing precious little, and that these establishments do not enjoy sterling reputations.

To my surprise, Tito is evasive and tells Hugo to call back later. It's probably just ego, but I expected Tito to be excited to see me. We hung out together quite a bit in Arica. One night he told me about having to identify his brother's body after a motorcycle accident. I'll never forget Tito's anguished description of the shattered bones as he held his brother's hand, nor the fierce look in his eyes as he asked me, "*Sabes que es eso?*" No, I said, I *don't* know what that's like.

Maybe Tito is embarrassed by his job. He moved to Santiago for economic reasons and now presumably makes decent money, but in a pretty low-rent business. Maybe Cara de Loco is simply not the nostalgic type. Maybe he has no interest in seeing some gringo from auld lang syne, especially since times turned dark for some of my Arica friends not long after I left.

Cocaine was the reason, or worse, its less refined form called *pasta base*. Because of Arica's proximity to coca-producing Peru and Bolivia, *pasta base* was cheap and plentiful in the 1980s, and the nasty, addictive stuff messed some people up. Two of them were Tito Soriano's roommate Chato Campbell, and Hugo's life-long best friend Julio Munizaga. I don't know where Chato lives now, or even *if* he does, but Julio is in Santiago and he comes to Hugo's apartment that first night. He's still the old Julio, smart, warm and funny, but he looks thin, almost gaunt, and has aged dramatically since I last saw him. A quarter of a century has passed, after all, though the years have taken far less of a toll on Hugo and me. Bad drugs age you faster than time.

Our only drug tonight is a two-liter bottle of Bodega Uno red wine. We offer toasts, laugh and trade stories, emulating the characters in Loudon Wainwright III's song "Old Friends" who "kiss the past's ass all night long." After Julio leaves and the wine runs out, Hugo and I stay up till three drinking *pisco* and Sprite and talking about anything and everything. The night feels hyper-real and surreal at the same time. Here I am, doing what I had done so many nights with my best friend in Arica, but somehow, I'm back in Santiago instead, where my life in Chile began. Not to get too mystical about it—I'm also loopy from lack of sleep after that marathon bus ride.

The next day we take the Metro downtown to the La Moneda station. La Moneda, originally the national mint (*moneda* means both "mint" and "coin") is the presidential palace. It was bombed and shot up by the Chilean military during the 1973 *golpe*, while inside its walls President Salvador Allende committed suicide. (I'd always assumed he was gunned down by soldiers, but most evidence today points to suicide—with a gun that was a gift from Fidel Castro—shortly after delivering a final radio address to the nation with explosions and gunshots audible in the background.)[30] When I lived in Santiago in 1978, La Moneda had been a symbol of horror and repression for many Chileans, and for outsiders like me as well. But over thirty years have passed since the *golpe*. The majority of Chileans today were not even born yet when it happened. For most people La Moneda is just a building again, three stories of imposing gray stone that hardly anyone gives a second glance.

At the moment, even a first glance involves effort. Because of extensive construction in the plaza in front of the palace, a safety fence surrounds the area and blocks the view. At my request, Hugo dodges traffic and poses across Morande Street in a gap in the fence where trucks rumble through, and I get a new memory on film. I'm not sure why I don't have a photo of La Moneda from my Peace Corps days. Maybe it was off limits to photography, the way military buildings were. Maybe I was intimidated that it *might* be forbidden, that if I got caught my camera would be confiscated, or worse. Maybe the picture had been in my camera when it got stolen near the end of training.[31]

---

30 The speech begins: "Surely this will be my last opportunity to address you. The Air Force has bombed the antennas of Radio Magallanes. My words have not bitterness, but disappointment. May they stand as a moral punishment for those who have betrayed their oaths." It ends: "The people must defend themselves, but they must not sacrifice themselves. The people must not let themselves be destroyed or riddled with bullets, but they cannot be humiliated either. Workers of my country, I have faith in Chile and its destiny. Other men will overcome this dark and bitter moment when treason seeks to prevail. Go forward knowing that, sooner rather than later, the great avenues will open again and free men will walk through them to construct a better society. Long live Chile! Long live the people! Long live the workers! These are my last words, and I am certain that my sacrifice will not be in vain. I am certain that, at the very least, it will be a moral lesson that will punish felony, cowardice and treason."

31 I left the camera in a restaurant on March 16, 1978, and when I returned two hours later, of course it was gone. Beware the day between the Ides of March and St. Patrick's Day.

It was months before I got a replacement, time during which I grew accustomed to Santiago and therefore less likely to consider my surroundings unusual and worth recording.

Hugo and I walk to the American Airlines office to confirm my flight, then to the tourist bureau off the Plaza de Armas. A friendly girl answers my questions about public transportation to the National Stadium and to La Reina, my two major pilgrimages in the city. Hugo and I each take a city map and head out in the heat to the plaza.

There's a Plaza de Armas—"Weapons Plaza"—in hundreds of South and Central American towns. The words sound more euphonious in Spanish than in English, but the popularity of the name illustrates the mind-set of the *conquistadores* and their descendants. I'm curious and excited to see again what for me would always be *the* Plaza de Armas. All Chilean PCVs were familiar with it, because when we were in Santiago on official business the Peace Corps would put us up at the one-star Hotel de France half a block away. Why it was called the Hotel de France and not the Spanish *Francia* was a mystery, but a moot point because no one in the place spoke French. Every PCV had Hotel de France stories and had heard plenty of others, many of which were actually true.

Across the street from the hotel back then you'd often see an old blind man in a fedora, with a white tin cup attached to his accordion. He would slowly walk as he played, left shoulder brushing the stone of the post office wall till he reached the corner, right shoulder touching the building as he returned. Hour after hour he'd plod back and forth, squeezing out the same tune that could fray your nerves if you listened long enough. It was the rare PCV who didn't drop a coin in his cup at least once.

The blind man is gone now, of course; he probably has been dead for decades. I hold out a slim hope of seeing the Hotel de

France but find instead a gleaming skyscraper where my memories had been. The Plaza de Armas, the size of a city block, is the same teeming bustle of tourists, artists and hustlers that I remember. One of the last evenings before leaving Santiago in 1980, to amuse Katherine (more on her soon), I paid a caricaturist fifty pesos ($1.25) to draw my picture. You know the kind: tiny body, huge head. To her surprise, and at least apparent delight, I gave her the drawing. I wonder if by any miracle she still has it, fading forgotten at the bottom of some box, maybe, or pressed like a dried flower in the pages of a long-unopened book.

At my instigation, Hugo and I try to locate Tito Soriano. Hugo says the guy didn't call back and we should just bag it, but he humors my nostalgia crotchet and several phone calls and fruitless searches later we find Cafe La Selva in a shopping *pasaje*, an alley like a small mall. Music thumps through a wall painted in amateurish jungle motifs. With the stereo blaring like that, patrons obviously don't come for conversation.

I have zero desire to go in, but we're only here because of me so I can't bail out now. The miniscule, dimly lit *cafe con piernas* oozes desperation and desire. I add to the desperation by desperately wanting to leave. Two bored waitresses in high heels and skimpy lingerie carry trays and look like they haven't smiled since Christmas. A bouncer tells us Tito isn't there. Hugo leaves his card; if Cara de Loco can't be bothered to call, the hell with him. We get out of that miserable place and drink a welcome beer at a sidewalk cafe.

That night Carlos Correa picks me up at 8:30. We embark on a long, maniacal drive down Avenida Vicuña MacKenna to his house on the far south side of the city. They're widening the road under the soon-to-be opened elevated Metro line out to that sector, but in the meantime the narrow lanes, numerous buses, and harried, hurried, honking drivers create a white-knuckle bedlam. I frequently fight not to do that wussified (and utterly useless) move of pressing an imaginary brake pedal with my right foot. Carlos says he's accustomed to the insanity of Santiago but detests it and plans to return to Arica as soon as he retires.[32]

In his house there's no secret where Carlos's heart lies: dominating the living room is a large oil painting of Arica's Morro and harbor. It's a treat to see Carlos's wife Sonia again, and to meet his son. We have a wonderful time talking of old times and new. Arica's *Infantil* (Little League age) team had won the Chilean championship the year after I left, which I knew, but Carlos filled in many details. What I hadn't known was that later Arica hosted a South American championship for players up to sixteen years old. Nine countries sent teams, and the games were played under the lights at a packed Carlos Dittborn Stadium, capacity almost 18,000 (though I bet the baseball games only drew a few hundred).[33] Chile even managed to snag third place, after Brazil (every player of Japanese ancestry) and Venezuela (with possibly some future major leaguers on the squad). How I'd have loved to see that.

I'm surprised at how much emotion I feel, largely because Carlos keeps emphasizing that none of it would have happened without me. I've seen Carlos in action and am certain that championship never would have occurred without *him*. Still, though, I remember arriving in Arica, no baseball programs in place, nothing organized—yet within three years the kids were national champions. I'm proud of that, even if most tangible evidence of

---

32 English speakers tend to chuckle when they learn the Spanish word for retirement is *jubilación*.

33 Chile hosted the World Cup in 1962, and Carlos Dittborn Stadium was built as one of the Cup venues. Brazil repeated as champion, despite Pelé being sidelined with an injury.

my work is gone. Yellowed newspaper clippings are about all that's left, with some photos and a few cheap trophies on dusty shelves.

At 11:00 we're eating Sonia's delicious pot roast and sausage, with rice and tomatoes. We started the night with a beer, then moved to a pisco sour before wine with dinner. I'm not drunk, not even close, but when I ask, "*Qué pasó*, Carlos? Why did it die?" there's a hint of melancholy in my voice I'd rather have kept buried.

I hear pain and exasperation in equal measure as Carlos explains how economic support had eroded, a symptom of the government's general neglect of public education in favor of privatization. Most of the coaches were teachers, and teachers' salaries were abysmal. Many took second jobs to survive and gave up coaching, especially since the hours they spent with their teams went largely unremunerated and unappreciated. Not having someone like me there meant no impartial cheerleader and advocate, no one who could at least potentially hold the situation together. Enthusiasm fizzled.

Carlos breaks out the *guinda*, a home-brewed liquor Sonia had made. A clump of fermented brown cherries lines the bottom of the bottle, and I fear that to be a good guest I'll have to fake enjoyment of the vile stuff—but not so much that I can't politely decline a second glass. Fortunately, the *guinda* is tasty and I'm spared the etiquette dance.[34] We cap the night with a little whisky. Drinking with an old friend after a long separation is one of the great joys of life, especially if you stay just this side of overdoing

---

34 A similar drink called *ginja* or *ginjinha* is popular in Portugal. One night an off-duty cop we met in a restaurant drove Christine and me on a tour of Lisbon, then proudly served us homemade *ginja* at his apartment. We smiled and thanked him, then took turns distracting him with his caged parakeet and pouring the liquid torment down the kitchen sink.

it, then get a lift home in the back seat with your friend while his son does the driving.

Carlos and I hug outside Hugo's apartment building, and he gives me a kiss on the cheek before getting back in the car. I hadn't expected that in the slightest and am remarkably moved by it. Carlos is one of the truly top-notch people I know. I never hung out with him much outside of work, though; he and Sonia were part of the married crowd and I was logically enough more interested in the singles scene. Parties with paired-off couples and me were fun but lacked a sense of excitement and possibility, that feeling that you never knew what (i.e., who) you might find.

The next day I walk to an internet cafe, find three e-mails from Christine and immediately write back. She's worried at not hearing from me, even though it has only been three or four days. Easy, instant communication is a gift, but can actually create extra stress, because we're so used to being in touch that a sudden lack of connection makes us suspect the worst. How different than when I was in the Peace Corps and wrote home every three weeks or so. My parents didn't expect more frequent contact, so anxiety took a lot longer to kick in.

I catch a bus north on Providencia then down Tobalaba and west on Principe de Gales toward the cordillera, hoping to locate our Peace Corps training center. I had taken that same bus time and again when I lived with Violeta Wood, Veronica Inostroza's mother, during our ten weeks of training. It's not truly the same bus—the new ones are far less polluting than the smoke-belchers of 1978—but it reminds me of the countless hours I spent on buses in Santiago, and what a slow way it is to get around the city.

Not that I care about speed today. Just as I had on my return to Arica, I'm constantly comparing Santiago's new reality to my memories, and this bumpy crawl through the streets is perfect for that. There's the San Carlos Canal, water as gray as paint, flowing to join the equally toxic Mapocho River. We must be in barrio La Reina (The Queen) by now, named for Queen Victoria. Here's Avenida Principe de Gales (Prince of Wales Avenue), a block from the sprawling Prince of Wales Country Club where fellow PCT Jocko Vertin and I once sneaked on to the clay tennis courts. Actually, it was less sneaking than walking on as if we belonged there, the *chutzpah* approach that works more often than not. Two young ball boys shyly told us that white shirts were required attire, so we gave them ten pesos each to trade *camisetas* with us and hit for an hour and a half wearing T-shirts so small we could barely breathe—but which didn't stop us from laughing at the world, while the kids chased balls with our shirts flapping around their knees.

So much has changed, though, that on memory lane I hardly recognize any landmarks. I stay with the bus up Principe de Gales, peering out the window for clues. Finally, I see a military base ahead. "*En la esquina, por favor,*" I tell the driver, and get off at the corner. The training center had been across the road from an army base. And the street name, Valenzuela Llanos, sounds familiar. The military complex has greatly expanded and looks far less austere than I recalled; in fact, it has rather a country club air about it. I head down Valenzuela Llanos, almost certain this is the spot.

After walking way farther than I remember, though, I begin to have doubts. There are all sorts of new houses out here; maybe the training center was torn down and built over. I keep going until I'm absolutely sure this is too far, then start back, checking every fence and wall I can peer over or through.

Then I see it: *el centro de capacitación*. I have no idea how I missed it the first time by, but there it is, the two-story former private residence, looking a bit forlorn and unused, but not decrepit. The site of ten weeks' worth of challenging Spanish classes, fascinating lessons on Chilean culture, deadly dull lectures on Peace Corps policies—and enough social drama to power a junior high school. Our training group had twelve women and five men. Subtracting Philip and Karen the married couple left eleven women and four guys, none older than mid-twenties, all feeling various degrees of dislocation and vulnerability—and horniness. Within a month the social dynamics got weird, got complicated, sometimes got uncomfortable, especially for someone like me who grew up with three brothers and was clueless about women. But man, it was an education.

Looking through the locked driveway gate of the center, thinking about all of this stuff and a lot more besides, out of nowhere I nearly break down. Without warning, my hands gripping the iron grate like prison bars, I feel the weight and wonder of the past, and tears well up.

They don't spill over. Instead, I scrawl on the folded piece of paper I always carry to write notes, "I might cry if I didn't have to take a piss so bad."

Call it a pratfall from the sublime to the ridiculous, but never have I been more aware of the dual nature of humanity, of the give-and take between our physical and mental selves. "You can't philosophize on an empty stomach," Plato said, at least according to Dr. Grassi, my professor of ancient philosophy in college. Art and philosophy require some level of prosperity and comfort, because otherwise you spend every hour just trying to survive. Similarly, when your bladder is bulging, it's tough to think about anything but looking out for number one. I take some pictures and head back to Principe de Gales.

On the corner is a gleaming new quickie mart called On the Run, where I waste time in a fruitless search for a public restroom. I walk west on Principe de Gales through prosperous neighborhoods, sticking to the shade when possible, eyes peeled for an impromptu outhouse nook. Eventually I slip behind a relatively private hedge and hope that its roots are grateful for the watering in the heat.

Relieved of my burden, I begin to enjoy this walk I had made so many times during training, sometimes alone, sometimes with one trainee or another who lived in the neighborhood. The nostalgia is pleasant now, not overwhelming. I reach Plaza Salvador Izquierda, where one long-ago morning I'd photographed two ragged boys sleeping under a shrub, huddled together on scraps of cardboard. Now I photograph signs advertising the Ripley credit card and McDonald's, whose McMenú includes McFiesta con queso, McPollo Jr., and Hot Dog Palta Tomate.[35]

I veer a block north off Principe de Gales along the plaza and turn left on Nocedal, toward Veronica's old house. I know she's not there, and hasn't been for years. She married former Nebraska Cornhusker football lineman Bill Startzer and moved with him and her two kids to the U.S. in the early eighties. I haven't seen her since 1988, when Christine and I spent a night at their southwest-style house in Eagle, Colorado while driving to Connecticut from Salt Lake City.[36] Vero and I stayed up till past midnight after everyone else had crashed, drinking wine and speaking Spanish on the patio. I recall verbatim one thing she told me: *"Tu tienes suerte, Tomás. Christine es un amor—mucho mejor que tu mereces!"* ["You're lucky, Tomás. Christine is a sweetheart—much better than you deserve!"] She laughed as she said the last part, but I think we both knew it was true.

I walk down quiet, residential Nocedal, checking driveways on the left side of the street. My pulse quickens. Veronica's little

---

35 *Queso* is cheese, *pollo*, chicken, *palta*, avocado.

36 In 2004 Eagle got its fifteen minutes (OK, more like three weeks) of fame as the site of the Kobe Bryant rape trial.

house had a lot to do with the man I've become. I learned much about love there, and later was reminded what a broken heart feels like. I saw the pain and strain and rancor as two friends' marriage broke apart. I heard stories of Chile in the old days, and under Allende, and of the *golpe* and the early Pinochet years. I met actors and painters and poets and writers, who treated me as an equal and made it seem possible that someday I might also be an artist. They encouraged me to sing them the songs I was writing, which I would never have presumed—or dared—to do without their asking. Since most of them made little or no money from their art, I learned that truth as well. In a real way, that house was a bridge for me between youth and adulthood.

Just as I had with the training center, I walk too far and have to turn back before finding the house. After standing a while outside the low gate I worry about being perceived as a stalker or a pervert. I imagine a neighbor wondering what this gringo is gawking at. Ring the bell, *hombre*, or drag your *poto* out of here. Whatever you're selling, I don't want any.

The wooden louvers are closed in Veronica's bedroom window. With a last look at the front door, I shuffle away, thinking about one August night on her living room sofa. I had often slept on that couch, for Vero didn't want her two kids to wake up with me in her bed, but this time was different. We weren't lovers anymore. I had spent the evening alone with her, pretending that I was fine just being friends. I wasn't.

> These painfully chaste goodnight kisses are torture, and
> I hate kissing through the mask I have to put on to do
> it. I left about 11:50, but was back at midnight when no
> bus came. I kicked myself for hoping none would come.
> I even had thoughts, as I rattled her [bedroom] shutters

to let me in, of saying *"Te amo tanto que no me pude ir,"* [37] taking her in my arms and kissing her as if I meant it. What I did—out of cowardice, or admirable restraint?— was say just that, jokingly; she smiled and brought the blankets then I sat alone in the living room, thinking. I hadn't even touched her.

The house was dark later, everyone asleep, when through the picture window I saw headlights creeping up the driveway. The lights went out; a car door shut; the gate hinge creaked. I heard a knock at the door. I waited, hoping someone else would deal with it. It was 1:30 in the morning; I was just the gringo guest. A second round of rapping, diffident yet insistent, then a third. I got up to answer. If the knocking had been harsher, more intimidating, I doubt that I would have left my covers.

A short, slight young man stood on the porch. Behind him a taxi was parked. *"Buenas noches,"* he said. *"Estará la Panchy?"*

"Sí."

He apologized, saying he thought they usually stayed up late. I led him down the hall to Vero's sister's room. He tapped on the door.

"Quién es?" she asked groggily.

"Fernando."

"Fernando! *Entra no más!*"

The delight in her voice kick started my brain, and as he closed her door behind him, I recognized Fernando Ubiergo, who six months earlier had won the International Song Festival at Viña del Mar.

---

37 "I love you so much that I couldn't leave."

Seaside Viña is Chile's toniest city, and in the pre-internet and cable TV (in Chile, even pre-color TV)[38] days of early 1978, La Festival Internacional de la Canción was a huge deal. Chileans were astonished to learn that I'd never heard of it; most of them were gaga over the festival and tuned in for every minute of the competition. When Ubiergo won first prize the nation celebrated, and for a while he rode the wave and was big in Latin America. He even played Madison Square Garden, on a bill with other Spanish-language performers.

Fernando spent only ten minutes or so in Panchy's room, then from the couch I saw his shadow figure pass through the dark and open and close the front door with scarcely a sound. The taxi backed away, its headlights shining through the window onto the wall above me, illuminating a wonderful painting of Valparaíso that Vero had done when she was just thirteen. The strangest part of the incident is that it barely felt strange. Soon after I'd arrived in Santiago and was living at her mother Violeta's house, Panchy showed me some photos, including a small black and white shot of a curly-haired young man with a guitar. "That's my old boyfriend Fernando," she said. "He's a really good musician. I mean *really* good. He writes great songs."

A few weeks later, on February 6, Ubiergo's ballad "El Tiempo en las Bastillas"[39] won the Viña competition and he became famous overnight. We were the same age; I had turned twenty-two three days before. I watched the festival with Violeta on February 5, interested in Fernando because of Panchy. His song was pretty cool with a catchy chorus (not that I understood much after only a month in Chile), but most of the tunes were

---

38 Part of the festival was broadcast in color, Chile's first-ever color transmission, though almost no one had a color TV yet.

39 "Time in the Hems," is a literal but clunky translation.

boring so I skipped the final night to write letters home and play my guitar instead. All these years later, walking the few blocks to Violeta's house, I wonder if Ubiergo is lucky enough to still make a living doing what he loves.[40] I remember several of Veronica's friends, poets and writers, who worked in advertising and hated it, but in 1978 Chile it was the only paying job they could find that offered at least some degree of creativity. What are they doing now?

I hesitate, peering through Violeta's wood and iron gate to the *casa*, maybe fifty feet away. It looks the same, a solid, well-made single story covered in off-white stucco, with a red tile roof, surrounded by the same exotic (exotic to a kid from Connecticut, anyway) palms and cactus plants. I ring the bell, suddenly almost as nervous as I'd been in high school calling up Leah Davis for a date. Slow seconds pass. A maid in an apron opens the door, leans out and stares at me suspiciously, probably expecting a salesman or a Mormon missionary.

"Buenos días, señora," I call out. *"Estará la señora Violeta?"*

Even at this distance I can see the surprise on her face. *"Momentito,"* she says, and disappears inside. Soon a woman around sixty steps onto the porch. I tell her that I used to live here and am hoping for news of Violeta. Without coming nearer, she says that Violeta moved away twenty years ago. That's all she knows.

Often under similar circumstances in Chile I've been invited in to visit, but not this time. I thank her; the door closes. I wait at the familiar bus stop bench a few feet from the gate, the gate whose key used to be in my pocket, the gate Jocko Vertin

---

40 Later I Googled him and discovered that he's still quite popular. There are several Ubiergo performances on YouTube, including "El Tiempo en las Bastillas" at the festival, as well as a recent up-tempo, more rocking version.

and I had hid behind the night we "challenged" the 2:00 A.M. curfew after my birthday party. I expected little from returning to Veronica's and Violeta's houses, and I pretty much got just that. But I'm glad I went. It would have been unimaginable to be in the neighborhood and not stop by, even if I knew they were long gone. On the ride back, a guitar player with bushy hair and a mustache somehow stands and plays three songs despite the lurching bus. Quite a few of us give him coins, less for his singing than for his ability to persevere and stay on his feet.

Two days later I return to the National Stadium, for many the main symbol of Pinochet's murderous repression. It was—and is—that for me as well, though only at second-hand. I went there to coach kids playing baseball, and our practices were never inside the stadium itself, but in a corner of the large, gated compound, the only baseball diamond among numerous soccer fields. In fact, the only time I ever entered the actual stadium was to attend a revival meeting by the American evangelist Rex Humbard. I didn't go hoping for enlightenment, I went out of curiosity to see this place I had heard and read so much about. Respectful curiosity, not morbid curiosity, though propped up by a flying buttress of irony that Humbard would be trying to save souls and collect cash on a killing field.[41]

The day of my return to the National Stadium, I take a north-south Metro line that didn't exist yet when I lived in Chile. I get off at the Ñuble station and walk east ten long blocks under blazing January sun, the familiar fluttery sense of anticipation building with every step, stronger even than when I'd been in the Peace Corps. Or maybe it's just a different kind of anticipation.

---

41 Humbard was the first televangelist to have a weekly nationwide show in the U.S., who by the time I saw him had the largest ministry in the world. Elvis Presley frequently watched his show, and Humbard spoke at Elvis's funeral in 1977.

Back then, I naturally enough saw everything through the lens of my job. On my first trip to the Estadio Nacional during training I felt indignant and curious and a little scared, but those emotions were mitigated by my nervousness and eagerness to see Chilean baseball and get a taste of what I'd be doing for the next two years. Whether we want to admit it or not, everything we do begins with the personal—the "I" and the "me."

During language training Jocko Vertin lived across the street from the stadium, in an apartment on Calle Marathon. In my novel *In the City of the Disappeared* I had the main character living there. Harry Bayliss looks out his bedroom window at the *estadio*, wondering what it was like to hear machine guns executing prisoners, wondering if the cries of the tortured would have carried that far. Now, as I cross Marathon on a sweltering Sunday afternoon, the area is practically deserted. I ask the gate-keeper about the baseball field and he points to the far corner of the grounds, well past where I can see from here. I thank him and head inside.

I detour to walk by the stadium. The generic concrete oval is smaller than I remembered, and shabbier, with plenty of rust and peeling paint. After a circuitous route around trees, walls and fences I find the fields (plural! four of them!), but all of the gates are locked. There was no barrier around the old field, an indication of baseball's negligible importance to the Chilean sports bureaucracy. I stand like a kid desperate to play, fingers grasping the chain link fence, chin pressed against the metal. If this is as close as I can get, at least it's a decent look. After coming all this way, though, I have to try every possibility. Feet and sandals dusty from the parched summer dirt, I exit to Pedro de Valdivia Avenue, on the opposite side of the compound from Marathon, then go south past the *velodromo*, the maniacally banked bicycle racing track, and turn right on Dr. Guillermo Mann.

It's a better view from here. I can see all four fields through the iron fence, so stick my wide-angle lens through the bars and take a picture. Better than nothing. I gaze for a few minutes then start back toward the metro. It's beastly hot, and I've seen all I can from the outside.

One minute later, a miracle: someone had removed a bar from a section of fence. It's a tight fit, but sideways I can just slip through. I wander around the fields—some for Little Leaguers, some regulation-size—thick grass underfoot like an overgrown golf green. There are plenty of brown patches, but enough green to show that the fields have been at least intermittently watered. What a contrast to my first trip to the National Stadium in 1978, when the single field was mostly just dirt and scraggly weeds. Now there's not only decent grass, but dugouts, outfield fences, sturdy backstops—even an electric scoreboard on the main field, though upon closer inspection I find it bereft of light bulbs and sprouting various disconnected, derelict wires. Still, what a mammoth improvement from the old days…my days.

I amble over to a pitcher's mound. Toeing the rubber and staring in for the sign, I shake off the imaginary catcher until he puts down two fingers for a curve. As a teenager I had a good curveball but lousy technique, which is why I iced my elbow after every game I pitched, and to this day can't completely straighten out my right arm. I'd heave that hook straight at the batter's head, and if I snapped my wrist violently enough most would bail out as the ball broke over the plate. A major league hitter—hell, a college hitter—would likely drill it four hundred feet, but to fifteen-year-olds in Babe Ruth League it was a feared pitch.

I go into the stretch position, check the runner on first, pick up the catcher's target. From the mound, the sixty feet six inches to home plate seems far away. It would be tough to fool the hitter from here, even harder to get the ball by him. I never throw that imaginary pitch; neither my cranky back nor my cold arm needs that, even in slow motion. Instead, I step off the rubber, careful not to balk (absurd, but there it is), and walk to the batter's box. I take my usual closed stance, front foot even with the back point of the plate. Strange—somehow the distance has shrunk. The mound seems close; the pitcher has the advantage. I have no idea whether other players feel the same way, but I've had this perception for years, at least since I was twelve and moved up to adult-size fields.

Time to go. It's a scorching day, and though I found more than I'd hoped for here, this isn't my world anymore. I squeeze through the fence and head back toward the Metro, my sunbaked brain mulling over and over how perspective can be everything in this life.

In December 1988, Christine and I drove east over the Connecticut River to visit Elizabeth Tashjian, a.k.a. the Nut Lady. She lived in Old Lyme, the first town across the bridge, and was creator and curator of the Nut Museum in her house. I'd heard about her for years. People tend to notice local eccentrics and even be weirdly proud of them, especially if like the Nut Lady, they get on the Johnny Carson and David Letterman shows.

It was a decaying old Gothic Revival house, with an organ in the front hall. Tiny Elizabeth Tashjian was a New England version of a cross between Miss Havisham from *Great Expectations* and Emily Grierson from "A Rose for Emily." Dominating the living room was a portrait of Elizabeth painted many years ago, posing in what appeared to be that same room. The effect was cute but creepy, like a doll left behind in a ghost town.

The museum was housed in a single downstairs room and turned out to be surprisingly meager. The only real highlight was a 35-pound coco de mer from the Seychelles that looked like massive black buttocks. The cases contained mostly basic stuff like acorns and chestnuts that any kid could have gathered. We pretended to be impressed. Elizabeth shared her extensive nut knowledge, every fact of which I have of course forgotten. She invited us to the living room to see a video of her on Letterman. She brought us cider, and wafer cookies that were remarkably stale. The cups were none too clean, so we took only a sip or two and a polite nibble. We appreciated the gesture, though, and chose to interpret the geriatric cookies as a sign that she rarely gave such goodies to her visitors, so she must have taken a shine to us. The other possibility was that she barely *had* any visitors, but since a family from South Carolina arrived as we were leaving, that seemed unlikely.[42]

Christine and I drove five minutes to the Old Lyme Little League field, over by the railroad tracks. I knew she wouldn't be bored; we're always fascinated to see pieces of each other's past. But this time there was no past to see. We found only an empty, overgrown lot, with nary a trace of the place where I had hit a home run in my last at-bat of the regular season when I was twelve. The grandstand was gone, and the backstop, the dugouts, the green-painted wooden fence, the scoreboard out beyond center field. It was pretty much the opposite of my return to the National Stadium, with its huge improvement in facilities. Presumably there's an impressive new (well, not so new anymore) Little League field elsewhere in Old Lyme, where kids play blissfully unaware of a long-gone diamond where their fathers and grandfathers had played once upon a time, just as blissfully, just as unaware. But it meant nothing to me to find it.

I was in St. Louis as the present Busch Stadium was being constructed, and in Chicago as the new Comiskey Park (later

---

42 The Nut Lady died in 2007, after being forcibly removed to a local nursing home for the last few years of her life. Her nut collection is now housed at Connecticut College.

renamed U.S. Cellular Field to rake in the advertising revenue) was going up. In 2009, the Yankees and the Mets moved into successors for Yankee Stadium and Shea Stadium. In all four cases, the new park was built right next door to its doomed predecessor. There's something vulture-like about a replacement structure rising in the shadow of the old, and soon casting the taller shadow. It's like a condemned prisoner watching as a gallows is erected outside his cell. But in all of these situations there's a countdown to extinction, a sad (or bittersweet) inevitability that you can prepare for. It's quite different to come back to a complete, unexpected transformation—especially when that transformation involves the utter disappearance of something. Outside of memory, it simply no longer exists.

Returning to Santiago, and in particular to the training center and the National Stadium, made me think about not just going back, but *how* you go back. Nowadays, I normally fly and/or drive when I travel, and stay in decent hotels. As a young man I was more likely to ride a train or bus; plenty of times I hitchhiked.[43] I'd stay in fleabag hostels or sleep under a bush or behind a stone wall. It didn't always make for a good time, but it always made for a good story. I'm glad I traveled that way then, because there's no way I'd do it now.

I'm also glad I took a bus to get back to Santiago, and glad I did it with Hugo. It's the first time I've been with him outside of Arica and its environs. Even during the long trip, with its boredom and discomfort, I was glad. Riding the bus put me closer to the person I had been. And if I was too big a wimp to

---

43 Hitching can be miserable if the rides don't come and the rain does, but can also pay off big. Once in Villars, Switzerland, Greg Abell and I caught a ten-mile ride in a chauffeur-driven Mercedes. That's nothing, though, compared to my friend Brian Duffy, who scored a lift in a chauffeured Rolls Royce Silver Cloud all the way from London to Paris.

handle twenty-nine hours on the road, especially when it meant reaching a destination so important to me, I didn't much like the person I had become.

My friend Bill Hennessey tells a story of going to a New York Yankees Old Timers game. After the player introductions, Hall of Fame pitcher Waite Hoyt stepped haltingly off by himself to the mound. Standing alone where he had once been a star,[44] Hoyt scanned the crowded Stadium for lingering moments before shuffling back to the dugout. I can only imagine what his thoughts were; maybe he saw the ghost of Babe Ruth grinning in right field. But his feelings? Each one of us knows them. At least you know them if you've ever gone back to a place that was once central to your life, yet now is central only to your history.

In September 2008, after a weekend with high school friends on Fishers Island, New York, Jay Clark drove me via the back roads to the Old Lyme Little League field site. Jay had played first base for the Westbrook Indians our last game there; I had pitched. He warned me that a house is there now, and has been for years, so I wasn't surprised when we arrived. Jay pulled off the road and I got out for a view of the prosperous, pleasant house, with a garden green and healthy in the sun. Railroad tracks still ran behind the property. I wondered how often a train rumbles by, whether the people in the house hear its mournful whistle blow, whether it disturbs their sleep. I wondered if they're glad they live there. Then I went back to Jay's truck, and we two old friends crossed the bridge over the Connecticut River and headed home.

---

44 Hoyt was 22-7 for the 1927 Murderers Row Yankees, considered by many to be the best team ever.

CHAPTER FOURTEEN

The Concatenation Connection

Later she remembered all the hours of the afternoon as happy—
one of those uneventful times that seem at the moment only
a link between past and future pleasure, but turn out to have
been the pleasure itself.

—F. Scott Fitzgerald, *Tender Is the Night*

Hugo, Any and I sit at the kitchen table in their Santiago apartment, sipping wine and not saying much. It's nearly 8:00 P.M.; my suitcase and daypack wait near the door. The "transfer" (I have no idea why the English word is used) is due any minute to take me to the airport. I wonder if it will arrive *hora chilena* or *hora inglesa*. I actually hope it shows up on time because prolonging this goodbye is no fun for any of us.

The phone rings. Any answers then hangs up. "*Llegó*," she says.

Hugo insists on carrying the bigger bag. We take the elevator down three floors, cross the parking lot and pass through the gate to the street. As the driver stows my suitcase in the back of the van, there's time for heartfelt hugs.

Still gripping my arms, Hugo smiles. "OK, Gringo, here's an idea. Consider not waiting twenty-three years for your next visit."

He claps my back as I step into the van. Through the window I smile and wave and watch my friends grow smaller, until we turn a corner and there's nothing to see except what's up ahead.

The van picks up only one other passenger before heading to the airport, where lines are long and slow and the flight is full. But that's all there is to it. The plane takes off on time at 11:15, and just like that I'm en route to Gringolandia.

What a difference from the first time I left Santiago. I've been in Chile two weeks, not two and a half years. I'm returning to my wife and established life, not a wide-open, unsettled future. I'm flying straight back, not meandering my way home via any path that strikes my fancy, taking as long as I please.

We climb quickly into the night. The lights of Santiago vanish from sight. I look out into the night sky and think about concatenation.

"Concatenation" means a linking up or chaining together. I learned the word in college from an essay by D. H. Lawrence that called Edgar Allan Poe's tales "a concatenation of cause and effect." Until I was in the Peace Corps, though, concatenation was just another word to me. A cool word, yes, visual and concrete and fun to say, but still only a word. Only in retrospect did I discover how important the concatenation connection is to virtually everything that matters in our lives.

Start with ancestry. Each of us exists because of a chain of life receding into the yawning maw of the past. Even if you can trace your family back to Genghis Khan, Ethelred the Unready, or Charlemagne's sister, there's a hell of a lot of history before that. Existence might seem self-evident, a truth simply to be accepted, but the longer the chain is extended the more astronomical the odds grow against any of us happening the way that we did. Every birth involves two parents getting together, whether for a few minutes or for a lifetime, two people out of however many millions of others are on the planet. Multiply that incredibly small likelihood times dozens, even hundreds, of generations, and the concatenation that leads to each of our lives is amazing, astonishing, overwhelming—and mostly unknowable. DNA tests notwithstanding, early links are lost to us like dreams unrecalled from the deepest waves of sleep, then sunk to the murky bottom of the sea.

Luck and chance play major roles in forging any chain of human connection. But luck and chance are only raw material. We are also the blacksmiths of our lives, or if you prefer a more delicate image, we are jewelers trying to fashion links of luck and chance into something beautiful.

In Arica I met tourists from all over the world. They were mostly backpackers, people who frequented the same no-star joints I did. We'd spend minutes, or hours, or days doing something together, building memories and friendships no less real and important for their brevity. Possibly even more so *because* of their brevity. There's something so random and beautiful about connections made while traveling, with the world waiting around every corner if you dare to make the turn. And every person you meet would have been someone else if you had taken a different turn—or if they had. You exchange addresses, hope to cross paths again, and on rare occasions you do. Mostly, though, those addresses aren't transferred when you replace your tattered book many years later, though maybe you send a postcard on the extremely off chance they're still there, and wonder if you'll ever get to Lagos, Nigeria or Spitsbergen, Norway, or even Saskatoon, Saskatchewan.[45] Odds are long, and the clock is running.

How did I end up in Chile at all? Because I happened to have played high school baseball, happened to have mentioned it on the résumé I sent, and my Peace Corps recruiter in New York happened to say on the phone one day, "With your sports background, here's one you might be interested in: baseball coach in Chile." Sports background? Sure, I'd played varsity soccer, basketball and baseball at Westbrook High, and one season of soccer at Fairfield University (after getting cut at baseball tryouts), but I never considered that a "sports background." It was just stuff I did. What if I had gone to a high school with a really hotshot baseball program? I might not have made the team, baseball wouldn't have been on my résumé, and my recruiter probably would never even have mentioned the job to me. One of the major links of my life depended on chance (no, a chain of chances) to occur.

Yet that chance wasn't entirely random. I had to apply to the Peace Corps in the first place or it never could have happened. I also had to accept the opportunity, just as I had declined the first Peace Corps assignment offered to me, in Afghanistan. I'll never know how different the chain of my life would have been if I'd said goodbye to my family and flown to Kabul instead of Santiago. Would I have transferred to another country after the Russians invaded in 1979, and the Peace Corps pulled out? Would I have gone home? Probably I wouldn't speak Spanish today, and to me Chile would just be that odd string bean of a country, rather than my second home. I never would have met so

---

45 These days you probably trade social media information, and it's simpler to re-connect.

many people who influenced my life, though of course I would have met others, who would have influenced me in who knows what different ways.

Everything in our lives is interconnected. Alter any link and there will be consequences, some of them obvious, others unforeseeable. Investigating my chain further into the past, I first became aware of the Peace Corps from commercials I saw as a child on our black and white TV set, featuring the memorable slogan, "The toughest job you'll ever love." The Peace Corps lingered somewhere in the recesses of my brain over the years. Then, while at Fairfield University I had my first experience outside of the U.S., a junior year in Switzerland that profoundly shaped the way I view this planet. It made me aware that the world outside of the United States *exists*, not as a theoretical somewhere like heaven or the fourth dimension, but as actual places where people live and you can go. Maybe I'd have done something similar at another school, but quite possibly not. And without the taste for traveling I acquired in Europe, maybe the Peace Corps would never have entered my radar screen. Even then, I might not have followed through on the idea if I hadn't taken Dr. Randall Schaffner's English class my senior year, and been inspired by tales of his Peace Corps experience in Thailand.

Jump ahead to the concatenation of my departure from Chile: Wednesday, July 16, 1980, the middle of winter but mild and dry in Arica, as usual. I stood at home plate holding a microphone, about to read the *juramento deportivo* to open the Chilean national baseball tournament, *infantil* (10-12 years old) and *juvenil* (13-15) divisions. The crowd was gratifyingly large in this soccer stadium, converted to a baseball field for the occasion. When I had come to Arica less than two years ago many of these folks had never even heard of baseball. With a combination of pride and a bit more nervousness than I'd expected, I read the "sportsmanship pledge," ad-libbing the coda, "*Que gane el mejor, entonces.*" May the best team win.

Delivering the *juramento* meant a lot to me. Fernando Viné,[46] whose son André was one of the *infantil* pitchers, had nominated me two days before to do it, and the rest of the Arica baseball people immediately agreed. At past tournaments a player had always read the pledge; I was taken completely off guard, but gratefully accepted the honor. I won't try to improve on the simple comment in my journal: "That kind of gesture really makes things worth it."

Arica's *juvenil* all-star team flamed out and was eliminated in two games, but the *infantiles* won three straight to reach the final on Sunday. Amazing: a national championship game versus perennial Chilean baseball powerhouse Tocopilla. Even more amazing, they had already dispatched Tocopilla with ease in the opening game, 16-8, so had to be considered the favorite. The Arica kids played like champs, dominating the game and taking a 14-6 lead into the bottom of the seventh inning—only to self-destruct, cough up nine runs and lose, 15-14. Under Little League rules they would have won in a romp, for Little League games are only six innings. But that's like saying Bucky Dent's pennant-winning home run to beat the Red Sox in 1978 would

---

46 Three student "radicals" were expelled from the Arica branch of the Universidad de Chile in 1973. All three were friends of mine. Luisa Viné was married to Fernando Viné. Pitina Varas was married to Lucho Varas, one of my earliest and most dependable contacts with the sports world in Arica. I lived with Lucho, Pitina, and Lucho's parents for several weeks when I first came to Arica, before I found my own place. Eduardo Cortéz was involved with baseball coaching until financial necessity forced him to quit. Later, while working at the airport in Iquique, Eduardo once scored me a free lift home to Arica in a two-seater prop plane used as a spotter for fishing boats. On a glorious sunny day, the pilot flew out over the Pacific, and radioed information down to boats about where to set their nets. The pilot even drove me right to my door after we landed.

have been caught in Yankee Stadium. True or not, it doesn't matter one bit. The game was played in Fenway Park; Dent's pop fly sailed a few feet over the fence. Under Chilean rules the team I trained for this tournament had to play seven innings, and they fell apart in the last one.

I hadn't coached the Arica team during the tournament, nor even sat on the bench. PCVs working in baseball were expected to stay impartial during national *campeonatos*. Outside of the obvious politeness factor, there could be jealousy and accusations of bias from cities that didn't have free help from a PCV. Human nature being what it is, though, beneath our placid demeanors we of course rooted for the kids we knew and had helped develop. I suffered silently through every error, walk and lucky bloop single in that last-inning meltdown. Though I hope my face betrayed none of it, my journal admits that "I was numb after the turnabout."

There was a post-game barbecue for the players, their parents and baseball federation folks at the Club de Huasos. (A *huaso* is a Chilean cowboy, similar to the *gaucho* of Argentina, Uruguay and Brazil.) It was a superb feast and a festive few hours. The kids took the defeat remarkably well. Afterward, the PCV gringos and federation officials met to select the all-tournament team and the winners of individual awards. Despite the sting of blowing that game, I was gratified that many of "my" kids were chosen. When the job was done, I moseyed back to my abode at 7:00, only to be greeted by Susan Gregory.[47] Not that it was a total surprise, because you never knew when a fellow PCV might show up at your door. Susan was stationed in southern Chile. She was from Montana and taught me what she said should be the new state motto: "Don't Californicate Montana." Little did I know that

---

47 Not her real name.

the following year I'd be living in California, then two years after that in Utah, and from Salt Lake City would take a road trip to Montana—with my girlfriend from California.

But that's a different set of concatenations. After surreptitiously installing Susan in my room (hoping to avoid being busted by my landlords on a morals charge,) and giving her an extra key, I went with Neil McFadden (he of the Arica jail story in the "Gringo Advantage" chapter) to the post-tournament banquet. I had a blast as one of the presenters giving awards.

A lot of happy kids. Big night for me: Aldo [Picozzi, the president of the national baseball federation] gave me a plaque from the Fed, Lucho Sakurada a leather photo album from Arica, the *selecciones* [all stars] a big postcard signed by all, and Caracho passed me a personal card. Signed many a pennant for my players. Is anyone so dense that I have to describe how I felt? Such moments make everything worth it, even 15-14 losses to Toco. Said goodbye to many a baseball person whom I'll never see again. It's been a good 2 1/2 years. I have no regrets.

Split with Guido at 11:30, took my leave of Kons and others at the hotel, headed home. Susan was asleep, but I woke her and talked for a while. After switching off the light I reconnoitered the territory. Little coaxing was necessary to convince her that my bed was plainly superior to the floor. Hope we didn't keep up Maria [the maid who lived in the room above me].

Aldo mentioned the possibility of returning later this year on a Comité Olimpico [Olympic Committee] contract for 6 months. For 1/2 year, I'll consider it, but Jimmy the Greek says the smart money is on yours truly to bolt. An era has ended, and with it a notebook. Later on down the line,

T.H.

My handwriting on that entry from July 20, 1980 shrinks to fit into the last line of the last page of a journal I had begun on November 11, 1979.

I spent the next day with Susan and other friends. We walked to the beach, had a great lunch at El Fascinador overlooking the ocean, and generally acted like people on vacation—which we were. That evening PCV Patty Stern stopped by my room with an Israeli guy named Itzhak. We three and Susan sipped our way through two bottles of wine, while Itzhak and I took turns on my guitar and our four voices raised a joyful noise. I taught him Dylan's "It Takes A Lot To Laugh, It Takes A Train To Cry"; he reciprocated with Victor Jara's "Te Recuerdo Amanda." (I still have the paper with Itzhak's handwritten lyrics and chords.) Our guests left at 1:30, though Susan stayed with me. The alarm shattered the morning at 5:30, for Susan had to catch a 6:30 bus to Putre. That's the last thing I remember till Bob Maurer's knocking woke me at nine. How Susan made it out in time is beyond me, except for the obvious answer: you do what you have to do.

A week passed, a blur of packing, last minute arrangements, and heartfelt, often alcoholic farewells from many groups of friends. On Sunday, July 27, Fernando Viné treated me to lunch and a Club Deportes de Arica professional soccer game from the best seats in the house. Fernando had just driven me home and I was settling down for a siesta when Susan returned from her trip to the mountains, accompanied by a lovely, highly intelligent

219

and personable blonde woman, Katherine.[48] I was smitten. Katherine was from southern California but disliked it there; she was in South America on a Watson Fellowship. I hadn't the foggiest notion what a Watson Fellowship was, but it sounded impressive and I was sure glad she'd gotten one and that events had somehow led her to my door. We three arranged to meet that night at ten to see *Kramer vs. Kramer*, after which I took Katherine and Susan to Maipú Street for fresh-squeezed juices, and we talked for more than an hour. It was 2:00 A.M. by the time I walked them to their hostel, and we exchanged addresses and hugs outside the Residencial Piquer.

I had a serious hankering to spend more time with Katherine. The odds were against that ever happening, of course. Who knows how many people I had connected with on the road, and never seen again? The women headed south the next morning. I left Arica a day later on a last, leisurely bus trip to Santiago, with several stops to see friends along the way. (At La Serena I flagged down a bus on the Panamericana and got a cut-rate fare by quietly asking the driver the *sin boleto*—without ticket—price, which he promptly pocketed.) It was raining buckets when I pulled into Santiago a week later, so I splurged on a taxi from the bus station, forgetting that cabs charged double on Sunday. It cost me a princely 160 pesos, around four bucks, to get downtown to the Hotel de France, where PCVs stayed courtesy of U.S. taxpayers whenever they were in town on official business.

You don't just blow a farewell kiss and put the Peace Corps in your rearview mirror. There's a daunting gauntlet of red tape before they cut you loose: medical and dental exams, blood tests, X-rays, a forest of forms to fill out. (The exam showed I had intestinal worms. Four poison pills quickly did them in.) I kept

---

48 She asked me not to use her last name.

running into other PCVs, which led to last minute socializing—a phenomenon I later named the Urgency of Endings. Time is slipping away; go for it now or the chance will be gone forever.

Accordingly, after two nights at the Hotel de France I spent the next two at Veronica Inostroza's house, thrilled to see my *amiga* again and hopeful that the Urgency of Endings would rekindle passionate memories. Terrible timing for me, though; it was strictly the snows of yesteryear. Vero had just returned from the States, a visit to former PCV Bill Startzer. She had nearly married Bill during the trip and was deeply focused on their relationship. I was hopelessly mired in the Just Good Friends zone.

Still, thoughts of Veronica dominate my journal entries of those days. After a mid-afternoon walk to Vero's in a cold rain, "I bused downtown, chilled to the bone.... I tried to define my feelings for V, especially the difference that not making love to her makes. That is, just how important to me is that facet of our relationship? It's not crucial, but for me it would be an intensely lovely culmination of a friendship that has probably affected me more than any other." There's plenty more, but you get the idea. I was thinking about Veronica, well, not constantly, but a hell of a lot. And then I discovered something about karma, concatenation, and how profoundly shallow a person I can be.

Friday, August 8, was the busiest day of all. I finished (aided by liberal skimming) Thomas Hardy's *Jude the Obscure* and left it in the Peace Corps library, went to the U.S. consulate for extra passport pages (I had so many stamps from border crossings that my passport was nearly full), then the Argentine *consulado* for an entry visa, since Buenos Aires would be the first stop on my open-ended return voyage to the States. I played some guitar at the hotel before walking eighteen blocks to meet Veronica for lunch at the Matadero, a clean and amazingly cheap market, despite its name: the Slaughterhouse. It was a gorgeous sunny day; we had a great time. I bused to the Clínica Roman and received a clean bill of dental health, then caught another bus to the Peace Corps office, starting Burroughs' *Naked Lunch* en route (the ultimate antidote to *Jude the Obscure*). I took the Foreign Service Institute language exam with Patty Polanco, one of the Spanish instructors, and received a 4 instead of the 4+ I'd expected (5 is the highest score, signifying native proficiency; I'd gotten a 2.8 at the end of training). But Patty had been our toughest teacher, and I requested her to be my examiner, so I couldn't complain.

By the time I left the office around seven, most of the termination rigmarole was history. At the hotel I was drying off after a shower when I heard a knock at my door.

"Lo buscan en la recepción," said a hotel employee. Someone was waiting for me at the front desk.

"Muchas gracias." Curious, I hustled into some clothes and down the stairs—and found Katherine standing there, smiling like sunlight on still water. I invited her to Veronica's welcome back party that night, and for the next eleven days, until I left on a bus for Argentina, we spent most of our time together.

I'll give myself credit for one thing, at least. I didn't hide from my hypocrisy. Journal entry, August 8: "I realized what a false bastard I am. Know thyself. Practically all thoughts of Vero as lover tumbled out the window. So be it." I can only imagine Veronica's amusement at my canoodling with Katherine when I'd so recently been mooning over her.

Five days later, Katherine and I rode a bus to the coastal resort city of Viña del Mar. We wandered about, lingered tenderly on the beachfront rocks, then took a ten-minute bus ride on the shore road south to Valparaíso, our real destination. Valparaíso is all heart and humanity, compared to Viña's commercial flash. We had lunch at a joint called Don Lucho's, took a funicular up one of the hills and spent the rest of the afternoon walking and climbing. I'd forgotten that much of Valparaíso was shanties, precariously perched on the earthquake-prone hills. As is common in South America, poor people live up the hills, not the rich. We got lost, eventually descending by a crazy route through back yards and over plank bridges, braving slick mud trails and vicious dogs.

After a drink in the lively, funky port section of town, we strolled the dozen or so blocks to the station. The last bus to Santiago left at 9:30 so we hopped on one that was leaving then, at 8:30. Hardly five minutes passed, though, before we realized logistics would make sleeping together very problematic in Santiago. Hold it! I told the driver Katherine forgot something; we got out and caught a local bus back to the port.

At the Hotel Old Boy, I climbed creaky steps to the second-floor office while Katherine talked to three giggling women downstairs. The room was dreary and a bit expensive at 500 pesos ($12), but it had a double bed and I didn't feel like searching for a better one that might not come. I paid the ancient, arthritic *patrón* and hoped his overflowing ashtray wouldn't set the place on fire.

Through grins missing many teeth, the women offered their glasses of cheap white wine mixed with orange Fanta. I politely declined, as Katherine already had, and we returned to the street. At the Bar Inglés, a dive with half a dozen faded travel posters on the walls, we shared a split of 1975 Undurraga Pinot, then found a restaurant for a tasty fish dinner.

Katherine told me the women at the hotel weren't married; the oldest was only twenty-four, and they had eight kids among them. When I commented on their dental problems, Katherine said that in her village of Icalma in southern Chile, most people over 30 had no teeth at all. Toothbrushes were unknown until she brought a box of 100. Wealthier people with a few animals would very occasionally have meat, but most meals were bread, pine nuts and unsweetened *mate*. Sugarless *mate* is so bitter it's nearly undrinkable. It must be like coca leaves to Andean Indians, providing some energy while dulling hunger pangs.

Around midnight we returned to the Old Boy, climbing the steps just a bit unsteadily. There were cigarette burns in the bedspread and scary splotches on the peeling wallpaper, but before long they didn't matter at all.

This is a chapter about concatenations, not my last days in Santiago, so despite the fact that the Urgency of Endings redoubled for me once I met Katherine, that's it for details of my time with her. Except for this one. Katherine had done a fair amount of hitchhiking in South America—by herself. Yes, it was crazy. I don't care how confident and strong she was, a beautiful blonde woman thumbing solo was risky business. But somehow, she encountered no problems, at least none she couldn't handle. And her fearlessness forged a link in a chain that I'm still connected to today.

I don't remember where the Brazilian guys picked her up. In Chile, I think, a long ride on the Pan-American Highway. The place isn't important. What matters to the concatenation is that Katherine got along so well with them that they exchanged addresses. When she heard I was heading to Brazil, she mentioned three cool Brazilians who'd given her a lift. "You'd like them," she said, and gave me their addresses.

Two weeks later, on September 3, my bus rolled into Florianópolis, Brazil from the interior town of Lajes, seven hours through gorgeous mountain and lake country on a beat-up two-lane road. The weather had been abominable lately, heavy with rain, fog and overall gloom. The night before, I'd gotten a shock turning off the bare bulb in my ratty *pensión* room. It would have been ironic to die that way after somehow not being fried by the jerry-rigged electric water heater on the shower. At least I would have had a tasty last meal of meat pies and wine at the cantina next door, whose owner had a smashed-in nose and packed a pistol in his belt. He told me that robberies were common there. I thought of my camera half-assedly hidden under the *pensión* bed, and hurried back to my room with its swampy aroma of mildew and swarming microscopic life. I didn't need to have a third camera stolen in South America, in a third different country for good measure.

My luck seemed on the upswing in Florianópolis. First, the rain stopped. Second, when I asked in halting Portuguese the way to Rua Monsenhor Topp, the address Katherine had given me for Miguel Büchele, I found that it was right across from the bus station. I walked less than a block up the street to #33, where I didn't hesitate to press the buzzer at the gate. The woman who opened the door said Miguel wasn't there, but she immediately invited an unknown, unkempt gringo with a cheap green backpack into her home. Soon Mrs. Siquiera had fixed me eggs, sandwiches, milk and coffee, and I sat at the table talking with her son Paulo and daughter Neusa. It felt so fine to be with friends, in a house, after two weeks of cheap hotels and restaurants.

Is it possible to make friends so quickly, within minutes, especially when you barely speak each other's language? Under the right circumstances, without a doubt. But would I even do such a thing now, show up out of the blue at a stranger's door, someone who's only a friend of a friend? To my wife's chagrin, I probably would, though I'd certainly try to get in touch before-hand rather than arrive without warning. (Which is far easier to do today. Miguel had no phone, and of course e-mail didn't exist.) The Peace Corps "*mi casa es tu casa*" outlook on life is ingrained in me, as indelible as the dark spot of graphite in my left palm, where a pencil punctured the skin when I was in second grade. I can't even remember how the stabbing occurred, but that ghostly dot is proof that it did.

Ruing a road not taken is one of the saddest, and sadly common, human activities.

"If only I had done X when I had the chance."

"If only I had gone to Y before they tore it down."

"If only I had made time to see Z, but I got so busy."

"If only...."

"If...only...."

I doubt that we can exist without occasionally wondering what might have been, but I'm not talking about idle or fanciful speculation. I'm talking about actively regretting letting an opportunity slip by. Every time we find an excuse not to do something, whether from fear, laziness or some more lofty pretext (which if we're honest is probably based on fear or laziness), we lose the chance for a link to be created. We remain bound by the chains already surrounding us, rather than making new links leading to fresh connections.

There's always a degree of luck involved, pure roll-of-the-dice luck, but you have to capitalize on your breaks. As film producer Robert Evans said, "Luck is when opportunity meets preparation." If I find $100 on the street, then wave it around to show off, get mugged and have my own wallet stolen, I didn't exactly make the best of my good fortune. If I had lost Miguel's address, the concatenation would have been cut short. If I hadn't wended my roundabout route to Florianópolis, located Monsenhor Topp Street and rung a total stranger's doorbell, the tenuous possibilities couldn't have coalesced into a chain. The chain would also have ended if people had not generously opened their doors and welcomed an unknown traveler into their lives.

I spent twelve days in Florianópolis, twelve of the best days of my life. That first night Paulo drove me in his VW bug to the

Universidade Federal do Estado de Santa Catarina, where we found Miguel in a philology class. Miguel and I became instant compadres. At his apartment after class "he cooked up a soup of fresh vegetables, and we stayed up till 1:30, talking mostly of our travels. Spoke mostly in *castellano* [Spanish], but starting tomorrow I'm going to seriously apply myself to learning Portuguese. Gilberto Gil's Portuguese version of [Bob Marley's] 'No Woman No Cry' was the last thing I remember before nodding off."

Celibacy is all that prevents me from calling those twelve days idyllic. If I had stayed in Florianópolis, though, surely that problem soon would have been solved. Smart, beautiful women abound in Brazil. Believe me, I thought about sticking around—especially since I was continually being asked to. As hard as it might be for most Americans (including me) to understand, Miguel and my other new friends kept lobbying me not to leave. "*Fica um mes mais*," they said. "Stay another month. At least. Summer's coming, the beaches are amazing."

It was tempting. I had money, though I barely needed any. I could have earned my keep by helping Miguel with his artwork, preparing copper panels and etching the outlines of objects, leaving him to do the skilled, detail work. In the end, only the fact that I'd been away from home so long—nearly three years—caused me to get back on the road. I missed my family and friends in the Land of the Round Doorknobs—and to a far lesser degree, the U.S. itself. I wanted to return to lovely autumn in New England, not wait till the onset of grim, grinding winter.

I had no schedule as I rambled after leaving Chile, just a vague idea that I might fly back to New York from Rio de Janeiro, but plan or no plan I never anticipated spending twelve days in one place. On day three in Florianópolis I walked to the *rodoviaria* to check on buses to Curitiba, my next destination, not because

I was eager to leave, but because it was the obvious next step. Yet by day five I wrote:

> I feel so relaxed, so at home here. The idea of staying here for a goodly stretch is inching its way into my consciousness. Why not? It's a perfect place to write and compose (though I desperately need an axe [guitar]). Everyone here urges me to stay....
>
> It's 11 AM, Miguel works on a *chapa* (metal plate etching), an intoxicating Brazilian rhythm flows from the radio.

Day Six: This island has a great climate for working, fine people, and offers the chance to quickly learn Portuguese. I wonder if I should stay, and if I have the *cojones* to do it. So tempting. Summer must be a paradise. I doubt that female companionship would be lacking, either, and it's a good place to stay in shape.

Day Seven: Had lunch at Ju's, M got me a guitar, Ju lent me the new *Time*—hell, every day I spend here convinces me to spend another.... Tuned up the axe; it actually was a beauty. Fine resonance and timbre. Played, started a song [about Katherine][49] and another melody (didn't feel *too* good!).

Day Eight: Miguel and I thumbed (three rides) to Lagoa da Conceição to lunch at Miguelão, his father's restaurant, and the plates just kept coming (*caipirinhas* to drink; seafood soup; crab; three kinds of shrimp).

---

49 In December, 2008, I found the song "Katherine" in the back pages of my last South America journal. I changed the music to make it more up-tempo and polished the lyrics a bit. It's a pretty good tune.

Even if we had had to pay it would have only cost about 4 1/2 bucks.... [B]egan walking along the shore...saw an old islander chopping out a dugout canoe...lucked into a ride in the bed of a pickup all the way downtown.... [Tonight] P and J came over, and Neusa later to say goodbye—I'd said I was leaving tomorrow!

Day Twelve: Finally time to get a move on... M and I walked to the *rodoviaria* for me to catch the 10:30 bus to Curitiba... *Abraços* [hugs] between two amigos before I boarded the machine. What a tremendous good fortune to have met Katherine in Arica—and whom do I have to thank for it but Susan! Concatenation...all because I met Susan at Vero's one day before she split on her field trip. That's how this crazy world operates, and goes to show that every contact and experience is valuable not only in itself, but for the unpredictable results it may bring. Sometimes everything is triply worth IT.

I left Florianópolis on September 15, sleeping that night in a Curitiba fleabag aptly named the Revil Hotel. On the 18th, I spent six hours at "crashing, inexorable, wondrous" Iguaçu Falls (taller and wider than Niagara), where "lizards and butterflies abound—and above, by the Iguaçu River, so do gnats." Tomorrow I would cross the Friendship Bridge into Paraguay. But suddenly I heard rumors of a terrorist attack in Asunción; supposedly the entire Paraguayan border was closed. That seemed like a wild overreaction to me, and I expected the frontier to quickly re-open. Then I learned "that 'terrorist attack' was [former Nicaraguan dictator Anastasio] Somoza's assassination! They blasted the fucker's white Mercedes w/ a bazooka, then machine-gunned it for good measure. Dancing in the streets of Managua. I can't help but feel that the bastard only got what he deserved."

The border would stay closed indefinitely. I pondered my options and decided to skip Paraguay. (To this day I have never been there, all because a deposed dictator tasted his own murderous medicine.) I was far more interested in Brazil, anyway. Paraguay had been more of a "Hey, I'm this close, I might as well check it out" destination. The country rated only 18 pages in the 1978 *South American Handbook*, while Chile had 68, Peru nearly 100 and Brazil 140. I certainly wasn't going there to breathe the sweet air of freedom. General Alfredo Stroessner had been dictator since 1954, and with that much practice I'm sure he was at least as repressive as the rest of his strongman pals. After all, he had invited the loathsome Somoza to live a luxurious exile in Paraguay.

So, I stayed in Brazil, reaching Rio de Janeiro in the wee hours of September 25th. I caught a local express bus through a tunnel to Copacabana, just south on the other side of a mountain, and started looking for Aquiles and Luciene Pedrini Junca's apartment. Someone in Florianópolis (Jussara, I think) had given me their address. Copacabana was mostly tall buildings jammed into a narrow horseshoe of flatland between the mountains and the ocean. I walked past upscale high-rises, luxury boutiques and other prosperous shops. Unseen money was everywhere, glittering on mannequins in the windows, whispering promises behind the thick storefront glass. It was 6:30 in the morning. Ragged children slept huddled in nearly every doorway.

Carrying my backpack and a fresh, steaming load of guilt, I pondered a useless question: Is poverty worse when juxtaposed with wealth, or when it's segregated, out of sight—in a ghetto, maybe, or under a bridge? I only knew it was worse for me when poverty slept on money's doorstep, because I couldn't pretend it

230

wasn't there. Thousands of Rio street kids have been murdered in organized slayings. Their presence is not good for business, after all. Prosecutions for the killings are virtually unknown. I was tempted to take pictures—righteous, indignant pictures—but ironic contrasts between homeless kids on the sidewalk and Armani in the window seemed obscene, not artistic. My camera stayed in its case.

The address on Avenida Nossa Senhora De Copacabana turned out to be just one long block from the famous beach. It was too early to bother anyone, so I walked to the water and watched all manner of runners and walkers strutting by, covering the spectrum of corporeal conditions and athletic attire, from tracksuits to the briefest and tightest of Speedos. At 7:15, I called from a pay phone on the street. My Portuguese must have been halfway decent by then, because I made myself understood without the crutch of smiles and hand gestures that you have when talking to someone in person. I was immediately invited up, and though a guy named Marcos and his psychologist girlfriend (whose name I missed and was too shy to ask for again) were already staying there, Luciene insisted I was welcome. I didn't argue, and the concatenation continued.

I slept on their couch for four days, bookended around a three-day solo bus trip to Ouro Preto. Luciene and Aquiles took in an unknown foreigner who showed up unannounced. They fed me spaghetti for lunch, and fried snake for dinner. (Delicious; I thought it was fish.) The next day they drove me to the Corcovado, site of the giant Christ the Redeemer statue, for a gorgeous view of the city. Luciene even had a sweet Giannini guitar that I was welcome to play whenever I wanted, which was often. Then, after all they had done for me, Aquiles actually apologized on October first that friends from their hometown of Campos were arriving tomorrow, and there wouldn't be room for me in the apartment.

On October 2nd, I took leave of my hosts with profuse thanks, bused to Botafogo on the other side of the mountain tunnel from Copacabana, and tramped for forty-five minutes till I found a suitable cheap hotel, the Senador Veraqueiro. I spent my last night in South America nearly naked in my room with a roasted chicken and two bottles of warm, supermarket Brahma beer. As usual for me, this eve-of-transition produced no lofty thoughts. I read a bit, after washing my greasy hands, and wrote in my journal. As I drank the second bottle, I felt a familiar paradox: two years and nine months felt like forever, yet had passed so quickly.

The last link in the chain—for now, anyway—was about to be forged. On October 3rd I bought a one-way ticket to JFK. Braniff had carried me to South America, and Pan Am would take me home—two airlines currently grounded in the dustbin of history.[50] Paying the $650 fare was no problem: as a self-abnegating Volunteer I had accumulated over three grand in Peace Corps readjustment allowance.

I left my backpack at the hotel desk and walked to the beach. Leaving my valuables unattended seemed crazy, so I brought them in my green nylon daypack: wallet, watch, airline ticket, camera, pouch with passport and dollars. That could be risky, too; thieves in Rio were supposedly everywhere. With cameras already stolen in Chile and Peru, I had no desire to go for a hat trick in Brazil. Despite my previous screw-ups, I felt the best option was to put the important stuff in one place and keep it close. Although I

---

50 What other now defunct airlines have I flown? People Express, TWA, Western, Eastern, Swiss Air, Ladeco (Chile), British Caledonian, Northwest, probably others I'm forgetting.

hadn't read *Pudd'nhead Wilson* yet, I was taking his advice: "Put all your eggs in one basket and—WATCH THAT BASKET."

I laid my towel on the sand, sat down and tried to wrap my mind around reality. Somehow, I was on a beach in Rio de Janeiro, with the iconic cone of Pão de Açucar hill across the sparkling bay. Somehow, I had lived in South America for nearly three years. Somehow, that night I was leaving. Somehow, I was going home. It was time, definitely time to go, but that didn't make it feel any more real.

The sun was strong for early spring, and before long I was roasting. My *South American Handbook* warned that Botafogo's beach was "too polluted for bathing," yet people were swimming and no one was keeling over. I wanted to join them. But what about my pack? It would be lunacy to just leave it on my towel, easy prey for any punk to snatch and run, even if I kept my glasses on so I could watch it happen. I looked around for an honest face. A lady on a nearby blanket seemed to fit the bill. She was middle-aged, or what passed for middle age to me in those days—maybe late thirties. Even if I was wrong and she turned out to be a Brazilian Bonnie Parker, I figured I could catch her if she bolted with my bag.

I headed across the hot sand, rehearsing in my head the Portuguese request to watch my pack for a few minutes while I cooled off in the water. I had no illusions of fluency, but I think I delivered the question well. She smiled and pleasantly agreed to help me out.

"*Muito obrigado,*" I said.

"*Voce é brasileiro?*" she asked.

"*Não,*" I admitted. "*Americano.*"

She beamed. "Really? I'm from New Jersey!"

The concatenation continued. We talked for half an hour, by far the most English I'd spoken in six weeks. Za Za Clark was actually born in Czechoslovakia (I should have asked if she was from the Czech part, or the Slovak part like my father's parents), married an American and lived in New Jersey before moving to Rio. They had a beach-view apartment in a complex right behind us. When I told her I was flying out that night, Za Za invited me to dinner. Man, I thought, this is working out great right to the end. One more link in the chain. Without a worry I went for a swim.

After Za Za left, I sat watching the water and imagining Africa, somewhere far off over the waves. I kept the pack tight at my side or beneath my bent knees. A young guy lacking front teeth came up and asked me the time. I took out my watch and told him, aware even as I opened the zipper that I was making a foolish mistake. Never advertise anything you don't want to lose. The man thanked me and jogged away.

Ten minutes later I was lying on my back with the pack for a pillow, eyes closed against the sun. Something tapped my bare feet. A different young man, face etched with worry, asked in Portuguese if I'd seen a missing *garota*. "She was just here," he said, almost panicking. "Now she's gone."

I sat up, worried. I *had* noticed a cute little girl, maybe two years old, playing in the sand. We both scanned the beach. No sign of her. The poor guy was distraught.

I'll never know what told me to spin around. The toothless lowlife who'd asked for the time was unzipping my pack, one hand balled in a fist. I lunged and gripped his scrawny wrist.

"Desculpe, desculpe, e somente areia na mão." Sorry, sorry, it's only sand in my hand. His fingers spread open and sand sifted out of his palm. I let go of his wrist and he ran off. His accomplice was already long gone.

My heart started thumping like mad, one of those times you realize you *have* a heart. That fistful of sand was no pretext; it was a weapon designed to throw in my eyes. Only pure chance, or instinct, or luck—wheeling around at the right instant—saved me. That and my uncharacteristic aggression in grabbing his arm, probably the only time in my life I've done something like that. Still, if he hadn't tried to be stealthy and steal the watch unnoticed, I wouldn't have had a prayer. If he had simply seized the pack and sprinted off, I doubt I'd have ever seen it again. No money, no passport, no ticket, no watch, no camera.

In a blink the beach had gone from paradise to menace. I turned my back on the postcard-perfect scene and walked away with jelly in my knees.

At Za Za's apartment, I met her friendly husband and two kids, a boy and a girl. When I mentioned that I wanted to take home a bottle of *cachaça* and a Caetano Veloso album,[51] twelve-year-old Donny led me to the neighborhood booze and music stores. I had no inkling at the time, but that bit of hospitality likely involved an ethical dilemma for the family, for it emerged during dinner conversation that they were Mormons. Practicing Mormons don't drink alcohol. I knew this because of Jeannie, a PCV in Constitución who would go with Mike Welsh and me to bars and drink Fanta, which we considered strange until she explained the Mormon prohibition. We still thought it was strange, but at least we understood.

I was impressed that the Clarks didn't let strict scruples stand in the way of hospitality. They served delicious roast beef, with a somewhat odd dessert of miniature marshmallows embedded in lime Jell-O. Little did I know that three years later, at dinner with a Mormon family in Salt Lake City, I would lo and behold encounter the identical dessert. Less than a month after my

---

51 I'd been impressed by Caetano's *Cinema Transcendental* on vinyl at Miguel's in Florianópolis, and bought the cassette in Rio. It still plays, and I still like it.

arrival in Utah for grad school I learned the ubiquity of "Jell-O salad" in Mormon cuisine.

This Mormon connection tempts me to think it's a link in the chain that led to meeting my wife Christine, when we played on the same softball team at the University of Utah. But it's just coincidence, not concatenation. Concatenation meant the Clarks giving me a lift to nearby Santos Dumont airport, where I caught a bus to Galeão, the international airport outside the city. I lucked into a seat in the Clipper section, which got me a free gin and tonic, and quarter-bottle of French wine with my second dinner around 2:00 A.M., though I slept less than three hours. Flota Barrios bus seats were far more comfortable.

We reached JFK at eight in the morning. I wasted an hour, and half a dozen dimes, at a pay phone trying to connect with friends in New York before deciding to thumb to Connecticut. These days I read my journal with astonishment: so many matter-of fact details about courses of action unthinkable for me now. A friendly airport customs agent found me a piece of cardboard, and I walked maybe a mile with my CONN. sign before a Black businessman in a new Cadillac Coupe de Ville drove me all the way to exit 22 on I-95.

It was the exit I'd taken so many times to Fairfield University. I decided to visit a favorite English professor, who lived just a block away. Dr. Schaffner had been a PCV in Thailand, and was a major influence on me joining the Peace Corps. How cool would this be, dropping in on him today, the first person I know to see me back in the States? The karma was perfect. Fighting to keep a grin off my face, I rang the bell.

A stranger opened the door. I asked for Dr. Schaffner.

"Sorry," he said. "He's been gone two and a half years."

OK, the karma wasn't perfect, but the weather was. A gorgeous early fall day. At the on-ramp a dad and his eight-year-old son picked me up and drove me right to my destination: New Haven. They were going to Yale Bowl for the boy's first football game and he could scarcely contain himself. I could relate as I used my last dime to call my friend Phil Rieth from a gas station. I messed with him a moment before identifying myself.

"Tom!" he shouted. Five minutes later Rich Dwyer pulled up in his blue Triumph to take me to their place on Elm Street for reunion merrymaking.[52] The next day he drove me home with the top down, wind in our hair and sun on our faces, and I arrived unannounced to surprise my parents. They had no idea when I was coming home, and few memories of my life compare to my father's smile when he saw me get out of that car.

So, the chain continued, and I picked up my life where I had left it. Except, of course, that my life would never be the same.

---

52 I moved into that apartment in December and stayed till the following summer.

EPILOGUE

The facts are always less than what happened.

—Nadine Gordimer

Life has a lot in common with writing. Once a piece is done it can feel inevitable, but thousands of decisions went into creating it. Like all people looking back on their lives, writers read their work from years before and question some of their choices, wish they could make changes—or conversely, stand in awe of former powers and abilities, now atrophied or gone forever. Until the work is published, of course, writers have the option—and the responsibility—of revising and polishing, of making their words sing as best they can. Sometimes if a piece is reprinted, a writer has the luxury, or the curse, of returning to old work and tweaking or transforming it. Think of Walt Whitman, with his six editions of *Leaves of Grass*. Life is less likely to offer a chance for revision. No matter what you do to atone for a mistake, the mistake remains, an unfortunate fact frozen in time. There is no delete key for the past. Every act remains part of the chain.

I started a writer's notebook on June 1, 1977, a few weeks after I graduated from college. Keeping a writer's notebook while doing precious little actual writing is a dubious strategy, which I'll chalk up to naive enthusiasm and irrepressible, unearned confidence. Weeks, even months would pass without an entry. On June 21, 1978, though, while I was walking home from Veronica's in Santiago a thought slipped into my mind. Here it is, copied from the notebook:

> Time takes longer to erase the inscription from a tombstone
> Than it does to scatter the fluff of a dandelion.
> But it's the same principle.

Below that I wrote the first line again angling down at a 45-degree angle, followed by the words of the second line floating willy-nilly on the page as I tried to visually approximate dandelion fluff adrift in the wind. The third line I used as an epitaph on a crudely drawn headstone, with an equally amateurish daisy growing on the grave. The original three lines are written in the careful longhand I was still capable of in those days. The "visual poem" is printed in all lowercase letters, also carefully, stark evidence of the devolution of my handwriting over the years.

Was it chance that this idea came to me on the winter solstice, on the shortest day of the year? Winter was just beginning, yet the days would soon grow longer. It was my first year in Chile; a lifetime of June 21 as the summer solstice needed to be overcome, twenty-two years of experience turned upside-down. Christmas was in the summer here, Santa sweating in his padded suit.

Hardly a soul cared about baseball. Government of the people, by the people, for the people, *had* perished from the face of the earth. Disappeared. *Desaparecido.*

So much of what I "knew" to be true had to be left behind. *Chao pescao.* So long, farewell. Adios, adieu.

Goodbye.[53]

There are two kinds of people: those who say goodbye and leave with their eyes forward, focused on the future, and those who turn around and look back. Whenever I say goodbye—a real goodbye, that is, involving prolonged separation—I always look back. Whether from politeness or necessity, I look back. Sometimes people are waving to me, sometimes smiling or crying, staring up at the clouds or watching the ground.

And sometimes when I look back, they're already gone.

---

53 "Adios" and "adieu" both mean "to God." "Goodbye" derives from "God be with you."

IF YOU TURN TO LOOK BACK

APPENDICES

A PINOCHET PRIMER

"The road stopped like a dying man's signature
on a last-minute will."

—Richard Brautigan
The Hawkline Monster

Augusto Pinochet Ugarte, 1915-2006. If his name is Pinochet, where did Ugarte come from?

Ugarte was his mother's surname. In Spanish-speaking countries, the mother's last name is part of a person's full legal identity, though it's rarely used in informal situations. Think of the Nobel Prize-winning Colombian author, Gabriel García Márquez. He should be referred to as García, or García Márquez, never simply Márquez. Many people use just the initial of their mother's name when they write their signature.

How do you pronounce this dead dictator's name?

"Augusto" and "Ugarte" are straightforward: ow-GOOS-toe and oo-GAR-teh. "Pinochet" has more variety. Many Chileans say peen-oh-CHET, though peen-oh-CHAY is common as well. In private, "Pinocchio" is often used, a reference to the catalogue of lies in a typical speech by *Su Excelencia*.

In Spanish, an acute accent indicates the stressed syllable, not a change in pronunciation. If there's no accent mark, the stress usually falls on the second to last syllable. In the case of

Gabriel García Márquez: gah-bree-EL (an exception to the usual penultimate syllable stress) gar-SEE-uh MAR-kes (outside of some areas of Spain, where the "th" is common, "z" has the same sound as "s.")

What did Mama Pinochet, *née* Ugarte, think of the historic success of her beloved first-born child?

What's not to love? Commander-in-Chief of the Chilean armed forces. Savior of his country from the Communist Menace. *Presidente de la Republica.* Enormously wealthy man with numerous Swiss and offshore accounts for himself and members of his family. To think that her Augusto was such an astute businessman that on his humble government salary he somehow stockpiled many millions. Pinochet had numerous accounts and certificates of deposit with Riggs Bank in Washington, D.C., beginning in 1985 while he was still president. Riggs even allowed him to open new accounts to hide money while he was under house arrest in England. Pinochet's total assets with Riggs ranged between $4 and $8 million—and that's just the money he had with Riggs. All told he had over 125 accounts, many under fake names, with at least six U.S. banks.

It's wonderful to live in a country where every child, even those sleeping in alleys on scraps of cardboard, can dream of becoming president, and filthy rich besides. The American Dream writ large in a skinny land on the bottom side of the globe. For every true believer in socialism and equality, there are a hundred (a thousand?) people who'd love to trade places with a plutocrat. They don't hate the unfairness; they hate being on the wrong side of the divide. According to Emma Goldman in E.L. Doctorow's *Ragtime*, "I am often asked the question How can the masses permit themselves to be exploited by the few. The answer is By being persuaded to identify with them.... [T]he laborer goes home to his wife, an exhausted workhorse with the veins standing out in her legs, and he dreams not of justice but of being rich."

Why did President Salvador Allende appoint Pinochet commander of the army on August 23, 1973, just nineteen days before Pinochet led the September 11 *golpe*?

Because, in addition to being a ruthless soldier, Pinochet was a good actor and a shrewd politician.

When did Augusto Pinochet and Salvador Allende first meet?

Get ready for some irony. They met in Pisagua in 1947, during the first era that the prison was used for political detainees. Largely to curry favor with the United States as the Cold War was heating up, President Gabriel González Videla had outlawed the Communist Party in 1946, and a number of Communists were arrested and sent to Pisagua. Captain Augusto Pinochet was made commander of the prison. When a congressional delegation led by Senator Salvador Allende arrived to interview prisoners about their treatment, Pinochet tried to stop the investigation. Allende responded that he had come to do a job and he intended to do it.

Versions of what happened next diverge 180 degrees. Pinochet later wrote that when Allende persisted, Pinochet threatened to have him shot and the senator backed down. Another story has Allende scornfully telling Pinochet, "How dare a little lieutenant [*tenientillo*] obstruct a Chilean Senator? Out of my way!" Since Pinochet had been promoted to captain by 1947, this version seems to exaggerate for effect. Possibly, however, Allende either so scorned Pinochet that he intentionally misrepresented his rank, or was unfamiliar with military insignias and simply made a mistake.

247

There are even varying versions of the incident's aftermath. Chilean dissident and exile Ariel Dorfman, later a professor at Duke University, wrote in *Threepenny Review* that "the General was to worry that this violent confrontation would come back to haunt him, but Allende never again alluded to it, and certainly did not remember it when he designated Pinochet Commander in Chief of the Army." According to other accounts, Allende put Pinochet on the spot in La Moneda, the presidential palace, by saying he remembered an official by that name at the Pisagua prison. "Not me," Pinochet said. "That was Manuel Pinochet." Pinochet's memoir proudly mentions the lie about the non-existent Manuel as an example of his quick thinking.

Why is Pinochet better known to Americans than Argentinian military dictator Rafael Videla, although over 25,000 people died in Argentina's "Dirty War," compared to 3,200 in Chile?

Longevity, for one thing. Pinochet was leader of Chile from 1973 to 1990, one of many right-wing military dictators who had dominated Central and South America in the '70s and '80s, with considerable aid from the U.S. ("Hate commies? Then you're our boy, no matter how wretched a swine you are." Through similar amoral tunnel-vision, the U.S. backed Saddam Hussein at the time.) In 1982, Videla idiotically started a war with England over the Falkland Islands (*Islas Malvinas*), a tiny clump of rocks in the south Atlantic. Perhaps even more idiotically, he apparently expected the U.S. to side with Argentina. President Reagan, of course, chose to support England, with its own right-wing leader, Margaret Thatcher. Argentina's military was thrashed within days, and Videla left office the next year.

Unlike a dictator such as Stroessner in Paraguay, Pinochet frequently appeared in the pages of U.S. newspapers. He won a rigged plebiscite in 1980 and remained president until voted out in December of 1989 when Chile finally had a fair election, and to the amazement and relief of many, Pinochet abided by the result. But he remained commander of the army, as well as "senator for life," and continued to wield considerable power. Slowly, Chile's democracy asserted itself, and Pinochet's decrees that no soldier could be prosecuted for actions during and after the *golpe* were overturned by the government and the courts.

Pinochet continued to make headlines long after he wished he didn't. In 1998 he was arrested in England, where he had gone for back surgery (the best surgeons and facilities in Chile were evidently not good enough for *El Presidente*). Spain attempted to extradite him for the murders of Spanish citizens. After a protracted legal battle amid much international publicity, England refused Spain's request and cravenly allowed Pinochet to return to Chile on humanitarian grounds, claiming that he was too sick to face trial. To the disgust (but not surprise) of many, Pinochet arrived in Chile not infirm, but hearty and defiant. Meanwhile, numerous lawsuits against him were working their way through the Chilean courts, for corruption, civil rights violations and kidnapping. À la O.J. Simpson, he might escape prosecution for murder, but not for depriving the dead of their civil rights. Courts also ruled that amnesties decreed by the *junta* for "excesses" committed during the *golpe* only applied to murders; perpetrators could still be prosecuted for kidnapping. Pinochet stayed in the news, a stalwart symbol of the bad old days, so Americans even casually familiar with current events have heard of him.

Possibly most important of all: the U.S. government was complicit in Pinochet's *golpe*, and Americans died as a result. "Only" three, but even one is enough to undercut easy dismissal of the event as a bunch of crazy foreigners killing each other in some godforsaken corner of the planet. Like John Walker Lindh, the "American Taliban," or Rachel Corrie, martyred beneath an

Israeli tank, some Americans remember Charles Horman. Maybe not his name, but his story, in large part due to the popular 1982 film *Missing*. (Directed by Constantin Costa-Gavras, himself an exile after a military takeover of Greece in 1967.) Who could not be horrified as Jack Lemmon's character slowly realizes that not only has his son been murdered, but the U.S. government knows who did it and is covering for the murderers to protect itself?

Pinochet's murderers also dared to kill, not only in this country, but brazenly and virtually in the shadow of the White House. In 1976, former Chilean ambassador to the U.S., Orlando Letelier, died in a car bombing in Washington, D.C. A colleague, 25-year-old American Ronni Moffitt, also was killed. The hit was ordered by the DINA, Pinochet's secret police, and organized by assassin Michael Townley, an American formerly on the payroll of the CIA. (Townley is now free in the Witness Protection Program for ratting on the five anti-Castro Cubans he hired to booby-trap Letelier's car.) Pinochet, of course, denied any knowledge or involvement. This from a man whose most famous (infamous?) quote is, "Not a leaf moves in Chile without me knowing about it."

Many Americans mistrusted Richard Nixon, Henry Kissinger and the CIA. Having that troika connected to the *golpe* also helped to cement Pinochet in U.S. collective memory—as a villain. It's human nature to remember the bad guy. Besides, as people often complain, good news is no news as far television is concerned. Television in a democracy, that is, with freedom of the press. Chilean TV news under Pinochet in the late '70s loved disaster and sensationalism (I was eating at a little dive in Arica when pictures of Jonestown poison victims filled the black and white screen), but stories about the government were almost uniformly positive and supportive. You don't need to be a genius to figure out why.

How did Pinochet hold power for so long?

Fear and intimidation, while keeping his base of Chile's rich and upper middle class happy. Fear not just of the military and the 3 A.M. knock on the door, though that was important, but also fear of destabilizing elements such as leftist terrorists and Argentinian expansionists. After the chaos of the later Allende years, Chileans wanted stability. Most resented Pinochet's authoritarianism and brutality but rationalized it as the price you must pay for protection from the bad guys. Keep the people scared and you keep them submissive.

Not that all Chileans wanted Pinochet out of power. Pinochet had his supporters; thousands showed up at his funeral. Militant anti-communism will put some folks on your side, regardless of your methods. All Chileans benefited when he brought runaway inflation under control, though many suffered from the ways he reached that goal. He embraced the unfettered free market policies of Milton Friedman and the "Chicago Boys"; crushed labor unions; eliminated employee protections; and fulfilled many public services with grievously underpaid *empleo minimo* workers. The income gap between rich and poor widened into a chasm.

Did you ever see Pinochet in the flesh?

I did indeed have that brush with greatness. Ariel Dorfman has never seen more of Pinochet than one white-gloved hand giving a patronizing wave from a black-windowed limousine. On June 6, 1980 (the 36th anniversary of the D-Day invasion) I saw Pinochet in a phalanx of uniformed stooges march up 21 de Mayo, Arica's main drag, then descend later in a black Mercedes. The sidewalks were jammed with people on both sides of the street; there was tepid applause. Pinochet passed within twenty feet of me. I remember thinking that if I were a different person

251

IF YOU TURN TO LOOK BACK

with different skills and a different mentality, armed with a gun instead of a camera, I could easily have shot the bastard. Blood would have soaked his gleaming white uniform.

I not only didn't shoot Pinochet, I didn't get a photo. The car passed quickly; I had no chance to focus so had time for only one shot. Holding the camera overhead for an unobstructed view I'd have to guess about the framing. Still, though, what the hell, right? Go for it. The worst that can happen is you take a lousy picture.

Actually, that's not the worst that could happen. Out of cowardice, paranoia, or both, although I didn't see any Chilean Secret Service agents, I figured they were there. A quick move involving a shiny piece of metal might get my camera broken—or me broken. These are subtle ways that living under a dictatorship shapes your actions. There's an undercurrent of fear to everyday life. Many people are willing to be bossed around by their Big Brother, so long as he promises to protect them from schoolyard bullies. If those promises prove false, and Big Brother's "Mission Accomplished" claim just creates more bullies, people look for different strategies to defend their lunch money.

Michelle Bachelet [botch-eh-LET], who along with both of her parents was tortured after the *golpe*, was elected Chile's first female president in 2005. Who did Pinochet vote for?
No one. He was under house arrest in Santiago and could not vote.

How ironic is it that Pinochet died on December 10, International Human Rights Day?
No more ironic than that he was a devout Catholic born on November 25, St. Catherine's Day—and Catherine was tortured and killed by the Roman dictator Maximus. Or that he swore

he never ordered anyone to be killed, and claimed in a 2003 interview, "I am good, I consider myself an angel."

An "angel"? Is it possible to feel no remorse for the deaths of over 3,000 people?

We know from movie cowboys like John Wayne that "a man's got to do what a man's got to do," and from political cowboys like George W. Bush that a real man says, "Bring it on." Seeing the concrete results of those credos—children killed in a raid on a supposed terrorist hideout, people tortured and killed at the National Stadium—must create a tremendous psychic strain. Talk about cognitive dissonance. "I'm a good person. I believe in what I'm doing. Our cause is just. That mangled corpse is not a human being, it's collateral damage. Well, it *is* a human being, or it *was*, but...I mean, no one wanted this to happen. Don't you understand? Our cause is just. No one wants these things to happen, but...our cause...."

Only a few sick people want to kill other human beings. For everyone else, it's traumatic. Therefore, if they do kill, they must try to assuage their guilt by justifying it—and there's no better justification than God's will. This propensity is easy to lampoon, but seems impossible to eradicate. In Voltaire's *Candide*, priests on both sides of an impending battle exhort soldiers to slaughter the godless enemy, and slaughter they do, with clear consciences. In Jaroslav Hasek's *The Good Soldier Svejk* an archbishop prays, "God bless your bayonets that they may pierce deeply into your enemies' bellies. May the most just Lord direct the artillery fire on to the heads of the enemy staffs. May merciful God grant that all your enemies choke on their own blood from the wounds which you will deal them!"

God's nemesis, of course, is the Devil, the Evil One. If you're convinced that God is on your side, simple logic says the Devil is backing your enemies. The 9/11/01 hijackers struck at what they saw as evil: America and its influence around the world. The 9/11/73 Chilean military with CIA help struck at what they saw as evil: Communism. It serves no purpose to call either group madmen. They were not crazy; they were zealots, absolutely convinced of the rightness of their cause. Nothing on earth is more dangerous than fallible human beings sure that they know God's will and determined to force that "knowledge" on others.

Psychologically, there are three rationales for this:

1) We're doing it for their own good, to enlighten the benighted. (The classic missionary position.)

2) We're exacting vengeance in God's name, as an example to the wicked. (The death penalty as a deterrent to future criminals; Pat Robertson and Jerry Falwell claiming that 9/11 and Hurricane Katrina were God's retribution on America for its tolerance of homosexuality—as if it *is* tolerant—and general licentiousness.) The irony, of course, although lost on the televangelists, is that this "avenging angel" rationale mirrors that of the hijackers for committing the attacks in the first place. The Muslim zealot and the Christian zealot who hate each other and claim a hotline to God, are the same person despite surface distinctions of dress and dogma. Crusade and jihad are the head and tail of the same coin of self-righteousness.

3) The "other" by his actions has forfeited his position as a human being and thus can, and even should, be exterminated as vermin to improve the planet. (The Holocaust; ethnic cleansing of every type; Saddam Hussein's treatment of Kurds; genocide of native peoples in the U.S., Australia and elsewhere). Pinochet's "other" was the familiar Cold War bogeyman, the Communist, a category expanded to include anyone on the left.

Pinochet had recourse to all three of these rationales. Chances are he never read *Love Story*, or saw the movie, but being the righteous avenging angel definitely means never having to say you're sorry.

Did Pinochet die "dead dog"?

Yes, according to my friend and former colleague Domingo Arias. It's the first thing he said to me after Pinochet died. *Perro muerto* is Chilean slang for getting away with something without having to pay. Domingo had to flee Chile after the *golpe*, so he knows about both getting away and paying the price. If you bolt on a restaurant bill, that's *perro muerto*. If you trample on human rights for years, loot the national treasury while thousands go hungry, then die before the wheels of slow, slow justice finish turning, that's *perro muerto*.

Are you glad he's dead?

I suppose it's best for Chile. Consign Pinochet to the dustbin of history and focus on tomorrow. If there's any justice, the civil rights lawsuits can continue, suing his enormous, ill-gotten estate.

Funny thing, though. The death of a man I despised has brought the years home. Hearing the news has made me feel older. The kid who sprouted his first ratty beard in Chile is clean-shaven these days, preferring to scrape away the ghostly gray growing on his face.

You didn't answer the question.

Yes, I'm glad the son of a bitch is dead.

My father and Pinochet were both born in 1915. Why did a brutal dictator live seven years longer than a good man?

Because life is neither fair nor comprehensible.

THE PAST ON PAPER: ARRESTED DECAY

"The truth is that we all live by leaving behind..."

—Jorge Luis Borges
"Funes the Memorious"

Driving down the east side of the Sierra Nevada past Lake Tahoe, you leave the mountain evergreens and soon hit the desert. Not the absolute aridity of Chile's Atacama, but the cactus and tumbleweed sort of desert—the landscape of movie Westerns. This isn't most people's (including most Californians') image of California. It's not oranges or surfboards or wineries or redwoods or coastal cliffs or smog or traffic or sprawling suburbs or huge valley farms. Think of it this way: Nevada starts before you leave California.

Take routes 89 and 395 south from Tahoe till you're twenty-five miles north of Lee Vining, the town on Mono Lake that's the gateway to Tuolomne Meadows, the eastern part of Yosemite National Park. That section of the park gets a fraction of the visitors who go to the western Yosemite Valley to see the spectacular, big-name sights: El Capitán, Half Dome, Yosemite Falls. Mono Lake is famous for being saltier than the Great Salt Lake, and for its otherworldly tufa formations, some on land, some projecting from the water like weird white stalagmites.

257

See these things, but not quite yet. First, turn east on route 270 and drive to Bodie, hard by the Nevada line. There won't be much traffic. You might well be the only car. Hardly anyone takes this road who isn't going to Bodie, and hardly anyone goes to Bodie because it's a ghost town, a gold mining boomtown gone bust.

I went to Bodie in 1983 with my then-girlfriend Diane Hargrove. It's a California State Historical Park. Dozens of weathered buildings remain, dotted around the scrubby, dusty landscape. We felt like voyeurs, peering in the windows of tin-roofed houses and businesses, but of course we kept looking. It was fascinating to see which pieces of their lives people had left behind. A sagging bed, an open book, a calendar on the wall as if to pretend time wouldn't matter in the new place they were going. Most poignant for me were the cracked leather shoes, sometimes for small children, seldom in pairs, waiting on the floor for long-dead feet to return for them.

I haven't been back to Bodie, but if all has gone according to plan, it looks exactly the same today. Why? Because the town is being preserved as a sort of time capsule, what the park pamphlet calls "a state of arrested decay." "Arrest" is from the Latin for "to stand still," and the idea is that Bodie will not be restored, but also not allowed to deteriorate further. Whether this policy is admirable, hubristic, or both, is open to debate. Try as humans might to counter the ravages of time, it's a losing battle. Every homeowner knows how quickly a house moves toward ruin if not maintained.[54] Despite the best efforts of the state of California, Bodie will eventually disappear from the face of the earth. It might take a thousand years, but it will happen. Decay can never be arrested, never thrown in prison or put in solitary

---

54 "Maintain" comes from Latin meaning "to hold in the hand." So, when we maintain, we try to keep a grip on things.

confinement where it can only harm itself. But humans aren't humans if we don't give it a shot.

That night we camped at Mono Lake, on a secluded stretch of land near a tufa colony. The world was silent; lights were few and distant, just faraway flickers. I hadn't seen a sky so shot with stars since nights out in the Chilean desert, and the stars stayed thick until the moon rose in the east over the lake. The tufa columns were spooky, hulking figures in the moonlight. It was truly sublime until the ridiculous intruded—and ravenous mosquitoes drove us slapping into Diane's faded red Toyota. We ate cheese sandwiches and drank a bottle of zinfandel, listening to a nearly inaudible Angels-Yankees game on the radio before repairing to my brand-new tent.[55]

This chapter is going to jump around, because that's how memory works (or doesn't work). In 2001, my wife Christine and I visited our friends Jon and Jill Maney in Geneva, New York. We had all met in Salt Lake City while Jon and I were getting Ph.D.s at the University of Utah; later he and I edited a short story anthology, *A Celestial Omnibus: Short Fiction on Faith*. This trip was the fine time it always is when we get together: a gorgeous drive around Seneca Lake; stops at local wineries and antiques dealers (the past is on parade in upstate New York); talk of the (mostly) good old days; and more food, drink and laughter than was strictly necessary.

The morning we headed back to Connecticut, Jon and Jill put out a sumptuous breakfast spread. Jon also fed a crowd of cats on their back porch, many of them former pets of Hobart College students who'd abandoned them when school ended.

"Those sons of bitches," I said when Jon told me that.

---

55 That tent was stolen from a rental car trunk in Barcelona two years later.

"Spoiled, selfish sons of bitches," he said, and poured me more coffee. "Listen, there's something I want to show you." He walked over to an old dresser and picked up an old book. Virtually everything in their house is old. Jon is an expert on antiques and is so driven to connect with the past that he once took a tinsmithing course just to try to understand the way life used to be.[56]

We were all at the breakfast table. Jon handed me the book. "It's a soldier's diary. From the Civil War."

I started reading. Christine leaned over to see. The writing was legible and literate, with occasional drawings to illustrate the scenes he was describing.

"Where'd you get this?" I asked.

"A dealer I know." Jon knows lots of dealers. "He said the soldier was from around here, and after he came back from the war, the diary got passed down in his family. Eventually some heir with no sense of history sold it."

I smiled. "Lucky for you."

"Sort of. Let me see that for a second." Jon carefully turned some pages then gave the book back to me. "This is the most interesting part," he said.

There was going to be a battle the next day, probably a big one. The soldier was scared, but didn't dwell much on that. Mostly he described what he saw: the landscape, the army's preparations. I would have been worried for him if I hadn't known that he survived the war. I turned the page.

Halfway down, the writing stopped. The rest of the book was blank.

---

56 Jon's opposite would be a Tennessee woman Christine and I met at a B & B in Maine. At breakfast she seemed bewildered by all the antiques around us and confided, "I won't have anything in my house older than I am."

Slowly I looked up. "You said that he lived."

Jon nodded somberly. "That's what the guy told me. Sometimes these clowns talk out of their asses. It's probably what the seller said, and he never bothered to check."

Before I'd even started reading, I knew the writer had been dead for maybe a century. Why then was this revelation such a shock? I guess because when we read, whatever is "happening" on the page feels like present tense. As far as we're concerned it's going on right now, at the moment our eyes send the symbols (letters, pictures) to our brains to decode. And this diary was creating a very personal "now," from a once-living person's handwriting rather than a mechanically printed page. Someone I was getting to know and care about suddenly wasn't there anymore. Until the words ran out, the fact that he was dead did not mean he wasn't there.

This is one of the great advantages of writing over an oral culture. Socrates deplored writing for a number of reasons, including that human memory would atrophy. He was right. Surely our mnemonic skills have declined precipitously since writing has existed as a crutch, but I'm willing to pay that price for the ability to personally connect with someone no longer living. Storytellers and bards in cultures with oral traditions can pass along tales of the exploits of the dead, just as we can tell stories about friends and family who have died. The stories make us feel closer to them. But the stories are also secondhand, at least one remove from the person who lived them. The original voice is missing. Writing allows a person's voice to reach across the years, to be available to and connect with people in the future. Possibly far into the future: Plato, Aristotle, Marcus Aurelius and countless others still speak to us. Often in translation, but they speak to us. In human terms, this might be the closest thing to arrested decay we've got.

A photo *is* arrested decay—of people, of moments—that leads to an interesting issue: the ethics of selection. In photography, this can involve techniques such as airbrushing and digital manipulation, but I'm talking here about cropping and framing. Countless times I've adjusted my camera angle to capture a selective and misleading image. Bend my knees to banish power lines from the top of the frame; tilt the camera to exclude a house and make the beach seem uninhabited; wait for a gaggle of tourists to disappear behind a building before taking the shot. The photographs will lie by omission: the first two examples remove the hand of man; the third removes man entirely. I want the picture to be beautiful, so I misrepresent reality to improve on it. Alternatively, someone could misrepresent reality in the service of propaganda, from the relatively benign (a travel brochure showing a lovely beach on a rare day it's not raining) to the reprehensible (Third Reich photos of smiling Jewish children at play, nary a Gestapo gun in sight). Any viewer not familiar with the subject of a photograph has only that frozen frame to judge by. It's real, sort of, but a carefully chosen slice of reality. Feel free to enjoy it, but never completely trust it.

Let me give a few examples. In 1984 I was riding my bicycle in Salt Lake City. Spring runoff had been heavy off the mountains, and half of Ninth South Street for several blocks had been turned into a river. Sandbags lined the road and directed the muddy water down a manhole, where it eventually flowed to the Jordan River. Unusual and a bit extreme, but completely under control. The water was maybe two feet high, in no danger of overflowing the sandbags.

I continued on to the Silo electronics store on State Street. Inside was a bank of televisions all tuned to a network evening news program. To my amazement, on screen after screen I saw the Ninth South River I had just passed on my bike—but with a crucial difference. The news cameras had focused tightly on the rushing water and not on the wider scene, filling the TV screen with what looked like a flood worthy of Noah's ark. It was so alarmist that my mother called me that night, worried that Salt Lake was about to become Atlantis. News (that is, trouble) had been created where there essentially was none, through simple and cynical manipulation of which details were included in the frame, and which were excluded—and therefore for most people would never exist.

There's a well-known photo of Mark Twain standing at the doorway of his boyhood home in Hannibal, Missouri, taken in 1902. The 66-year-old writer was in the area to receive an honorary doctorate from the University of Missouri; it was the last time he would see Hannibal. The image shows the iconic Twain of later life, with bushy white hair à la Einstein and trademark white suit. What it doesn't show is the rest of the picture: while the local hero and national celebrity posed before the house, half of Hannibal was gawking at him outside the reach of the camera lens. Seldom-seen shots from different angles display what the May 30, 1902 *St. Louis Post-Dispatch* called "a large crowd of adults and children gathered about him."[57] I had seen the house photograph many times without the thought ever crossing my mind that Twain was looking out at a sea of admirers and curiosity-seekers, and posing for an audience. (A live audience, that is; obviously Twain knew these photos would be reproduced and viewed by thousands, because people like to look at celebrities.) It's reminiscent of the artificial "reality" of

---

57 Another headline from that visit: "MARK TWAIN WEPT AS HE BADE 'FAREWELL': Pathetic Climax of the Humorist's Visit to His Old Home in Hannibal—Men and Women Shed Tears With Him as He Spoke"

the cinema, with cameras, crew, microphones and all manner of gear just out of sight, creating the artifice.

Selection of detail is crucial to all art—and all propaganda. I'm constantly selecting which details to include in this essay, and which to leave out. Inevitably, later I'll recall things that would have been perfect for this or that section, and marvel at how what now seems obvious was veiled to me when I needed it. But not only artists and propagandists are selective. Everyone is. Humans are incredibly selective on both the conscious and unconscious level. Any piece of the past that stays with us has navigated two sets of filters: first, what and how our minds notice, and second, what and how our memories retain. Otherwise, we'd be drowned in so much information we couldn't function.

In Jorge Luis Borges's short story "Funes, the Memorious," a perfect memory is a curse—and therefore imperfect. For the unfortunate Funes, every detail of his life resides on the front page of his memory, unfiltered and overwhelming. He carries the burden of a total past: "Funes not only remembered every leaf on every tree of every wood, but even every one of the times he had perceived or imagined it." He has no escape from history, no shelter even for a moment in the foxhole of forgetting. For Funes, mental decay is completely arrested, though not so his body: his freakish memory began when he was thrown from a wild horse at age nineteen. He spends the rest of his life "hopelessly crippled" and dies at twenty-one. His memories die with him, for none of his past is on paper—except for what Borges's narrator says about him.

It seems terrible to us, but someone with brain damage who lives every moment with life as a blank slate might be happy, or at least not unhappy. Nothing is routine for that person; everything feels new, an adventure akin to a young child's relationship with the world when each day is a process of discovery—with the difference, of course, that children remember much of what they discover. But is this a human happiness, or something else? With no sense of self, which after all depends on a past to develop, is happiness possible? People talk about "living in the moment" and trying to truly appreciate life as it *is*, now, not as it was or will be, not to be constantly concerned with cause and effect. But before a moment can be grasped, the next one takes its place, then a next and a next and a next...until that self runs out of moments.

What's worse, forgetting everything or remembering everything? A handful of people have hyper-powerful, non-selective memories without filters to decide what's important. They can't *not* remember, so like Funes their brains are cluttered with trivia as well as what matters, and bad memories never fade. But forgetting is definitely worse—ask anyone familiar with the ravages of dementia. Our pasts are more than prologue, they're our frame and foundation. If my past were wiped away and I started anew tomorrow, I wouldn't be who I am. I wouldn't *know* who I am. Identities are constructed, not simply inhabited, and I would have to begin rebuilding myself. The process would be far different than the first time, though, because I would be actively and probably anxiously aware of it, unlike a child blithely progressing through Piaget's stages of development.

Sometimes people *want* to leave their past behind and start over with a new identity, or if not a completely new identity, at least a mulligan for past actions. Participants in the Witness Protection Program, for example, or Weather Underground fugitives. Robert Zimmerman changed into Bob Dylan; Steven Demetre Georgiou became first Cat Stevens, then Yusuf Islam, then Yusuf and finally the hybrid Yusuf/Cat Stevens. But deliberate decisions about identity can go only so far. Such transformations are never absolute; the past is neither erased nor

265

forgotten. It might be ignored as much as possible, or retained as a template for what *not* to be, but it's always a presence lurking in the background—and sometimes stepping straight into the path. What do people who know the old identity do? At least Dylan could still be "Robert" or "Bobby" when he returned to Hibbing, Minnesota. Did Marion Morrison's family greet "John Wayne" when he paid them a visit? If Bernie Schwartz went back to his old Bronx neighborhood did his friends call him Tony Curtis?[58]

We forget most of what we perceive; that's a given. But how much control do we have over what we *do* remember? Can we force our memories to be selective? Even if we fight to forget something painful, Freud claims the memory is still stewing in our subconscious—repressed, not forgotten, doing more damage beneath the surface than if it is resurrected and consciously confronted. Maybe my father spent eight months in a V.A. hospital psych ward attempting the impossible: to forget the war, but not the friendships forged in that war. Maybe Chilean dictator Augusto Pinochet woke at night sweating from dreams of screams and death, his subconscious attempting the impossible: to reconcile torture and murder with the decency and civilization he claimed to represent.

My father and Pinochet, polar opposites, bring me to the end of this rumination: friendship, death, and the past on paper. I have corresponded with six people who later died (six that I know of; I hope it's not more). One was my dad. One was Mary Pritchett, a former literary agent born in 1890, who lived a hundred yards

---

58 I've heard Frank Sinatra, Jr. refer to his father as "Sinatra," but that's a separate weird issue.

down the road from my parents' house.[59] The others were my friends Bob Maurer, Karl Hnilicka, Debbie Dixon and Brent Rutkowski. Each friend represents a different stage of my life: Karl (growing up in Connecticut); Debbie (college junior year abroad in Fribourg, Switzerland); Bob (Peace Corps); Brent (Central Connecticut State University). I have fond memories of all of them. Beyond my memory, though, the differences lie in varying degrees of the past on paper.

I emptied my oldest box of letters onto the floor of my office. Like a miser with a mound of bank notes, I slipped my hands under the unruly heap of my past and lifted, letting the paper sift and fall, shuffling my history for no reason that I understood. Diverse types and colors of paper, stamps from around the world (31 cents airmail postage from the U.S. to Chile in 1979), envelopes both thick and diaphanous, postcards, pale blue aerograms. Words jumbled on tumbled paper—adjacent, atop each other, upside-down—in varied hues of ink or pencil; disparate handwriting in three languages (English, Spanish, French). Even the typewritten letters have personalities: different fonts (a word we never used back then; fonts were for baptizing babies), different abilities and carefulness of the typists, different methods of correction (from Wite-out to XXXXXing out, from fixing with a pen to not bothering at all). An ink-filled "e" or "a" could be as individual as a handwriting characteristic, like crossing "t's" high on the staff or never quite connecting "o's" into a circle.

What began in a spirit of dispassionate historical inquiry soon devolved into a hike through memory's backcountry, a heavy pack of nostalgia digging into my shoulders. It didn't hurt, though,

---

59 She was Graham Greene's U.S. agent. She told me that Greene once came up from Cuba to work on a book in her quiet guest bedroom, while I was a clueless kid down the street.

except to "hurt good," as my father used to say. The past on paper brought my friends back to me. It brought *me* back to me.

I did some tallying. My most faithful correspondent (33 letters) was Brian Duffy. Eventually, Brian became a reporter for the *Miami Herald* and *Washington Post*, editor of *U.S. News & World Report* and managing editor of National Public Radio. Back then he was painting houses, driving a cab, working at a New Hampshire resort, reading like a fiend, writing fiction and trying to figure out what was next in his life. In second place (26 letters) was Bob Maurer, a fellow Peace Corps baseball coach in Chile and a former college professor,[60] who both encouraged my early writing and gave it the frank criticism it needed. I can never thank him enough for taking me seriously and giving me the confidence to do the same.

Unfortunately, I never did thank him, or just barely did, and now it's too late—far too late. Bob's last letter to me is dated May 19, 1983, mailed from Elizabeth, New Jersey (postage 20 cents) to my parents' house in Connecticut. I had just finished my M.A. at the University of California at Davis. Bob knew I was coming home for a friend's wedding but wasn't sure when. I arrived late the night of June 10 and was busy with the wedding the next day. On June 12, I finally read Bob's letter. As always it was typed, only the signature handwritten. At the beginning: "I'd better send this to your home, taking no chances. So, when you get this, you'll not be there, but elsewhere. All clear?" In the middle: "Where's it to be next, Utah or Japan? I need to be caught up on you. Drop me a line for sure when you get a chance, please." At the end: "I need to talk to you Tom. Let's try. Meanwhile, with hope that all's going well with you, My best, Bob."

---

60 Philip Roth, Bob's student at Bucknell, dedicated the novel *Our Gang* to him.

I called that night. His brother and housemate Harry answered. I asked for Bob.

"Who's this?" The voice sounded stricken and suspicious.

"Tom Hazuka. Bob's friend from Chile."

Silence. If I hadn't known before, I learned then that tension can travel phone lines.

"I hate to be the bearer of bad news, but Bob had a massive heart attack. He died last weekend."

Heart thumping, I said something understandably lame. "I wanted to see if he could get together next weekend, maybe see a Yankees game."

"I'm afraid that under the circumstances that won't be possible."

I could feel Harry trying for a smile in those words. We never met, but I liked him a lot right then. I soon hung up and called Neil McFadden, a Peace Corps friend who knew Bob well, to break the news. Then I lay on my bed and re-read Bob's letter.

Apologies for not having written to me in months. Comments about Pinochet's current repressive tactics and tough times in Chile ("depression, unemployment, bank and business failures, increasing resistance from the populace, peso devaluation, drops in exports and imports, quite a mess in all"). Advice about my novel, then titled *Asylum* but published years later as *In the City of the Disappeared*:

> Knowing that your novel is set in Chile makes me want to read it more. What publication does for you on a first novel simply can't be a major consideration, I've been telling fledgling writers for years—to no avail, I might add. Tom, I've known people and people who published first novels, and only one, Roth, hit it on first try, and flopped with his second book, <u>Letting Go</u>. Normally, neglect is

269

what you must expect. Then, if you stick with it, you get more notice, and with talent and luck ultimately catch on. The first usually doesn't get publicity by the publisher, gets sparse (often very sparse) reviews, and fizzles. That's hard to take, but practically inevitable. You need to prepare for the shock of neglect, like preparing for death, or a change of life in middle age. Except for death, things improve.

The irony soon compounded. Sentences that I'd blithely read a few hours before were now freighted with meaning, knowledge that hollowed me out instead of filling me.

I don't want to play you tennis now. I played this late winter and spring, indoors, and at 62 going on 63, I get feebler I'm afraid. I still hit it hard at times, and run after everything relatively fast, but my legs get heavier and my power gets reduced. Still, I'd take you on, just to see your improvement.

In two days I head up to meet Charlo and Lauren [his daughter and granddaughter] for a week in a cottage on Cape Cod.... It's great—in a cove backed up by salt flats that flood on the high tides and lock off the cottage from passage out by car. Clams, oysters, fish (I'm bringing my saltwater fishing rod this time) bought or caught, fires in the fireplace, baked beans in the oven. It makes one all alive again, believe me.

I hope Bob did feel all alive again one last time, with death waiting for him a week later. Bob never saw my improvement, in tennis or anything else. He never read my book. But I have him with me, today, on paper. He speaks to me, all alive again, appalled at "the mess in Central America, and the Reagan administration's half-assed approach to it all. It's so sad; the US could be helping. Instead, we consistently are on the wrong side."

My friend Karl Hnilicka is also with me. He only wrote to me in Chile twice, in June and September of 1979, but the letters are eight and ten pages long, loaded with laughs and abuse of our mutual friends in Connecticut for not writing often enough. The letters are also loaded with exotic information, for like me, Karl was living a world away from where we'd grown up, though at an opposite extreme of the Western Hemisphere: backwoods Alaska near the Yukon River. Ruby was the closest town, and the closest post office. As Karl says in his first letter, "My next trip to town, this [letter] shall be on its way." Visits to civilization were not frequent, especially in winter; even this letter dated June 10 was not postmarked until June 25.

So, three long, quick decades after the fact, I read about Karl's trek by pickup truck and boat to the outback. He lived with his brother Charly and friend Carl Schlott in a cabin they built, raising sled dogs and "trapping fur bearers. We catch innocent little critters, then liberate them from their skins, and sell them so they can be fashioned into garb for the disco and suave and debonair crowd. We didn't have a mass carnage, just enough were caught to help pay for some of our living expenses." On December 21 there were only two and a half hours of daylight.

Lighting is real bad, there get to be no shadows and you can't see depths at all. You could be snowshoeing along then all of a sudden fall into a big drift, totally unaware. This place is full of surprises like that. We see all kinds of wild game and critters, moose by the score, wolf, fox, mink, marten, otter, beaver, birds of all kinds.

...I plan to be here for some time to come. This life is a pretty neat way to go. You have few large items, you live a somewhat nomadic lifestyle, you shoot a lot of your food and eat a lot of beans, you're not rich with money, that's for sure, that's not easy to come by, you trade and barter, you don't have to answer to anybody, there are a lot of simple pleasures. I shot my first bear just about a month ago and boy he tasted some good. There is a lot of physical work to be done to get by. And it depends on whose eyes you're looking thru to say if it's a hard or a good way to live.

Karl stayed in Alaska. Eventually he got married, had some kids. We fell out of touch, though I saw him twice over the years on visits to Connecticut, the last time with his wife and kids at Jay Clark's house in 2000. Karl was gaunt from melanoma treatments, but his sense of humor hadn't lost any weight: "The doctor gave me three choices—chemo, chemo or chemo." I never saw Karl after that day and I never will; he died the next year. But he lives with me on nine roughly folded sheets of paper, in three colors of ink, written in a wilderness cabin and in a tent at his fishing camp on the Yukon River on "a super sleazy day, rain, snow, sleet and winds, just the pits." A woman he knew from town had unexpectedly shown up a few days before on a barge and asked, "Mind if I move in?"

I ask you, if you were out here all alone and a lady comes down river and asks you if she can move in, would you refuse? I think not. I took her in most gladly and since, all goes great. She is one hell of a worker and doesn't mind this life, so far. I only wonder what's going to happen when Charly and Carl come back when the barge lines close for the winter.[61] Stay tuned for the continuing saga of Yukon Karl and his Lady Suz. Next episode—Blood on the Snow or SUZ WHO?

I never got the next episode, but I'm grateful for the past on paper I do have, there to be unfolded and not just read, but held and touched, tangible pieces of my friend that remain with me, linking me to him. Thus, in a very real way Karl and Bob are still alive, for what is living but to make connections? Nothing else much matters; everything else is empty distraction.

I have no past on paper for Debbie Dixon or Brent Rutkowski. That's not quite true: I have a single fading Polaroid of Debbie, and in a box somewhere, two address books ago, there's a long-outdated address and phone number in her handwriting. A tenuous scrap of the past, just a toehold above nothing. I wrote to these friends, not frequently but often enough. So where is the evidence? What happened?

I screwed up royally and deleted my entire email in-box, that's what happened. I didn't pay attention, my brain cramped, and seconds later hundreds of emails had vanished in the ether. Had I made an email address book? Of course not, that makes too much sense. (Years later, I still haven't made an email address book...) I lost many letters from friends that, if they had been written ten or twenty years earlier, would have been on paper, waiting in a box for me. After a time, I managed to re-connect

---

61 Karl's brother Charly is still a barge pilot on the Yukon River. Carl Schlott returned to Connecticut decades ago.

with most of the people I wanted to, but Debbie and Brent? Impossible. They're not with me anymore, except in memory; I can't touch a piece of paper that retains part of them, a part that they shared with me. Of course, I couldn't touch it even before deleting my in-box. Email is email, after all.

Will anyone in the future read these words I'm trying to get right so I can put them on paper? It's wild to think that someone centuries from now just might read them, this speck of the past on paper, and wonder who this Tom Hazuka character was who was wondering himself way back then. A future someone marveling at how the present eternally slips past before we can grasp it, but that doesn't stop us from trying.

THE SECURE PAST

"The past at least is secure."

—Daniel Webster

Webster's assertion, of course, is charmingly naive but quite false. It reminds me of Emile Zola's description of his novels as scientific experiments, in which he placed his characters in situations like a scientist combining chemicals and reagents in a petri dish, then observed the results. I'm not sure whether to be impressed by Zola's humility vis-à-vis his creative process and artistic vision, or annoyed by his chutzpah in implying that his work is objectively and scientifically true.

In art, objectivity is impossible. To create anything, an artist makes a myriad of choices. Even "simply" observing and describing involves a host of decisions. For a writer, at the very least this involves two variable and idiosyncratic concepts: point of view (who does the observing?) and diction (what words will be used to describe?) No two writers would be the same, despite the

275

same starting point.[62] It's easy to disprove Zola's claim that his books are science. To be valid, a scientific experiment must be replicable. Results obtained a single time, no matter how spectacular, are useless. Yet give fifty writers the same raw material Zola used, the same characters and situations, i.e., the same chemicals and reagents, and fifty different books would result. The talents, limitations, proclivities, health, and who knows how many other factors for each individual would hopelessly muddle the experiment. The human element would result in some books written within months; others still unfinished after twenty years. Some might be slim novellas; others, tomes as hefty as cigar boxes full of sand.

Any discussion of the secure past will be riddled with nostalgia—and its opposite, bad memories. Or possibly we just need a wider definition of nostalgia, one that includes all aspects of its etymology. The word derives from the Greek "nostos" (to return home) and "-algia" (pain).[63] What if nostalgia included pain not only for what is gone, but also for what can't be corrected? Pain for guilt and regret, and what we can't undo? Not only a bittersweet longing for bygone days and ways, but also a yearning to fix or forget past mistakes?

---

62 In "Pierre Menard, Author of *Don Quixote*," Jorge Luis Borges' satire of literary pretension, Menard achieves his life's work by re-creating parts of *Don Quixote*—not by copying, but *ex nihilo*. The story's pedantic narrator claims that Menard's feat is even more impressive than the original, because Cervantes had the advantage of being a sixteenth-century Spaniard and was familiar with the material, while as a twentieth-century Frenchman Menard required far greater imagination! None of Menard's early drafts exist, which is a problem for cynical skeptics. Not for the narrator, though. He insists that he has seen Menard's notebooks, full of "his insect-like handwriting," but the great genius "liked to go for walks on the outskirts of Nîmes; he would take a notebook with him and make a gay bonfire."

63 Hence our word "analgesic": "an-" (without) pain

A good friend of mine went to his tenth high school reunion, intent on apologizing to a girl he had teased unmercifully in school. He hadn't seen her since graduation. What happens? She doesn't show up, and he's crestfallen. Decades more have crept by since that night, and he still hasn't seen her. Maybe the guilt has faded over time. Maybe not. As Tim O'Brien says in *The Things They Carried*, "Once someone's dead you can't make them undead." He's talking about soldiers, but it applies to everyone's ghosts.

The past can make us insecure. Remember anything you've done that makes you cringe now, be it as harmless as wearing a leisure suit or as dire as causing someone's death. In Ken Burns's film *The War*, survivors of World War II, both soldiers and civilians, show in interviews how insecure a place the past is for them. Nearly all of them falter at some point, voices breaking with emotion at memories sixty or more years old. These interviews are neither fiction, nor poetic. Yet they evoke William Wordsworth's definition of poetry ("the spontaneous overflow of powerful feelings...recollected in tranquility")[64] and Joseph Conrad's aim for his fiction ("to make you hear, to make you feel...before all, to make you *see*).[65] If you have something to say, and say it honestly, people will connect.

Compare that honesty to people who act as if they deserve a Purple Heart for enduring the opening of *Saving Private Ryan*, which depicts the D-Day invasion. So devastating, they say. So real, so disturbing. But we're safe in a comfortable seat, watching an artificial war on a screen, and only for twenty minutes. Our discomfort is a miniscule fraction of an actual soldier's surreal nightmare, trudging up Omaha Beach through swarms of lethal metal wasps trying to rip his flesh and make it dead.

---

64 From the preface to Wordsworth's *Lyrical Ballads*.

65 From the preface to Conrad's *The Nigger of the 'Narcissus'*.

I'm reminded of a California woman in Burns' film who spent long, hungry years in a Japanese POW camp, and after the war was disgusted by "spoiled Americans" whining about the awful hardships they'd faced, because food and gasoline were rationed, and stockings hard to find.[66]

Spoiled Americans and the insecure past bring me to Copacabana, Bolivia. The name conjures up nightclubs and Barry Manilow, but it's a real place, and a surpassingly beautiful one, on the shore of Lake Titicaca. Christine and I were in Copacabana for the last two days of 2004, staying in the new Hotel Rosario del Lago. Our comfortable room overlooked the lake. The lake trout lasagna in the hotel restaurant was one of the finest dishes I've ever eaten. With two glasses each of surprisingly good Bolivian wine, a shared dessert of fruit and ice cream, two cups of coca tea and 18% tip, the bill came to 132 *bolivianos*, around $17. Incredibly cheap by U.S. standards, such a dinner is beyond the reach of most Copacabana residents.

Sure, it's an example of the Gringo Advantage, but that's not my main point here. Just over a year later, on January 6, 2006, I was at Jussara Bayer's house in Florianópolis, Brazil, for a *feijoada* lunch.[67] We hadn't seen each other since 1980, when I spent

66 In the national myth that we prefer, Americans all heroically pitched in to the war effort to defeat the evil Axis (not to be confused with George W. Bush's Axis of Evil). Human nature being what it is, though, there are always opportunists like *Catch-22's* Milo Minderbinder to supply black market products. As demonstrated by the idiocy of Prohibition and the insanely expensive and utterly futile War on Drugs, if people want a product, someone will provide it if the price is right—ethical considerations and legal consequences be damned. The easier the process, the better, which explains why the most common black market commodity during World War II was counterfeit ration stamps.

67 Recipes vary for this Brazilian national dish, but pork and black beans are almost always the foundation.

twelve idyllic days in Florianópolis during my ramble north from Chile back to the U.S. Just a lovely accident, a chance encounter on the road when I met her and other Brazilian friends on the island of Santa Catarina.[68] I had no schedule, no commitments, and a pocketful of greenbacks from my Peace Corps readjustment allowance. Those six weeks between leaving Santiago and flying home from Rio de Janeiro were the freest time of my life.

Lunch wasn't quite ready, so Ju poured me a glass of white wine (Brazilian, and quite good) and I sat on a couch leafing through her photo albums. Jussara is my age, maybe a year or three younger. She spent a high school year in the States and has backpacked in Europe and various parts of South America. Flipping the crappy "magnetic" album pages, seeing people and places I rarely recognized, I still felt a heavy dose of nostalgia. As I wrote in my journal that evening, "There's nothing like traveling when you're 20, the world is new and you're loaded with energy and curiosity."

Then I turned a page and saw Copacabana. I immediately recognized it as the same place—except it wasn't really the same place, because the photos had been taken over twenty years before, in 1984. Copacabana was a village then, though built around an impressive seventeenth-century church. Despite significant expansion it's still a small town today. The difference is in the details, and you know where sages say the devil is.

My trusty, well-worn 1978 *South American Handbook* lists eleven Copacabana hotels, ranging from 75 cents a night to $6 (though for that inflated rate you got full board). As isolated as the town seems, obviously it had visitors. Here's what jumped out at me, though. The *Handbook* describes the Prefectural Hotel as "new, US $1.50 single, no hot water, only hotel with view of lake."

---

68 It wasn't *completely* an accident. See chapter 14.

That statement isn't true anymore, and not just because of the laughably low price. Several fairly upscale hotels overlook Lake Titicaca now, including the Rosario del Lago where Christine and I stayed. Undoubtedly, more such hotels are already there or on the way. In Jussara's photos, Copacabana is a tiny way station for commercial traffic and backpackers passing between Peru and Bolivia on miserable roads, most of whom were just looking for the cheapest bed they could find. In our photos, Copacabana has become a destination for tourists willing to pay for stunning views and nice restaurants, especially if with the Gringo Advantage they really don't have to pay that much (our room was $43.50 a night, tax included).

As the planet gets more crowded there are more gringos to *take* advantage, including folks like me who did the trips as a kid with a backpack (actually in Europe I didn't even have that, just a canvas duffel bag my friend Jim Kane gave me), but now wouldn't mind a bit more comfort. Many are married to spouses even less interested in roughing it, so we travel like middle class Americans, hopefully not the Ugly variety. This kind of tourist spends more than shoestring-budget backpackers, which must benefit at least some local people. Surely that's true. But I'm suspicious of trickle-down economic arguments. They sound like attempts to soothe the consciences of fat cats vis-à-vis the have-nots. Presuming fat cats have consciences, that is. The inescapable fact remains, though, that despite my self-image I *am* a fat cat compared to most people of the world.

On New Year's Day, 2005, morning rain broke in Copacabana and the day turned sunny and warm, as warm as it gets at that altitude, anyway, maybe 70 degrees. While Christine graded essays on the hotel balcony, I hiked up a hill overlooking the town. It turned out to have fourteen different markers of stations of the cross along the way, depicting Christ's crucifixion. The path was steep and I climbed it swiftly—with frequent stops to gulp the thin air—fearing I'd miss the bus to La Paz if I dawdled. I passed men in alpaca hats brandishing smoky censers and chanting incantations, an amalgam of Roman Catholicism and the indigenous religion it ostensibly replaced. At the summit were eight large stone monuments, their bases painted pale blue. Some were marred by graffiti; each was topped with a concrete cross. People, all Bolivians as far as I could tell, sat and rested after the effort of reaching the top. Indian women in colorful skirts and bowler hats sold soft drinks, cookies and votive candles, which burned by the dozens in smoke-blackened niches in the low stone walls.

The view was extraordinary in every direction. Titicaca was massive and impassive, a deep, primal blue like Lake Tahoe. I looked down on the tightly packed town and saw hotels; a few hundred people milling about on the shore; fifteen or so docks; and kayaks and boats dotting the water. The bay curved away gently toward empty farmland: waterfront property awaiting more hotels, or maybe villas for the wealthy. I turned around and saw a different world. On the other side of the hill was pristine coastline with hardly a sign of humanity outside of some agricultural terraces, probably much the same view a conquistador would have had in the sixteenth century. I wondered how long that would last. Copacabana hasn't been ruined by overbuilding and commercialism, but neither had Park City when I moved to Utah in 1983. Now most of the quirky people who gave Park City its character can't afford to live there. Still, Copacabana's isolation works in its favor, and it's a far, far cry from Aspen or Taos or even Fuengirola, Spain.[69]

Few of these ideas came to me while I was standing on that hill. Mostly I just reveled in being there, a hyper-alive feeling of strangeness and wonder, even awe: man, you're in *Bolivia*. Don't take a second of this for granted; breathe it in, try to notice everything. Only chancing upon Ju's photos a year later, seeing images of Copacabana as it used to be, led to these thoughts of transformation, of change, of gain and loss. I was particularly receptive to them after returning to a drastically altered Florianópolis twenty-five years later, differences that my friends hardly noticed because they had occurred gradually over time.[70] It wasn't just the profusion of buildings and cars. The elderly (at least to our eyes) man Miguel Büchele and I had watched hand-carving a dugout canoe from a log in 1980 was almost surely no longer alive. Who would consider doing such a backbreaking task today, especially without power tools? Does anyone even know how, or has that skill died? The knowledge is likely as lost to the past as that scrawny Brazilian man and his hand-rolled cigarette, not to mention the canoe itself.

Soon after returning from Brazil in 2006, I decided that I needed to read my South American journal for this book. I put off writing for a week and waded through three years' worth of entries, jotting dates and notes in a new notebook to give myself a condensed timeline with highlights, something more wieldy

---

69 I mention Fuengirola because its funky, historic El Gadinito restaurant has four large aerial photos on its walls, chronicling the town's transformation from sleepy fishing village with a few five-story hotels in the early 60's, to the glitzy, crowded tourist mecca of today.

70 A variant of this phenomenon happened when I asked Hugo Buitano about a new building in Arica. "*No es tan nuevo,*" he told me. "*Es que tu estuviste tanto tiempo afuera.*" ["It's not so new. It's just that you've been away so long."]

to work with. Among many surprises, one of the biggest was discovering that I had been in Copacabana before my stay with Christine—on August 21, 1979.

I don't recall that visit, and have no photos to help, because my camera had been stolen in Arequipa, Peru. In my memory's defense, I spent just twenty minutes in Copacabana. I came in by bus from Yunguyo, Peru, found another bus leaving for La Paz at two P.M., and got on. I remember absolutely none of these details; if not for my journal they would all be as gone as that man hewing a canoe. More so, for at least he remains in my slightly faded photograph, kneeling by the hollowed-out log, wood chips scattered everywhere, right hand resting proudly, almost lovingly, on the roughly carved gunwale of his creation.

If circumstances had been different, or even if I were alone, I might have tarried in Copacabana. The 1978 *South American Handbook* calls it "an attractive little red-roofed town," and describes fascinating Titicaca boat rides to see Inca ruins on the Island of the Sun and the Island of the Moon. But in Cuzco I had met Eyal,[71] an Israeli guy my age, and made plans to travel together to La Paz. I was going there anyway, eventually, to catch the train back to Arica. As Eyal and I talked, though, my final days of vacation began to harbor the possibility of exciting, unforeseen trips involving the hallucinogenic San Pedro cactus.

That probably sounds like a couple of college kids looking to get wasted. I swear that's not true. We may have been naive, but we were sincere. My journal says: "Spectacular ride to La Paz, complete w/ ferry at Tiquina. Eyal and I had a wonderful ride, discussing seriously our ideas (Castaneda and Don Juan)

---

71 All names associated with the San Pedro cactus are pseudonyms. I don't feel comfortable using their real names without permission, and outside of one brief visit to Arica I never saw any of them again.

and situations (he has to return in a week or so for his last year at school: electrical engineering), and we took to talking about the San Pedro cactus."

Eyal and two friends he'd met on the road had been instructed in the rituals of San Pedro by a *brujo* (medicine man) in Esperanza, Ecuador. The friends, a French man and a German woman, were going to be in La Paz, where the San Pedro cactus grows wild in certain sacred spots in the hills. After sounding me out, Eyal invited me to join them, but only if I was serious about the experiment, certain that I wanted to take this journey. He made it clear that San Pedro is not for everyone. Its power is not to be trifled with or underestimated. Sudden warmth tingling in my legs and arms, I said to count me in.

After debating at length how best to convey my Bolivian San Pedro experience, I've decided to let my (slightly redacted) journal do the job. Anything in brackets is me talking now.

Wed. Aug 22—I wonder if this entry will fill half this book, or if I'll despair of ever providing an adequate description and give it up after a page. The daytime events are easy. Walked to the *gare* to confirm my train to Arica.[72] Eyal showed up soon after, we ate breakfast and bought *salteñas* [meat and potato pies], then rode an Ñ bus to Cota Cota, realm of the San Pedro Cactus. They were there all right, and in abundance. Spent all afternoon cutting and scraping away the dark green flesh just below the rind, ending up with a decent accumulation apiece. At one

---

72 Irredentist posters on walls at the train station: "Bolivia Reclama Su Mar" (Bolivia Demands Its Ocean); "El Mar Es Y Sera Nuestro" (The Ocean Is And Will Be Ours"). Bolivia has been landlocked since losing hundreds of miles of coastline to Chile in the 1879 War of the Pacific.

point a large, curious cow came over to look, but soon lost interest. Cota Cota is a special place, a power place, with nearby cliffs that look like the Badlands, the Valle de le Luna [Valley of the Moon] behind, and La Paz nestled like a toy city among the mountains in the distance.

Returned to Hotel Italia at 7:30. Ran into Pascal and Inga, Eyal's friends he'd made in Esperanza, Ecuador. That settled matters as far as tripping went. We had to extract more pulp from cactus pieces we'd brought back, and of course they had some. Heavy trippers all of them, very serious about learning what the drugs have to offer. They have Eden-like memories of Esperanza [which means "hope"].

Took some time to prepare the trips in Pascal and Inga's room. Around 9:30 we had a foul green "omelette" on a plate, and we went around by turns eating spoonfuls and trying to wash it down with Oriental Cola before our gag reflexes could kick in. [I was surprised to learn this was the method taught by the Ecuadorean jungle *brujo*. What did *brujos* of old use to mask the horribly bitter taste, before cola drinks existed?] As a novice I did only 3 1/2, everyone else 5.

Consumed raw it takes a long time to react, better than two hours. Eyal and Inga soon got sick; I never did though I tried twice later on. The trip comes on gradually and by midnight I was shaking and feeling queasy but still functioning. Inga burned incense. The bizarreness was heightened by the strange agents parading past the open door: a tall dude in long underwear; a Bolivian with no underwear; an extremely fucked-up woman from Washington, whose tales of her ex-husband, six-year-old daughter, various men who've shafted her in South

America and her persistent vaginal infection labeled her a wacko.

I was buzzed by now, but with a rancid stomach. In fact, I was wondering whether the deal was worth it. The answer arrived like an anvil (always the bloody alliteration!). We four were alone now. The candle burned low and finally out. Someone killed the bathroom light. Only a mild starglow filtered through the green plastic window curtains, and the hallucinations began.

The window was [there's a small, puke-green San Pedro stain on the journal page here] like a movie screen with constantly changing projections, from exploding, scintillating colors to Incan and Egyptian designs. Closed eyes brought on Peter Max, Yellow Submarine, dazzling animated effects I feel so inadequate to describe. Suddenly, the entire wall to my right became a glowing, gleaming array of dials and screens like the control room of a Hollywood spacecraft. To my left, an Indian like Castaneda's Don Juan (or maybe one of those mechanical gypsy fortune tellers in an amusement park glass booth) knelt cross-legged on the floor. His cupped hands formed a black circle that somehow I knew was a portal. I got on all fours to see up close, put my face right up to the hole and was tempted to enter, but the intensity of abandoning myself to the blackness was too much and I had to withdraw and trip elsewhere. [I get the creeps thinking about what would have happened if I'd slipped into that tunnel, which I somehow knew I could do even though it was only as big as the man's two cupped hands—that were of course not "really" there. I also wonder what my experience on the floor would have looked like to anyone watching me.]

The vibes were so perfect, everyone felt wonderful and full of love. Occasionally we'd talk, and nothing but harmonious impressions, mutual support and awed loving comments about the trip would surface. Flashing colors, shapes and often recognizable figures fascinated me, and I could change the tenor of the trip simply by opening or closing my eyes. Never had I experienced anything approaching it.

Probably I dozed at intervals. Time obviously was an alien concept, but when the power part of the trip was over I checked my watch. 6:15. Though we were still tripping, the strong hallucinations were behind. All were exhausted. Eyal and I tried to go to my place to sleep but the Italia gate was locked, so we couldn't get out and settled for passing out on Pascal and Inga's floor. Around 7:30 I woke and relocated to my room at the Andes.

As Eyal and I were discussing this afternoon and tonight, San Pedro is not for everyone. The cactus *must* taste terrible and be difficult to find and prepare. Otherwise many would try it, and its power and "sanctity" would be greatly reduced. You must want to take it and try to learn, and be willing to make the sacrifices. I am a changed person after tonight.

Friday, Aug.24—Another in a series of unforgettable days, and maybe the craziest and most enchanted of all. We had five chunks of cactus and a borrowed stove, and spent most of the morning preparing the trips. Had breakfast in the market while the potion was brewing. Things got a bit heavy earlier when Interpol came, according to Brenda (weird chick from Washington), and she split while we prepared her trip. That just isn't done, and I'm uncomfortable with her vibrations anyway. But all works out for the best. In the late A.M., relighting the stove, Eyal set the gas bottle ablaze. Panic. Eyal heaved the canister at the closed window, but it smashed the glass and rebounded. Finally Brenda came through tremendously. She threw open the window, grabbed the flaming metal bottle with my hooded sweatshirt and heaved it out the window. Crisis over. It could have been disaster, especially if it had exploded or landed on someone two stories below. The hotel manager showed up, incensed, and we had to explain that we were making tea! (Meanwhile I stood blocking his view of the apparatus.)

We swallowed the vile, bitter green liquid that Eyal strained through one of Pascal's white socks, chasing it with Oriental Cola, then walked to the Plaza San Francisco to catch bus 130 to the Valle de la Luna. (By the way, Brenda didn't come—probably a good thing.) At the end of the bus line we lucked into a ride from a lady in a big Chevy van/wagon to a *pueblito* up the hill. Drank a toxi-cola in a tiny market because there was nothing else. We began to feel the trip when we exited. Guided by a map Eyal had we located a patch of supposedly great San Pedro cactuses, then entered the valley.

Spent the entire afternoon tripping in the sun on an eminence overlooking an almost otherworldly scene. I also dried San Pedro from Cota Cota in the sun. Nowhere near the intensity of a night trip. In fact, as the San Pedro power ebbed and flowed at times I nearly forgot I was tripping. But I was, and luckily not much heavier.

At sunset we started down the dangerous trail into surroundings that only got more bizarre. At my instigation, Eyal and I headed back to cut some San Pedro. An incredible rush ensued. A massive, satanic hound with blood-red eyes came bounding at us on the path to the cactus. It stopped only a yard away, slavering and barking viciously. Even the San Pedro vibes didn't deter the beast. [All these years later I wonder: maybe the vibes kept the dog from actually attacking.] After the initial scare we chucked rocks, the hellhound fled, and we made it to the plants. Pascal soon arrived and we filled his and my rucksack with cactus [cut into lengths of a foot or so].

We hiked down in tranquility, but with tremendous care because a slip could mean a broken leg or much worse. All were awestruck at the fantastic stone formations and the incredible aura of the valley. As darkness settled we sat for several hours, talking and lying back to gaze at the magnificent sparkling sky, the thousands of stars. Saw a red shooting star. My descriptions can never be adequate.

Then came the search for the road, picking our way along trails in the dark, often with chasms on either side whose bottoms are scarcely visible even in daylight. We paused frequently to look about in wonder. I've seen beauty in many parts of the world, but never anything so positively magic. We were transported. It strained the imagination to believe that this was part of the same earth we walk every day.

As the trail wound downward the stark hills loomed ever higher and more imposing. Phantasmagoric shapes surrounded us, cacti silhouetted against the stars. We crossed rickety wooden bridges that spanned black abysses, all in an unreal starlight that illumined the path just enough to make it passable. It was enchanted, but awesomely powerful. We felt to the bone a strength we knew could be terrible.

The walk was difficult and quite long, even when we finally regained the road. A stroke of luck rolled up in the shape of a Mercedes en route to Cochabamba. After that excellent lift it was easy to nip a bus into the city. The Esperanza (!) Restaurant caught the eye of my companions, so we split a few mediocre, expensive pizzas then walked home. Hung out at the Italia, where we had a few tense moments bringing in our sacks of cactus because of two Interpol agents lurking about like carrion birds, but with a bit of care no problems ensued.

Saturday, August 25—[I'll skip the pages describing a largely uneventful trip and include only the last two lines of the entry.] A somewhat disappointing but possibly an important trip. Only future trips can clarify this one.

3 A.M., Tuesday night, Wednesday morning—[I'm including this section out of chronological sequence because it was written first. In my journal it directly precedes the entry for Tuesday.] I know I'll be awakened in four hours, but it seems immoral to sleep when I feel this good. When you come through an incredible series of events with a group of folks that hazard threw together, something profound happens. A powerful bond develops among those who have shared the communion, and that unleavened bread is so sweet.

How do I go about recording the essence of a perfect day? Especially when I'm still immersed in it? With this delectable buzz, sleep seems such a waste. I'm ready for just about anything. Almost anything, amigo.

Vacation winds down. Aricaville tomorrow. If the dénouement sparkles in your eyes and pulls up the corners of your mouth, can a human legitimately ask for more? I love some of the people I've met. We've shared our lives on the move, and will always carry a piece of each other. That is as it should be. Amen.

Tuesday August 28—Hope I can record the essence of this most wonderful day in less than ten pages. We began cooking around 9:30. Boiled the bejesus out of that S.P. for almost three hours; took turns going to breakfast and watching the pot boil (disproves that theory...) to prevent incendiary incidents. Drank a 10-spoon trip around one. Lawd Gawd Almighty that liquid was gaggingly foul. We all had some tense moments for the next few hours, a bit of a battle to keep it down. Marcelo, an Italian Eyal had met somewhere on the road, showed up at the perfect time, lucked into a trip from the leftover juice and spent the day with us.

Split at 1:30 to return the tired stove to the lady at the market and collect our deposit. A quick chicken sandwich calmed my entrails somewhat. Caught a taxi to the Parque Central and zoo, which proved to be a mistake. Crowded and "Keep Off The Grass," the zoo was cramped and most of the animals sad, crammed into cages nowhere near big enough. By now the cactus was making its presence strongly felt, and its first manifestation rolled up in the presence of an off-duty city bus. We'd planned to take a taxi, but the driver gave us a free lift right to the gate of a botanical garden. The only price we had to pay was enduring several minutes of sloppy drunk drivel from a front-toothless passenger.

As if in a dream we entered the sun-washed, immaculately tended garden. I was gloriously tripping, so high that if it were night I think I would have hallucinated more than the first time. I've seldom felt so alive, so content, so vibrant, so enthralled, so exalted. I was in love with the world, especially my companions. We sprawled on the grass in the warm sun, gazing at the sky though the intricate maze of tree branches, sighing and smiling.

At 4:45 the bad-ass world intervened. A dour park guard roused us from our sublime indolence, ushered us out and locked the gate. Strands of barbed wire topped the fence. But all was too right for anything to go wrong. A block away we found a small park that had delightful grass to lie upon. A young boy, at first sullen but later friendly, and his lovely little sister had a monkey named Monacho that entertained us no end. [What I wouldn't give to have photos of all this.]

We relaxed there for probably an hour, then crossed the park to a handball club. There we were in mid-trip, a multinational group of gringos watching macho Bolivians swell their palms into puffy steaks by bashing a small, hard ball off a wall. Just one more fascinating incident, which for me included conversation and an explanation of the sport from a tumid-handed La Paz cop.

The mysterious Israeli sanctuary where Eyal was staying was nearby, so we decided to take a look. Local kids were playing netless volleyball in the street, and at first we watched them and ate bread and bananas. The Israeli house was bizarre. The ancient, white-haired *dueña* from Danzig speaks Yiddish and barely communicates in Spanish. She's pretty much off the wall but a good person at heart, and her weirdness blended perfectly with our tripping personalities. Two girls, one French, one Israeli, were staying upstairs, so we hung out with them till 7:30. A crazy old guy was wandering about, but his oddness bothered no one.

The San Pedro worked again, and a big empty taxi was parked on the street, seemingly waiting to take us downtown. [After various adventures] we all hoofed back to the Italia by 10. Four, two American and two English, were hanging out in "Jerry Brown's" room. (Actually a Brit named Simon who Eyal says looks like J.B., so we called him Jerry. He didn't seem to mind.) I volunteered to fetch my pot at the Andes, and by the time I returned Eyal was picking some good blues. Rolled it all, three bones' worth.

The weed on top of the cactus was delightful. (If you didn't know the slang and the drift of this entry, what a strange sentence that would be.) An American named Larry on banjo, Eyal and Jerry playing guitar. Later I took Jerry's ax, and from there we traded off. Vibes were excellent, and I've seldom been so into playing. Stayed till 1:30, then said good-bye to those folks and continued for another hour chez Pascal and Inga. Eyal and I took turns on the guitar (a nylon stringed one borrowed from a friend of Marcelo's). Such fun to sing.

We'd been through so much and grown so close that it was tough to part. Warm farewells. Pascal promised to pass through Arica in a month or so. Took my leave of Eyal on the street. I'm sure I'll see them all again.

Had to ring three times to rouse the porter, and had visions of a chilly night in an alley. Still tripping. Turn back a few pages for thoughts on the last night of an unforgettable vacation, born of a brain stimulated by the sacred San Pedro cactus and the tasty acrid smoke of marihuana.

Lawdy mama, what a vacation.

There you have it, a me who no longer exists, on a mission I would no longer undertake. Trying to connect with that former self is as easy as it is impossible. I smile at memories created by someone who used to inhabit my body, a person I know intimately yet don't understand. Would I take a San Pedro trip today? I doubt it, and not just because of the wretched bitter taste I can conjure up like muscle memory. As an adult[73] I have a heightened sense of human fragility, of all that can go wrong, of how many cracks there are in the foundation. So yes, I'd be afraid of the drug, of what it might reveal, and what it might unravel. Maybe that's prudence; maybe that's cowardice. All I know for sure is that in this case, I'm content with memories of a former me with a different sort of curiosity about life, and little sense of how tenuous that life is.

Pascal and Alain visited me in Arica seven weeks later. They were with Amanda, an Australian I'd met on my last day in Bolivia.[74] I was glad to see them, but the vibe had changed. This wasn't La Paz, pure freedom and adventure—not for me, anyway. In Arica I had responsibilities. For Pascal, though, Arica was just another stop on his travel odyssey, a continuation of his years-long wandering around the world. I had smuggled some San Pedro back to Chile, but I didn't suggest a trip. Arica was not the place for me to do it. Certainly, my single room was not the place, now crowded with three people sleeping on the floor for three nights. Breakfast becomes a project when it involves

---

73 I was twenty-three during my six days of San Pedro experiments in La Paz. Officially an adult, but I thought of myself as a kid then, and I still think I was a kid.

74 Rereading my journal, I wonder what happened to Inga the German, who had been with Pascal in La Paz. At the time, I didn't even give it a second thought. It was just the natural order of things: travelers meet, live together intensely until the road forks, then go their separate ways.

cooking for a group on a weak-flamed camp stove, so I got a late start on my job every day. On the fourth day, I escorted my friends to a bus stop and put them on the right bus to get out to the edge of town. They were armed with a map I'd drawn of the Pan-American highway so they could thumb south. We hugged. They smiled and waved through the window. I waved back, sad to see them go. But even more than sadness, I felt relief.

Several years later I called Eyal. We were both in grad school, he at Stanford, I at the University of California at Davis. To my surprise, he showed scant enthusiasm when I suggested getting together, as if he preferred to keep La Paz and the San Pedro experience locked in the past. Maybe it's just as well. The intensity of on-the-road relationships is tough to replicate in a quotidian context. We probably would have spent the whole time kissing the past's ass, drinking beer and waxing (then probably waning) nostalgic.

Possibly, Eyal hoped to keep the past secure. If not secure, at least *secured*, tied down, if not tied up. Captured. You can always reread a book or watch a movie again. You can't take the same trip again. Even if the itinerary is identical, the places will have changed, or at a minimum the human effects on them will be different, for good or ill. The Grand Canyon remains what my friend Roark Whitehead calls "God's stupendous pit," but its air quality continues to worsen, sightseeing flights disturb the peace, and a transparent observation platform juts out from the rim. The mighty Sete Quedas waterfalls that I saw in Brazil in 1980, the world's largest in terms of volume (even greater than Iguaçu Falls, and twice Niagara's) were destroyed by a hydroelectric plant dam in 1982, lost beneath the waters of a massive reservoir.

And the main variable as far as you're concerned—yourself—will have changed. Of course, you're a different person when you reread a book, but turning pages is virtually never as big a deal as taking a trip. Unless the book transformed your life, you're unlikely to recall how old you were, or *who* you were, the first time you read it. Travel is another story. Trips are landmarks in a life and stay with us like a first kiss. Or a first broken heart. I'll probably never travel with a backpack again. I *know* I'll never be twenty-two years old again, forehead pressed to a bouncing bus window as I roll through the desert to Arica—my new home. I'll never be twenty-three again, slicing San Pedro cactus in the Andes with a Swiss army knife. I'll never be forty-seven again and returning to Arica after twenty-three years away, or forty-nine and going back to Florianópolis after twenty-five years. Never again. Life doesn't work that way.

The past is back there somewhere, dancing like a child's balloon in the breeze. It's not tied down, not secure. Once when I was a kid we went to a carnival. My parents bought me a helium balloon. They tried to tie the balloon's string to my wrist, but I refused. I was a big boy, not a baby. I got the balloon home, bouncing it against the ceiling of Dad's '51 Ford, but playing in the back yard I somehow let go. The string leaped out of reach. The balloon wanted to fly. I cried as I watched it soar high and fast into the endless sky, receding from me forever, shrinking to a fragment of itself, then to the barest pinpoint, and finally to nothing at all.

"You wouldn't listen," my parents said, and they were right. I think—I hope—that I've learned to listen. Maybe this book is my attempt to bring back that balloon, to loop the twine securely around my thin, five-year-old wrist before it's too late, though I know by now that even if it doesn't float off into the heavens, soon enough the limp, empty skin of the balloon will be all that's left of our laughter at the carnival.

LANGUAGE AND OTHER APPROXIMATIONS

"When everybody's lost, everybody's listening."

—Derek Trucks

Three friends of mine tell funny stories about misadventures with foreign languages. I'd pass along some of my own, but they're not as good as these. Jack Hicks, a professor at the University of California at Davis, forgot his leather jacket at a club in Paris. Worried, he went back to retrieve it. "*C'est cuit,*" he told employees, trying to explain that it was made of leather, but all he got was confused looks. That's understandable, because "*C'est cuit*" means, "It's cooked." Eventually Jack got his point across, and his coat back, when folks realized he meant, "*C'est du cuir.*"

During our Peace Corps training in Santiago, Mike Welsh pointed to a cake on a Chilean family's table and asked politely, "*Es caca?*" After the laughs subsided, he learned that the Chilean word for cake is *torta*, and *caca* means *mierda*.

Nilda Cabral, a Brazilian who speaks superb English, said of a man who'd lost his job that, "He got laid." She soon discovered that omitting the word "off" creates quite a different meaning.

The common thread connecting these three stories is that Jack, Mike and Nilda tell them in a self-deprecating way. They don't mind a laugh at their expense, which is a sign of a secure person. Good luck picking up a language if you're afraid of making an error. I have first-hand experience with two totally different approaches to learning a language. I had studied French for eight years in school before going to Switzerland for my junior year in college, so was fairly proficient. To some extent, though, that ability hindered me. With my background I expected to speak and write French extremely well, and this perfectionism got in the way. I created my own barrier. Instead of just talking unselfconsciously, too often I'd let my brain (and my ego) parse everything before I'd speak. Partially I feared looking like a fool, but mostly I just expected too much of myself. It's hard to do something when you focus mainly on your mistakes. It's certainly a lot less fun.

Learning Spanish was an entirely different process. Before leaving for Chile, I studied a bit with a workbook Westbrook High School Spanish teacher Bob Sinnott had given me. That was my entire Spanish background. I knew I was a beginner, that mistakes were inevitable, so I put minimal pressure on myself. Just go for it, just communicate—what the hell, you're doing pretty well, considering. Plus, I was a bit older and starting to realize that life is way too short to worry about screwing up a verb tense. I learned Spanish quickly. Six hours of language instruction five days a week certainly hurried the process, as did living with a Chilean family, but if I had held off speaking until I could do it proficiently, I would have been mute for many months. Not to mention, I wouldn't have been able to do my job.

Language is one of the most powerful human barriers. It's also, of course, a crucial means of connection and communication. Language plays a determining role in both self-definition and how others define us. Though language can unify people, that unity can create new barriers: "Speak English or go back where you came from, you goddamn foreigner."[75] Looked at from the other side, if you live for years in a foreign country and never learn the local language, you're making it clear how little you value the host country's culture, how little you care about being part of it. It's also an indication of some pretty severe laziness, and probably a large dose of fear as well. No matter which angle you approach the language issue from, barriers crop up. Then it becomes a question of how hard people work to surmount those barriers—or if they try at all.

Barriers don't have to come from a completely different language; sometimes just an accent is enough. There's a TV commercial with some New York Yankees fans at work discussing last night's game in stereotypical New York accents (one actually says "fuhgeddaboudit"). A new employee is brought into the room. He tries to be friendly, but speaks with an exaggerated Boston accent, the language of the hated rival Red Sox. The New Yorkers react with sullen, hostile silence; they won't even look at him. The ad is supposed to be comic, but I find it sobering. The newcomer is shunned simply because of his language. A few words create a huge barrier, in this case not even because of the words themselves (he doesn't mention the Red Sox, or anything remotely inflammatory), but because of his way of saying them. His accent is like the biblical shibboleth that distinguished friend from foe by whether or not he could pronounce the "sh." The dilemma now for the Boston guy is, Do I try to change my accent to fit in? (Or, far more drastically, root for the Yankees—at least in public?) Maybe he sees that as a betrayal of his roots.

---

75 I'm reminded of the strange unity of smokers clustered outside a building, a motley pack who would normally never all socialize yet find themselves together, bonded by addiction and pariahdom. When people quit smoking, do they still hang around with the crowd outside? I doubt it.

Maybe he'll do so for convenience, then switch back to his native accent on trips to Boston—though inevitably people there will remark that he sounds like a New Yorker now. And another barrier starts to rise.[76]

In cinema and television, ignorant or stupid characters often speak in exaggerated southern drawls, harsh Brooklynese, or Speedy Gonzalez Mexican accents. Meanwhile, in costume dramas ancient Romans sound like BBC newscasters, unless the film is a comedy that tries for laughs by playing against expectations (Zero Mostel, not Richard Burton, in *A Funny Thing Happened on the Way to the Forum*). Ways of speaking can be easy shorthand for clichéd characterization: the flaming gay man, the ghetto thug, the inbred aristocrat, the insipid like, you know, like, whatever, Valley Girl. The problem, of course, is that the same clichés and prejudices exist outside of the movies, which is why over the years so many Americans have struggled to erase their regional accents. Of course, if you're a NASCAR driver from New Jersey, chances are your speech develops a southern lilt in order to play the role, and it's amazing how politicians start dropping the final "g" of words when addressing a blue collar, "jes' plain folks" audience.

Some of the most basic, human moments of my life have involved communicating with someone whose language I didn't speak. It's frustrating, sure, but there's virtually no artifice in the relationship. It's a return to almost childlike purity (and makes us recall how difficult being a kid can be). We usually take words for granted. Without their help, suddenly we have to truly pay

---

76 My CCSU colleague Marty Capper has relatives on Long Island and in Boston. In New York he says he's "Mawty," in Massachusetts he's "Mahty." Only in Connecticut is he "Marty." Of course, this being the United States, the "t" is pronounced "d" in all three places.

attention to the other person, to read body language, to read expressions, to try to make sense of unfamiliar sounds that for this other person miraculously have meaning.[77]

A musical analogy might be useful. I once talked to guitarist Derek Trucks, whose band was known for extended, intricate improvisations, about how they manage to return to the original song after an especially "out there" jam. "Don't you ever get lost?" I asked.

Trucks nodded and said something profound. "Sure, sometimes. But when everybody's lost, everybody's listening."

Thus, in a lovely paradox, the language barrier can remove other barriers—if all parties are willing, that is, if they're attuned to the other(s) and trying to connect. Conversely, no barriers will fall for an Ugly American (or any other nationality) who's affronted by someone's inability to speak English (or any other language) and expects that shouting the words a bit more slowly will somehow resolve the problem.

My sweetest memory of communicating without a common language took place on the Greek island of Ios. It was April of 1976. I had met up with my friend Greg Abell on Ios after ten days of traveling by myself in Italy and Greece. The island's single town was lovely but a shade touristy, so according to my journal the next day we "moved to a place cheaper and close to the beach." ("Cheaper" meant 40 drachmas instead of 50; $1.11 instead of $1.39. Don't laugh. Those 28 cents were enough for a hot loaf of bread straight from the bakery, and a Greek salad with the world's tastiest olives, goat cheese and tomatoes.) The hostel was tiny, just two spare but spotless rooms, with a view

---

[77] I saw a print ad once that at first glance seemed to be composed of words, but actually was just random groups of letters. "Now you know how it feels to be illiterate," it said at the bottom.

high above the turquoise Aegean. Two girls from Vancouver had the other room.

Elena ran the place. She was in her late thirties and spoke nary a word of English. My Greek was equally non-existent, but somehow we managed to do a lot of laughing.[78] Elena taught me that in Greek "Thomas" is pronounced with the theta "th" sound, like in "thick." On the inside back cover of my journal, she inscribed my name in Greek beneath several lines of Arabic that a Sudanese traveler had written for me on the boat to Greece from Italy. More than three decades later, I look at those handwritten letters from alien alphabets as I type these words and remember the connections I made—the barriers we breached—with an African man and a Greek woman, neither of whom I ever saw again.

Different Spanish accents also show where someone is from, both country and region, and of course people make fun of others' accents. Same with the Portuguese of Brazil and Portugal. Brazilian jokes love to feature dim-witted "Joãozinho" from Portugal, and I've laughed heartily at ten-year-old Isabela Nutti's spot-on imitation of the sibilant Portuguese accent of the Cariocas, the natives of Rio de Janeiro. (Lots of "sh" sounds, like in the Portuguese of Portugal, or Argentine Spanish.)

---

78 Speaking of laughing, my favorite story about Greek comes from my Swiss friend Hans Meier. He and some high school classmates went to Athens with their Greek teacher. The teacher confidently spoke to the locals, who responded with blank stares. Turns out they were utterly ignorant of *ancient* Greek. The Swiss kids all knew English, though, and communicated with the Athenians that way—then translated for the hapless teacher, who didn't speak English!

English doesn't have both a formal and informal way to say "you" since "thee" and "thou" bit the dust centuries ago.[79] Many other languages do, and it can be an immediate indication of class distinctions and personal attitudes. Spanish, for example, has the informal *tu* and the formal *usted*. I would use *tu* to show friendship to someone I know, but if I say it to a store clerk, I'm claiming a superior social status to that person.[80]

When I visited Florianópolis in 2004, I found that people in Santa Catarina state still use the informal *tu* for "you" as well as the formal *voce*. *Tu* has disappeared from Portuguese in São Paulo state, where I'm used to speaking, so I never learned the *tu* verb forms. (Similarly, the informal Spanish plural "you" *vosotros* is used nowhere in South America.) My Florianópolis friends understood, of course. They were surprised that I spoke decent Portuguese at all, since I didn't when I'd passed through the first time in 1980. Still, I felt weird when they called me *tu* but I responded with *voce*, like some tight-ass twit standing on ceremony.

It's an all-too-common phenomenon to hear Americans sneer at immigrants to "talk English," or to ridicule foreign accents. To quote Arlo Guthrie in "Alice's Restaurant," it shows "a lot of damn gall" to mock a foreigner's attempt to communicate when you don't speak another language yourself. The irony is how often these self-styled patriots butcher their supposedly beloved English language. H. L. Mencken satirized this hypocrisy (and

---

79 Though it sounds pretentious to modern ears, "thou" is informal. That's why in *For Whom the Bell Tolls*, Hemingway's use of "thee" and "thou" to render the informal Spanish "*tu*" sounds weird and stilted.

80 *Tu* is noticeably more common in Chilean Spanish now than when I was in the Peace Corps. This informality is likely a corollary of global capitalism's influence on the society, especially through advertising. No matter what the medium—print, radio, television or Internet—*tu* appears in ads far more often than *usted*.

a lot more) nearly a century ago in works such as "The Declaration of Independence in American," which opens with the stirring words, "When things get so balled up that the people of a country got to cut loose from some other country, and go it on their own hook, without asking no permission from nobody, excepting maybe God Almighty, then they ought to let everybody know why they done it, so that everybody can see they are not trying to put nothing over on nobody." Little has changed today except for the slang *du jour*, the countries most immigrants come from—and the ease of disseminating ignorance, via the internet, ubiquitous telephones, Twitter, etc. From what I've seen, wherever I've been, inconvenient facts rarely hinder folks who could use them the most.

Language chauvinism is far from a strictly American phenomenon. Where there are people, there are prejudices, and for better or worse, language is a powerful component of identity. A friend of mine in grad school, determined to maintain his New Zealand identity while in the States, insisted on using Kiwi terms such as "tea" instead of "dinner." Meanwhile, an Australian friend who reinforced his identity by chowing down on Vegemite (a brown, salty paste loved by Aussies and abhorred by almost everyone else), taught me that a "whinging pome" is a whining Englishman. Said with a smile I don't think "pome" (pronounced "pommy") is necessarily offensive, maybe on a par with "Limey."

Another relatively benign example is a Chilean slang phrase for pretending to be ignorant about something, *hacerse el gringo* ("to become a gringo"; literally, "to make oneself a gringo"). It's derived from the frequency that gringos in Chile don't speak Spanish, and even if they're learning, their most common phrase is probably *"No entiendo"* ("I don't understand"). Lord knows how many times I've said *"No entiendo,"* but whatever the number it's only a fraction of the times I've actually not understood, yet kept silent either not to be a bother or not to be seen as stupid. After all, a Chilean slang synonym for *hacerse el gringo* is *hacerse el tonto* ("to make oneself/pretend to be a fool").[81] *Hacerse el gringo* is often construed as funny, not mean-spirited. Still, humor at someone else's expense can get tricky. Ana Maria Buitano once said to a group, "*Me hice la gringa,*" then remembered I was there and felt embarrassed. I laughed; it didn't bother me at all. If anything, I took it as a positive sign, that to her my main identity was "friend," not "gringo."

Two Chilean ways of saying "Don't be stupid"—*No seas indio* ("Don't be an Indian") and *No seas boliviano* ("Don't be a Bolivian")—are more problematic. On the surface, these expressions at the expense of gringos, Indians and Bolivians might seem identical, but the latter two are definitely stronger, more scornful. There's an enormous difference in Chile between being a gringo and being an Indian or a Bolivian. Gringos might be begrudged their material prosperity, or expected to answer for actions of the U.S. government, but in general Chileans like Americans. On the other hand, Indians and Bolivians (most Bolivians *are* Indians) aren't highly respected—hence the warnings not to be like them. Probably most important, *hacerse el gringo* involves an act of will. A person *decides* to do it. It's hard to imagine a Chilean admonishing someone, "*No seas gringo*"—especially when in terms of language the exact opposite is happening. Gringo-speak is conquering the world.

English is far and away this planet's most important language. (I don't buy the claim that one day it will be Chinese; English is easier to learn and has a massive head start. Besides, there's a nationwide campaign in China to teach their kids English.)

---

81 Not until I went to Chile did I realize that the name of the Lone Ranger's sidekick, Tonto, means "fool."

Almost everywhere, fluency in English is increasingly seen as essential to economic success. Some Americans resent and even fear the increasing importance of Spanish in the U.S., but this chauvinism is not only misplaced, it's misguided. Spanish is rising from below; English is the boss and is going to stay that way. In Latin America and the rest of the world, however, English is imposed from above. Not officially, necessarily, though that's often true as well, but de facto. English is the lingua franca not only of business, but of practically every field. It's the language of the political, cultural and economic superpower, as well as other A-list countries such as the United Kingdom, Australia and Canada, and everyone else must either adapt or be left out of the party. That's a greater reason for resentment than the presence of Spanish in the U.S. We're a nation of immigrants, a polyglot mongrel of a country—even before Europeans arrived. My father spoke only Slovak until he went to school, but soon English took over, as it nearly always does. Eventually, he hardly remembered a word of his first language.

When American diplomats or businesspeople visit Latin America, it's a plus if they speak Spanish, but rarely a requirement. The usual expectation is that the locals will be able to speak English, or as a last resort will provide a translator. Now imagine the reverse, that someone coming to the U.S. expects Americans to speak anything but English. Not very likely, is it?

In the Santiago subway I saw an advertisement showing a girl with two clothespins on her lips. The caption read, *Así te vas a sentir si no hablas el mejor inglés. El mejor inglés es el inglés de MANPOWER.* [This is how you'll feel if you don't speak the best English. The best English is MANPOWER English.] Someone should tell Manpower that their sexist name might not go over so well in the States, especially for a company teaching people English, but that's a separate issue. The point is that the battle concerns where and how to learn English, not whether students need to. It's simply taken for granted today that without English, people are at a disadvantage.

What *is* the "best English"? The English of Australia? South Africa? Canada? Scotland? Jamaica? Ireland? Kenya? The United States? Bermuda? New Zealand? England? Liberia? Belize? Which of the manifold accents and dialects in these countries is best? Manpower's claim to provide the "best English" is as silly as it is spurious (as well as rather weird, since it's made in Spanish). The fact is, though, that students of English today usually want to learn an American accent, and are more likely to do so because of ubiquitous American music, films and TV shows. Most Chileans my age were taught English with a bad British accent by incompetent teachers, and therefore actually learned almost nothing.[82]

South America has innumerable private schools that teach English (and often other languages as well, though English is by far the most common). They're a bit like SAT prep classes in the U.S., where many middle-class families feel compelled to send their children to keep up with their peers. Tutors are also common. Hugo gives individual English lessons (*clases particulares*) in people's homes for a much higher hourly wage than he receives at his public school job. There's competition for admission to the best schools, after all, and competition for jobs in the global marketplace. Parents don't want to see their kid lose that competition. How much of this is true concern for the children, and how much is an attempt to forestall parental

---

82 In Lima, Peru, in 2009, I heard an English language instruction CD playing from a store that was trying to sell the course. The instructor was carefully pronouncing the months of the year—with quite a strong Spanish accent. Even if students managed to learn English from this model, their pronunciation would be skewed.

embarrassment if they *don't* succeed? It's a complicated question of human nature, human psychology and human behavior.

So is language itself. Take the issue of incorporating words from other languages. The Académie Française foams at the mouth when the French speak of *le weekend* or *le drugstore*, but the people do it anyway. Chilean Spanish is interlarded with English words: Coca Cola Light (Diet Coke), jeans, shorts. English has done the same with Spanish words: canyon, mesa, mesquite (which the Spanish got from Native Americans). Given the opportunity, people cherry-pick the best language options, as we did in the Peace Corps once Spanish became familiar. When PCVs got together, our English was peppered with Spanish words, sometimes because we simply liked the word better, but more often for efficiency's sake. For example, it was rare to hear a PCV say "watermelon" instead of *sandía*, or "avocado" instead of *palta*.

That was the idea with Esperanto, except that it was created rather than developing organically. Despite the name, it was hopeless to think that Esperanto would catch on. People bring parts of other languages into their own because they're useful, not because someone tells them to.[83] Think about sidewalks. Except in parks or other places of leisure, where taking one's time is the point, sidewalks should never be laid out according to some abstract, curving idea of beauty. Instead, make sure they follow the shortest distances between points, because that's the route most people are going to take. Defy human nature and soon dirt paths will cut through the grass, courtesy of pedestrians who are either lazy, in a hurry, or both.

---

83 My neighbor Peter Kiss, who immigrated from Hungary at age fifteen, assures me that he has willfully forgotten as much as possible of the Russian that was forced on him in school.

Most of the time language is like a sidewalk, a means to get somewhere. Few people speak ten words when five are sufficient, and those who habitually use ten (or twenty, or thirty) instead of five acquire reputations as blowhards, bores or politicians. (Not mutually exclusive categories, unfortunately.) Language isn't always strictly utilitarian, but no matter how artistic or poetic it's still a means of getting somewhere. Even a doctrinaire belief in literary *ars gratia artis*, art for art's sake, requires language to get there, to create the art.[84]

Here are a few memory snapshots of people using English to try to get somewhere:

A nine-year-old boy in Lima: "Meester, one money, plees."

A prostitute on Calle Thomson in Iquique: "Hey joo, American, fooky fooky?"

A sign in a bus in Arica: "PLES DO'NT SMOKIN".

A Chinese beer label: "The Taishan beer is made of German high quality yeast and taishan's sierra 280 meters deep places high quality natural water, fermet according to the German pure zymotechnics, the taste puregentle, low sugar pale with crisp, it has the brand-new German flavor."

And finally, a T-shirt in Santiago: MELTIN' POT.

I couldn't have said it better myself.

---

84 A brilliant artistic use of language to create identity appears in Henry Roth's novel, *Call It Sleep*. To indicate when the narrator's immigrant mother is speaking Yiddish, Roth puts her sentences in beautiful English. To show when she speaks English, he makes her language fractured and ungrammatical.

I AM ALMOST MEDIEVAL [85]

"In midevil times everyone was middle-aged"

—student bloopers

The relation seemed invisible at first: a dusty 1973 *National Geographic* in an Avon Products box, a musty 1974 *Sports Illustrated* swimsuit issue in a garbage can, an 1802 house on the mend in upstate New York. But this strange triangle has spun into a circle, found a center somewhere behind my eyes, grudgingly made sense. Or at least forced me to try to find a middle ground. For the farther my thinking took me, the more progress I made, the deeper I waded in the muddle of the middle.

The 1802 House

To get anywhere, I had to go backward; as is often the case, travel was the catalyst. Trips make our brains remember what they're for. And the longest trip we can take with any luggage is to the past: the future, however long, must be faced naked. Returning to Connecticut from a car trip west, death rattle in the throat of our Toyota's clutch, my wife and I stopped to visit friends in Geneva, New York. We four had met while acquiring

---

85 First published in *Under the Sun*, Summer 2002.

various degrees from the University of Utah in Salt Lake City. About a year ago Jon and Jill bought a house on Main Street, the oldest residence (and second-oldest building) in town, and he is in the long process of restoring it while she finishes her Ph.D. and joins him in the hideous hunt for college English teaching jobs.

The house project is enormous. Jon showed me the scars of generations of questionable taste—the brick fireplace resurrected from behind a wall, the hardwood floors rescued from glued-on floral carpet. I asked about traces on the living room floor and ceiling, odd indications that it had once been partitioned into half a dozen tiny cubicles. Who would do that?

Jon glanced up at the marks on the ceiling. "A doctor lived here for years. These were his examining rooms. When I'm done it'll look good—like they never were there."

He spoke with the pride of a craftsman, confident in his ability to mask the unwanted past, to bring the worthy past to light. Was there similar pride in the craftsman who, Montressor-like, walled in the fireplace? Or did he regret it, do the job for the same reason most of us do—to be able to eat next week, or go to the tavern or hide cash under the mattress? I looked out the window at Seneca Lake below, primal gray and deep and beautiful, unchanged since the last time I saw it, probably unchanged since the trees were felled to build this house, unchanged since the Iroquois settled its banks—maybe on this very spot—who knows how long after craftsmen glaciers carved out these Finger Lakes. I looked at Jon and remembered when he had a beard, remembered when I did not, thought of how long my hair was once, when I was in college and living in Switzerland and hiked on glaciers in the Alps. Styles change, people change; I argued with my parents over long hair that I sheepishly smile at now in my college yearbook. Melville could hardly give *Moby Dick* away when he wrote it; Van Gogh's paintings went begging as hard as collectors beg now for anything with his signature on it.

Obviously the "worthy past" is a fluid concept, no less so than any era's myriad contemporary judgments of itself and its players. During just the course of my formal education, Christopher Columbus devolved from unquestioned, pedestaled hero to a controversial figure considered by many to be a genocidal monster. Richard Nixon somehow managed to leave this world a more or less respected "elder statesman" rather than a disgraced crook we won't have to kick around anymore. Stalin's twisted version of history (show trials, Katyn Massacre) has been purged from Soviet—sorry, Russian—history books. The erstwhile "merciless Indian savages" of the Declaration of Independence are now acknowledged victims of Manifest Destiny, and in twisted recompense a lucky fraction of their ancestors is growing robber-baron rich running gambling casinos.

Heinrich Schliemann found many layers of Troy, as present after present built on and over and eventually became the past. In the summer of the year Jimmy Carter was elected President I worked on an archeological dig in western Switzerland. There were many holes on the site, of varying depths and dimensions, undressing different layers of history. The deepest one had exposed pilings from a Bronze Age house over four thousand years old, once prime lakefront property, now a hundred yards from the water and fifteen feet underground. Every day we would find pottery, tools, evidence of craftsmen and pride in a job well done. Every day after work we would swim in Lake Neuchatel and watch the sun's rays filter through distant clouds like the gaze of God and gleam on the mountains that seemed as if they'd been there forever and always would. I'd float in the water, totally relaxed, meditating thoughtless at the sky until it slowly sank all the way to my hopeful face and I was buoyed up, supported, surrounded by warm, perfect, forever blue. That was eighteen years ago, more or less the mathematical middle of my life so far.

"What's past is prologue," and "Those who cannot remember the past are condemned to fulfill it": Shakespeare's and Santayana's trenchant observations have all but been rendered clichés (by people, not time; as Martin Luther King insisted in his "Letter from Birmingham Jail," time is neutral) but like most clichés they contain a degree of truth, or at least sense, that is not as simple as it seems. They invite examination and thought. Clichés arise because they provide ready-made responses to save people the bother (or pain, or embarrassment) of thinking. But if we *do* think about it, the questions don't disappear, they multiply. How many Americans today have looked a horse, gift or otherwise, in the mouth? Or put all their eggs in one basket? Or done something till the cows come home? These images from a vanished agrarian society linger in our language, atavistic signs further removed from their origins with every passing year, relics of a frequently idealized worthy past that never existed when twenty-four hours was enough time in a day, nobody locked their doors, and everybody knew their neighbors. What does it mean that we refuse to let them go?

The 1973 *National Geographic*

I also refuse to let things go. I hold on to the past (and its remnants), not in the fatuous hope of continuing to live it, but to not forget it, for it to live *now*. The past *isn't*—it is not, anymore, that's what makes it past. Which makes the concept of reinventing the past that much more bizarre. We recreate what no longer is for the use of a present that constantly joins the past in non-existence. Which is why I save things, why I like museums, why my shelves are stocked with books on worlds that no longer exist, from ancient civilizations to the Great Society to the Watergate era. And why I marveled at the serendipity this spring when my mother prevailed upon me to haul away boxes of magazines that had been stored at my parents' house for two decades and more, and there on top of a stack was that April 1973 *National Geographic* with Chile as the cover story. The article was guardedly optimistic about the country's future. Five months later, on September 11, 1973, general Augusto Pinochet grabbed power in a *golpe de estado* and became military dictator.

The CIA was involved, Nixon and Kissinger were involved, because democratically elected President Salvador Allende was a Marxist, and democracy dies under the Monroe Doctrine when a person you don't like wins the election. Brutal repression, suspension of civil liberties and thousands of *desaparecidos* resulted from the military takeover, but that's a small price to pay for installing a despot who's virulently anti-communist. He may be a creep but he's our creep, and that's good for business.

This essay isn't about Chile, and military dictators. But it is about the past, and making sense of its role in the present, and for me the past includes Chile, where I was a Peace Corps Volunteer from 1978-80, and I want you to know how I feel about those events of 1973 that at the time I hardly noticed—if I noticed at all, for I don't remember. On September 11, 1973 I was in the second week of my freshman year of college. Books, girls and beer were my primary concerns; Chile was some skinny country on the other end of the world, more remote to me than the Plato I was reading in Ancient Philosophy, in a used copy irritatingly marked up by a previous owner in neon pink hi-liter (for the first forty pages or so; after that the pages were as virgin as I was). On January 8, 1978, I arrived with my Peace Corps group in a country with the world's friendliest people—and a curfew, a censored press, and a Presidential building downtown still pocked with bullet holes from the *golpe*.

So, this place that had been at most a footnote to me, became home for two and a half years. And it has been over fourteen years since I flew from Rio de Janeiro to JFK, and hitchhiked to New Haven with October leaves just beginning to blaze. I stayed with old friends that night, celebrated appropriately, met my college roommate's future wife, got a ride from him the next day in a Triumph with the top down to my parents' house. They had no idea when I was coming home, and my father's smile when he saw me get out of that car is a highlight of my life.

I felt like I'd made progress when I returned. Not in any linear sense like passing Go and collecting $200, but in terms of growth, in terms of happiness and appreciation for what matters. Progress is a mistrusted word these days, with connotations of ecological devastation and empty materialism that make me want to wiggle the first two fingers of both hands like snails' antennae each time I say it, to put it "in quotes" and show that I'm not naive, that I realize how problematic a concept it is. It needs defining to be useful. Santayana claims that "progress, far from consisting in change, depends on retentiveness," and I think it is at best foolish and at worst perilous for a person, a nation, or a planet to ignore that. Progress is not solely a matter of retention, of course; otherwise, we would be consulting Galen before attempting a heart transplant or using the Bible to calculate the precise date for the creation of the universe. But we should always bear in mind what has come before, if not for emulation, then for humility. For surely future humans will cringe at our crude medicine the way we do at medieval barber-surgeons with their leeches, and with shaking heads will attempt to repair some affront to taste that we have perpetrated, the way our age has removed the prudish loincloths and gravity-defying flowing robes that epigoni foisted on Michelangelo to give the Sistine Chapel a PG rating.

Medieval means middle age; according to that sadly hilarious collection of student bloopers most teachers have seen at one time or another, "In midevil times everyone was middle aged." At thirty-eight I suppose I am almost medieval, according to actuarial tables. But thirty-eight was old in the time of Charlemagne, and still is in Chad. Labels, always suspect, become increasingly so as time moves on. There can be no 'middle" without boundaries of some sort, or at least surroundings: left/right; youth/old age; beginning/end; an ocean, a desert, a road, a universe. And "middle" implies a place with more or less equal areas around it—one step from the finish line is not the middle of a race. In a thousand years, or five thousand, or ten, will people still refer to the time of the Crusades and Richard the Lion-Hearted as the Middle Ages? I heartily doubt it. Our definition, so accepted and useful today, relies on our current historical perspective and will inexorably change as the centuries pass. It is a middle stage in itself, a transition, one that later perspectives will modify or abandon like the vestiges of the doctor's office Jon is eliminating from his house. Quite possibly our era, so self-evidently modern to us, will become the thirtieth century's Middle Ages, complete with AIDS or some even grimmer virus as its Black Death.

The lawyer who narrates Melville's "Bartleby the Scrivener" considers himself "rather elderly" at fifty-eight. Maybe this held true in 1853, but it does not square at all with American life today. Many of my colleagues at the university where I teach are in their fifties, and the word "elderly" would never come to mind to describe them; even their talk of retirement involves *doing* things: going places, not to seed. My father is seventy-nine but doesn't seem old because he doesn't act old—and this is from the perspective of a child of the '60s who was temporarily brainwashed not to trust anyone over thirty, when that age denoted virtual senescence to a naive teenager who also believed protest demonstrations would end war forever.

"Your old road is rapidly fading/So get out of the new one if you can't lend a hand/For the times they are a-changin'." So sang Bob Dylan in 1963. The image of the road is long and venerable and will never wear out; people will always respond to it, in books like *On the Road*, poems like "The Road Not Taken," songs like "On the Road Again." But returning to clichés might provide only a path of quicksand. Dylan warns the unuseful to get out of the road, and "middle of the road" is a well-worn description for insipid moderation, with overtones of dullness and cowardice for good measure. Yet a moment's thought shows the middle of the road to be far more dangerous than one side or the other: that's where the traffic is. The film *The Program* was bowdlerized because it began a crazy fashion of proving one's manhood by lying in the road as cars whiz past. To return to Santayana a final time: "For an idea ever to be fashionable is ominous, since it must afterwards be always old-fashioned." But fashions can certainly return, like 50s retro in the 80s, bell bottoms and tie-dye in the 90s.

Those who do not remember the leisure suit will be condemned to wear it again.

The 1974 *Sports Illustrated*

My wife and I have bought a house in Connecticut. It is a 1950 house, not an 1802 house, built in a former asparagus field, not on a historic main street. Yet it is not without history, a past, traces of those who came before. It is not without ghosts.

Stalin was still in power in 1950, Thurgood Marshall had not yet argued *Brown v. Board of Education* before the Supreme Court and rockets had never left the earth's atmosphere. The Normandy invasion and Hiroshima bombing were still terrifyingly real, just beginning their imperceptible fade to the remoteness of Bull Run or The Battle of New Orleans or Bunker Hill—or Waterloo or Agincourt or Thermopylae. Willie Mays hadn't made his famous catch off Vic Wertz. My parents hadn't met at the factory. I wasn't born.

And in the house we would buy over four decades later, someone put up wallpaper that somebody somehow thought looked good.

Somebody was mistaken.

Removing it was nothing like the job we had in a rented house once in Salt Lake City, where we eventually dug through seven layers of wallpaper in a bedroom, each one reluctantly yielding to the next like strata of Troy under Schliemann's shovel. Which is where the ghosts come in: realizing that each paper-thin layer represents human effort, human selection and human work, a deliberate decision to bury the past to create a better present. People we would never know anything about, successions of them, generations of them, had lived here, worked here, done the things people do in a place and now were gone. Each brand-new present had glued over the past, covered it up, forgotten it—and waited for its turn. Southwest Indians call their ancient, unknown forebears the Anasazi: The Old Ones Who Are Not Us. It is a very useful word. My wife, stepdaughter and I momentarily released the traces of our Anasazi, their ghosts, then threw them away. Tastes change. Times change. People change.

That was six years ago. The walls of that rental house, which we painted antique white after the paper had been stripped and stuffed in that week's trash, might be covered with something else by now. If not, the paint is surely feeling the years, for dirt and stains are inevitable in this life.

Like the malodorous ones on the 1974 *Sports Illustrated* swimsuit issue I found staring at me when I lifted the garbage can lid this spring. Redolent of kerosene or paint thinner, the magazine had stiffened and the pages crinkled when pried apart, but it was eminently salvageable so I did, to my wife's dismay. She, after all, had been the one who dumped it and a dozen similarly damaged magazines into the can in the first place.

"It stinks," she said.

"It's history," I said.

"Sometimes history stinks. Please don't bring it in the house. I notice you didn't save the ones that don't have a bikini on the front."

"True, but these only come once a year. Like Christmas."

"Perpetual adolescent," she said smiling, which I took as at least a partial compliment. I also took the magazine in the house, after a few days of airing it out in the garage, and displayed it on the living room coffee table. Everyone who came by took a look at this once racy, now almost quaint piece of the past, a mere seven pages of swimsuit photos from the days before *Sports Illustrated* dumped its "girl next door" image for glamorous supermodels in fifty-page, ad-interrupted spreads, with glossy videos and pricey calendars just an 800 number and a credit card away.[86]

---

86 The fifty-page spread has since gone the way of the girl next door. Today the swimsuit issue contains no sports and is published as a stand-alone entity apart from the weekly magazine. [Update: in 2020 *Sports Illustrated* became a monthly publication.] Subscribers have the option to not receive the swimsuit issue, instead extending their subscriptions. This courtesy had the unfortunate consequence of eliminating the always entertaining "cancel my subscription" letters a few weeks later. Guess which issue is—by far—*Sports Illustrated's* best seller every year.

Our friend Martha even noticed that Cheryl Tiegs's neck strap was twisted in the lead picture. "That wouldn't happen today," she said, and of course she was right. Now they pay attention to details. No way that photo would get in. And yes, somehow, impossibly, Cheryl Tiegs is middle-aged now—more middle-aged than I am.

On the cover of the January 28, 1974 swimsuit issue a smiling, sunny-faced model peeks back at us over her left shoulder; behind her, tiers of out-of-focus waves crest offshore, frozen forever a few feet from the beach. The bottom of the page is cropped at mid-thigh, while the horizon bisects the rest of her, two-thirds of the way up—admirable composition. Shades of blue complement each other—sky, sea, shimmering swimsuit—though her eyes are green. In today's quest for perfection a blue-eyed model would probably take her place, or she might wear colored contact lenses to make reality come out right. And certainly, her contemporary swimsuit would not have a prominent seam in its seat.

The title of the issue is "What's New Under The Sun." It's not a question, but if this essay has shown anything it might as well be, and here are a few answers. Chile was enduring a military dictatorship that began less than five months before. I was enjoying a college career only two weeks older than that. And every person alive at that moment, each one of us, was in the middle of something.

We still are.

CITY OF GLASS [87]

by Martín Espada

For Pablo Neruda and Matilde Urrutia
La Chascona, Santiago de Chile

The poet's house was a city of glass:
cranberry glass, milk glass, carnival glass,
red and green goblets row after row,
black luster of wine in bottles,
ships in bottles, zoo of bottles,
rooster, horse, monkey, fish,
heartbeat of clocks tapping against crystal,
windows illuminated by the white Andes,
observatory of glass over Santiago.

When the poet died,
they brought his coffin to the city of glass.
There was no door: the door was a thousand daggers,
beyond the door an ancient world in ruins,
glass now arrowheads, axes, pottery shards, dust.
There were no windows: fingers of air
reached for glass like a missing lover's face.

---

87   From *The Republic of Poetry*, W.W. Norton, 2006.

There was no zoo: the bottles were half-moons
and quarter-moons, horse and monkey
eviscerated with every clock, with every lamp.
Bootprints spun in a lunatic tango across the floor.

The poet's widow said, *We will not sweep the glass.*
His wake is here. Reporters, photographers,
intellectuals, ambassadors stepped across the glass
cracking like a frozen lake, and soldiers too,
who sacked the city of glass,
returned to speak for their general,
three days of official mourning
announced at the end of the third day.

In Chile, a river of glass bubbled, cooled,
hardened, and rose in sheets, only to crash and rise again.
One day, years later, the soldiers wheeled around
to find themselves in a city of glass.
Their rifles turned to carnival glass;
bullets dissolved, glittering, in their hands.
From the poet's zoo they heard monkeys cry;
from the poet's observatory they heard
poem after poem like a call to prayer.
The general's tongue burned with slivers
invisible to the eye. The general's tongue
was the color of cranberry glass.

324

GRACIAS A LA VIDA

by Violeta Parra

Gracias a la vida que me ha dado tanto.
Mi dió dos luceros que, cuando los abro,
perfecto distingo lo negro del blanco,
y en el alto cielo su fondo estrellado
y en las multitudes el hombre que yo amo.

Gracias a la vida que me ha dado tanto.
Me ha dado el oído que, en todo su ancho,
graba noche y día grillos y canarios,
martillos, turbinas, ladridos, chubascos,
y la voz tan tierna de mi bien amado.

Gracias a la vida que me ha dado tanto.
Me ha dado el sonido y el abecedario,
con él las palabras que pienso y declaro:
madre, amigo, hermano, y luz alumbrando
la ruta del alma del que estoy amando.

Gracias a la vida que me ha dado tanto.
Me ha dado la marcha de mis pies cansados;
con ellos anduve ciudades y charcos,

playas y desiertos, montañas y llanos,
y la casa tuya, tu calle y tu patio.

Gracias a la vida que me ha dado tanto.
Me dió el corazón que agita su marco
cuando miro el fruto del cerebro humano,
cuando miro el bueno tan lejos del malo,
cuando miro el fondo de tus ojos claros.

Gracias a la vida que me ha dado tanto.
Me ha dado la risa y me ha dado el llanto.
Así yo distingo dicha de quebranto,
los dos materiales que forman mi canto,
y el canto de ustedes que es el mismo canto
y el canto de todos, que es mi propio canto.

Gracias a la vida que me ha dado tanto.

THANK YOU TO LIFE [88]

by Violeta Parra

Thank you to life that has given me so much.
It gave me two bright stars that let me, when I open
them, distinguish perfectly between black and white,
and in high heaven its starry background,
and in the multitudes the man that I love.

Thank you to life that has given me so much.
It has given me hearing that in its amplitude
records night and day, crickets and canaries,
hammers, turbines, barking, rainstorms,
and the tender voice of my loved one.

Thank you to life that has given me so much.
It has given me sound and the alphabet,
with it the words that I think and declare:
mother, friend, brother, and light illuminating
the path of the soul that I am loving.

---

88 The translation is mine and I bear responsibility for any infelicities. I have made
no attempt to maintain the rhyme scheme of the original song, which is far easier in
Spanish with all those words ending in "o."

Thank you to life that has given me so much.
It has given me the steps of my tired feet;
with them I walked cities and puddles,
beaches and deserts, mountains and plains,
and your house, your street and your patio.

Thank you to life that has given me so much.
It gave me the heart that shakes its frame
when I see the fruit of the human brain,
when I see the good far way from the bad,
when I see the depths of your clear eyes.

Thank you to life that has given me so much.
It has given me laughter and given me tears.
Thus I distinguish between happiness and grief,
the two materials that form my song,
and the song of you people that is the same song
and the song of everyone, which is my own song.

Thank you to life that has given me so much.

EL ULTIMO POEMA DE VICTOR JARA[89]

Joan Jara: *"Cuando más adelante me trajeron el texto del último poema de Victor, supe que él quería dejar su testimonio, su único medio de resistir ahora el fascismo, de luchar por los derechos de los seres humanos y por la paz."*

Somos cinco mil
en esta pequeña parte de la ciudad.
Somos cinco mil.
Cuántos seremos en total
en las ciudades y en todo el país?
Solo aquí
diez mil manos siembran
y hacen andar las fábricas.

Cuánta humanidad
con hambre, frío, pánico, dolor,
presión moral, terror y locura!

---

89 Victor Jara was murdered in the Estadio Chile on September 15, 1973. His corpse was tossed with others by the side of a road, then taken to a city morgue. He would have been buried in a mass grave had not a morgue worker recognized the beloved folk singer and dared to inform Jara's wife Joan, who in peril of her own life claimed his badly beaten and machine-gunned body. When a soldier came to take him away to be tortured and shot, Jara managed to slip this poem to a fellow prisoner, who courageously kept it and eventually smuggled it out to be published.

Seis de los nuestros se perdieron
en el espacio de las estrellas.

Un muerto, un golpeado como jamás creí
se podría golpear a un ser humano.
Los otros cuatro quisieron quitarse todos los terrores.
uno saltó al vacío,
otro golpeandose la cabeza contra el muro,
pero todos con la mirada fija de la muerte.

Que espanto causa el rostro del fascismo!
Llevan a cabo sus planes con precisión artera
sin importarles nada.
La sangre para ellos son medallas.
La matanza es acto de heroismo.
Es este el mundo que creaste, dios mío?
Para esto tus siete días de asombro y trabajo?
En estas cuatro murallas solo existe un numero
que no progresa,
que lentamente querrá más muerte.

Pero de pronto me golpes la consciencia
y veo esta marea sin latido,
pero con el pulso de las máquinas
y los militares mostrando su rostro de matrona
llena de dulzura.
Y Mexico, Cuba y el mundo?
Qué griten esta ignominia!
Somos diesz mil manos
que no producen.

330

Cuanto somos en toda la Patria?
La sangre del compañero Presidente
golpea más fuerte que bombas y metrallas.
Así golpeará nuestro puño nuevamente.
Canto que mal me sales
Cuando tengo que cantar espanto!
Espanto como el que vivo
como el que muero, espanto.
De verme entre tanto y tantos
momentos del infinito
en que el silencio y el grito
son las metas de este canto.
Lo qu veo nunca ví,
lo que he sentido y que siento
hara brotar el momento...

(Estadio Chile, Septiembre 1973)

VICTOR JARA'S LAST POEM [90]

Joan Jara: "When later on they brought me the text of Victor's last poem, I knew that he wanted to leave his testament, his only way now to resist fascism, to struggle for human rights and for peace."

There are five thousand of us
in this small part of the city.
There are five thousand of us.
How many of us are there altogether
in the cities and in the whole country?
Here alone
ten thousand hands sow seeds
and keep the factories running.

So much humanity
starving, cold, panicked, hurting,
morally stressed, terrified and crazy!

Six of us have been lost
in the space between the stars.

---

90 Again, the translation is mine; so are any errors.

One dead, one beaten like I never believed
a human being could be beaten.
The other four wanted to escape all the horror.
One jumped to his death,
another slammed his head against the wall,
but all had the fixed look of death.

The face of fascism causes such terror!
They carry out their plans with crafty precision,
with no regard for anything.
Blood for them means medals.
Slaughter is an act of heroism.
Is this the world you created, my God?
For this your seven days of wonder and labor?
Inside these four walls exists only a number
that doesn't progress,
that slowly will want more death.

But soon my conscience strikes me
and I see this tide has no heartbeat,
just the pulse of a machine
and the soldiers showing the face of a matron
full of sweetness.
And Mexico, Cuba and the world?
They should cry out against this atrocity!
We are ten thousand fewer hands
that produce nothing.

How many of us are there in the entire homeland?
The blood of our companion, our President

hits stronger than bombs and bullets.
That's how our fist will strike again.

How badly I sing when
I have to sing terror!
Terror like the kind I am living,
like the kind I am dying, terror.
Meanwhile, to see myself and so many
moments of infinity
in which silence and cries
are the goals of this song.
What I see I never saw,
what I have felt and am feeling
will make the moment bloom...

(Chile Stadium, September 1973)

FICTION

Nowhere Station

I was alone in a second-class car on a train out of Madrid, bound for Barcelona. Yesterday I'd spent twenty minutes standing in front of Picasso's *Guernica*, which was black and white like old war photographs and far larger than I expected. I was twenty years old. No painting could make me cry back then, at least on the outside.

It was springtime in Spain. Franco had died last fall after 36 years as dictator, which meant little to me till I saw *Guernica*. I couldn't stop thinking about the painting.

The train stopped at some nowhere station. A short, scrawny man around sixty hesitated at the door of the compartment, then sat across from me by the window. I smiled and he smiled back.

There was a five-day beard on his sunken cheeks. He took a pack of Fortuna cigarettes from his shirt pocket and held it out to me.

"*No, gracias.*" That was about the extent of my Spanish, along with "*Buenos días*" and "*Una cerveza, por favor.*"

He shrugged and lit one for himself. He blew out foul-smelling smoke and made what seemed to be a friendly remark.

I knew one more thing in Spanish. "*No hablo español,*" I said apologetically.

He nodded. Easy math told me he was around twenty years old on April 26, 1937, the day Guernica was bombed. I wanted to ask—oh so carefully—about his life, what it was like to be twenty during a civil war rather than a college student traveling from across the ocean. I wondered if he had fought, and for which side. I wondered if he'd been to Guernica.

For many miles he smoked and I looked out the window, until without a word he touched my knee and left my life at another nowhere station.

DEAD LETTER

For Bob Maurer

Her dead lover's letter has waited on the desk since yesterday, unopened, the unripped envelope partially hiding the snow leopard on the cover of this month's *National Geographic*: June 1986. The postmark is dark and smeared, the stamp a standard issue, nothing special. "Ms. Charoltte King," reads the typed address, the "a" and "o" fuzzy, ink filled. Rory always typed his envelopes, even when he wrote the letter out longhand, and rarely managed it without a mistake. "He was funny that way," Charlee remembers out loud.

A typo. A typo in my name. "Charoltte," she says, pronouncing it with two syllables, then three. "Carlota. Gibraltar." No return address.

It's one of those small, stationery-size envelopes and is bulkier under the stamp, as if he'd used bigger paper like lined stuff ripped out of a spiral notebook, or maybe a page from a yellow legal pad, then folded it double on one side to make it fit. He'd used all those sources before, after all, and plenty of others, too. Theater programs. Campaign posters. Jackets to long forgotten and immediately remembered record albums. You never knew what to expect in a letter from Rory.

Sunshine streams through the window. Thigh touching the hard oak desk, Charlee presses the letter between her fingers

339

("Every month," Rory told her once in bed. "You lie on your back and feel both of them, check for lumps. Like this."), then holds it up to the morning. But the warm sun is no X-ray. She can't penetrate the solid blankness of the envelope, can't know if the letter is typed, nor even the color of the paper. Is that newsprint rustling on top? An editorial? A good *Doonesbury* she might have missed? Maybe one of his cartoons on a cocktail napkin, maybe a page ripped from a romance novel, with underlinings and exclamation points, and mock-serious literary commentary.

Maybe.

She aligns the letter with the front corner of the desk, careful to make it perfect. Her parakeet watches silently from his cage, head tilted toward the sun, then flutters his wings and squawks a little. Charlee pokes a finger between the bars but pulls out before he can peck it.

"You men are all alike, Terence." She gives him some sunflower seeds, which he ignores until his dignity runs out. Charlee smiles sadly.

She opens a drawer, bottom right. The news clipping of the accident is on top. The whole page, actually, folded once down the middle, because the scissors shook when she tried to cut it and besides, it's too small by itself. Three short paragraphs, a third the size of the shrimp scampi recipe on the refrigerator. That's not right. Buried on page three of the local section, under an ad for high-interest IRA's. But it happened far away.

Charlee has seen Becky's picture: in Rory's wallet behind his driver's license, in a framed 8-by-10 on his bedside table. It's not like he tried to hide it, or told her any lies. Charlee knew the score from the beginning, knew Becky was his girlfriend though she was three hundred miles away at graduate school and Rory only saw her once a month. He told her all this the first time they met, last summer at the pool in their apartment complex. And she had seen the picture the first time she entered his bedroom, a few weeks later, with plans he probably hadn't even considered yet. Still, it hurt to see the photo, his smile as wide as hers, on a sailboat deck with drinks in their hands and their free arms around each other, tanned and easy. It hurt to see that Becky looked as young as a college girl, hurt to see her in a bikini no woman would dare to wear unless she could wear it right.

Charlee sets the clipping on the coffee table and sinks into her couch. She likes her furniture soft, even her bed. "When I'm on it with you it doesn't matter," he said once, "but I like things firm."

"Like commitments?" she asked, feeling a great weight disappear as she said it but already sorry, watching Rory immediately lock himself the way men do. His jaw set and she knew he wouldn't answer. He stared at the ceiling, hands clasped behind his head. She felt like a nag; she thought of her mother bitching at Dad, and how many times she'd told herself I won't be like that, no matter what.

"I'm sorry," she said, touching his shoulder.

"No problem," he said to the ceiling.

"Want to go for a drive this afternoon?"

"Sounds good, but I told the Spiders I'd play softball." He turned to look at her. "Sorry."

She couldn't help it. "That's OK. There'll be plenty of other perfect sunny days to spend with me. Do what you want."

He stared back at the ceiling, then got out of bed and left the room. Charlee heard the radio in the kitchen and wanted to cry. Instead, she punched his pillow, twice, three times, then carefully smoothed out the depressions, put on a robe and followed. Halfway down the hall she smelled coffee, the good, strong, morning smell of coffee.

Rory was scrambling eggs, bopping a little to "The Great Pretender" on the oldies station. Toast popped up and he started

341

buttering. "I'll leave practice by one, Charlee. How about a picnic down by the delta?" He handed her a piece of toast. "If you take off your shirt on a levee, I'll take off mine."

Charlee is chewing on her hair. She knows it and doesn't care; it's not hurting anybody, not even anybody's sense of propriety. Mother is not in the room to tell her to stop, with a lengthy catalogue of reasons why. A thirty-year-old woman has earned the right to chew on her hair if she wants to. Across the room, his softball glove sits on the bookshelf next to a Swedish ivy. She'd asked if she could borrow his baseball glove and he'd said sure, but it's a *softball* glove. Bigger pocket. She was terrible at softball, afraid of the ball to tell the truth, but it was her first office picnic at the new firm so what the hey. Then it rained most of the day and the glove never left her back seat. That was Saturday, four days ago. Today is sunny, warm and beautiful. Charlee walks over and slips her hand into the glove. The leather is stained dark with oil and smells like why she liked him. She reads his name scrawled in ink on the thumb. She punches her fist in the pocket and thinks, Go ahead, throw it as hard as you want. Of course, I know how to catch. I wouldn't be out here if I didn't know how to catch.

It wasn't Becky's fault. Nobody disputes that, least of all Charlee. Like any lawyer, she expects she knows something about blame and who should wear it. Foggy road to the airport, Sunday afternoon and some high school kids joyriding with bourbon and beer, still celebrating a big win on Friday. Charlee has done the same, and more recently than high school. The other driver was hardly touched. His back seat teammates in traction, his front seat girlfriend, Becky and Rory dead. That was it. Charlee always refused to drive until he buckled his seat belt, and with a laugh he always would. It was just a stupid game; he could be such a child. But it wasn't Becky's fault he wasn't strapped in. She wasn't his mother. No one can blame her.

Charlee leans her head back against the couch, on the white crocheted whatever-you-call-'ems Rory brought her one time after he'd been out of town. They aren't mats and they aren't covers; the only word she can think of is antimacassar, but that's what her mother used to call them and there has to be a better word than that. Charlee wonders if he had been going to bring her something this time. She wonders about Becky's reaction when he broke the news. God, what if she was so upset that it contributed to the accident? Surely it was a tense ride to the airport. Charlee closes her guilty eyes. Would *I* have driven him to the airport if he'd told me we were through? She realizes she's chewing her hair again. Would anybody? Her hair tastes like someone else's as she stares at the letter, still flush with the corner of the desk, lying in a square of sunlight from the window.

Charlee sits near the back of the church, in the rainbow light of a stained-glass window. How do Catholics ever learn all this stuff? Stand, kneel, sit, kneel, stand, cross yourself, bow your head, sit some more, stand—all on cue from certain prayers or tinkling bells or some mysterious signs from a heavenly third base coach that only the initiated can understand. There's a big white casket in front of the altar, at the end of the center aisle, on some kind of trundle device with rollers so the pallbearers don't have to carry it. Charlee thinks that was a sensible idea. She is doing a lot of thinking, most of it to avoid thinking. She hopes that Catholic funerals always have a closed coffin, not that Rory's is shut for a reason. Everybody kneels, and she kneels too; wait, they just genuflected then stood up again. She scrambles to follow. Rory never went to church, but he never took the Lord's name in vain.

He'd never said so; Charlee simply noticed after a while, and though she didn't mention it, ever, she liked him better for it.

"Roark was a fine man, loved by all who knew him, who lived a life blessed in the sight of the Lord." The young priest looks down at the podium, whether for inspiration or to read his notes Charlee can't be sure. Rory hated to be called Roark, said it sounded like a lion with a seal's vocal cords.

"He has been called away, and we grieve at his departure from this life, but let us accept the wisdom of God's eternal plan and rejoice that Roark has found his heavenly reward." He goes on, and on, and Charlee listens, screams and laughter dueling in her skull. Damn this generic eulogy! She doubts that this man ever *met* Rory. He probably wasn't even ordained before the last time Rory went to church. Still, the priest is handsome. You can't help noticing that. But she's ashamed for noticing. In a front pew, Rory's mother cries silently. Beyond many heads, Charlee can see her shoulders trembling. Charlee crosses her arms and presses them tight against her breasts, reliving a last kiss at the airport and crying just a little as she waits for this to end.

"Send a postcard," she had called out with a wave, as Rory winked and disappeared down the tunnel. How do men learn to pretend so well, or does nothing *really* bother them? It has to be pretending. Pretender to the Throne; the Great Pretender. Rory could pretend with the best of them, and her shut eyes smile until she remembers the letter.

"All are cordially invited to the White home, 512 Boyden Street," the priest announces. His hand traces a cross in the air. "Go in peace to love and serve the Lord."

"Amen," Charlee hears all around her.

"Amen," Charlee says. Family members are the first to leave, Mrs. White in front leaning on her husband's arm. She isn't weeping any more, just staring straight ahead to avoid the sympathy each person exudes in case she looks their way. Charlee had done the same thing at her father's funeral, six years back. Back when she was Becky's age.

On the church steps, Charlee squints in the sunshine. As she checks her purse for sunglasses a hand touches her shoulder. Rory's younger brother Jack is smiling at her.

"Coming by the house, Charlotte?" He shifts a step to block the rays and shield her face. "Is that better?"

"Thanks, Jack. I don't know. I don't know anybody."

"You know me. Really, it would mean a lot to Mom. And Dad. They like you; you know, they really do." He smiles again and she wonders if he is making fun of her. But Jack would smile at a firing squad, she tells herself; it's not so hard when you're twenty-two and still believe in everything.

"Becky liked me too, I suppose?"

"No lie. Mom and Dad wanted Rory to marry you and settle down in the hometown. You're stable, you're a good influence. Becky was too wild for them. Rory never told you any of this?"

Charlee finds her sunglasses and puts them on. She knows Jack can see himself in the lenses.

"Okay," she says. "If you think I should."

Jack touches her arm again and turns away. Charlee watches him cut across the grass to his parents' sedan. She does not see Rory in his walk, did not see Rory in his face. No one would have picked them for brothers. Their features are—were—so different. Thinking about the meaning of a closed casket she walks to her car, and curses herself for the trouble she has getting the key into the lock. It's a short drive to the cemetery, and an even shorter one from there to the house where Rory grew up.

"Someday when my parents are out of town," he said once over a bottle of wicker-basket chianti, "we'll throw a huge party

345

then sleep in their bed. I'll be back where I began, and I want you there with me. What do you say?"

"I say go for it," she said. But his parents never went anywhere. Only Rory left town.

Charlee has been to these things before. The men stand around looking doleful, not knowing what to say, and the women all help in the kitchen to fake business-as-usual and feel they're doing something useful, and soon everybody's had a drink and the host is mixing more, and numbness sets in and it's not as bad as at first and maybe you shame yourself at some point when you laugh at a joke and forget for a minute why you're there. She stands at Rory's open grave, sun baking the back of her neck, until the priest finishes his benediction and the mourners shuffle off. She watches the last car roll away down the hill, then walks up the slope, a slow slalom among the headstones, back toward the trees in the far north corner. It's peaceful, actually, except for the plastic flowers. How could no one replace them before they bleach to such a dead white? She thinks of the letter and says, out loud, "You'd better get over to the house." She doesn't take away the dead plastic flowers, because she has nothing to leave in their place.

"How are you, dear?" Mrs. White is wearing the same black dress she had on at the funeral, but now a freshly washed apron protects it. "Thanks so much for coming."

A white-haired lady bustles up. "Rest, Evelyn. There's no need to knock yourself out. You've been through so much." She peers at Charlee. "Terrible, isn't it? Just terrible. Who are you?"

"None of your business," trembles on the end of her tongue, but she can't say that—Rory's mother is listening as if it matters to her too.

"A friend of Rory's," she answers. The words taste stale and inadequate.

"Friend, my foot." Mrs. White turns to the woman. "This girl was the best thing my son had in this world, and I pray to God he realized that before it was too late. *That's* who she is."

"Oh," the woman says.

Charlee feels as close to good as she has since Jack called with the news. She would love to hug this woman, this mother like you read about and some lucky people manage to have.

"Is there anything I can do, Mrs. White?"

"Take things one day at a time, Charlotte. That's all any of us can do."

"I mean anything I can do for *you*, for the family."

"I know what you mean," she says, and Charlee sees Rory in her glinting green eyes.

"Evy, take a load off your feet," coaxes the white-haired woman.

"Go soak yourself," says Rory's mother, and now Charlee knows where he got that dopey expression. "There's plenty of liquor, dear. Who knows who won't be here tomorrow to drink it. Excuse me. Hello, Mark, hello Connie. Thanks so much for coming. It would have meant a lot to him."

"It was a beautiful service," Connie says. "Evelyn, if there's anything we can do..."

Charlee moves to the bar. Jack is mixing drinks like someone with a lot of practice. "What's your pleasure?" he asks her.

"It doesn't matter."

"Manhattan it is," he says, and pours her something brown out of a big pitcher. It crackles over the ice cubes.

"Thanks, Jack."

"I was beginning to think you wouldn't make it."

"Sometimes you don't get to the place you were headed for."

"That's what I'm saying. Cheers, Charlee."

"Cheers."

347

They both drink, then avoid each other's eyes. Charlee feels most of her weight on her right foot and knows she is slouching, just a little but enough to have prompted a comment from her mother: "Do you want to go through life stooped over like your father?" The jagged realization hits that Rory is really gone, that she will never see him again. Of course, she has felt it before, but it would dull before stabbing home again; her mind had to close circuits or overload, like those icy moments when her own death becomes as real as fear, and she fights to picture fresh snow or sex with Rory or anything at all that might trick her brain into believing everything is all right. Throat tight, she drinks again, filling her eyes with details to keep from thinking as she tells herself, Don't cry. Damn you, don't cry. There are maybe twenty-five people in this room. They are all dressed up. This drink is strong. I should stand up straight. Rory says women should take calcium pills, and drink milk. His graduation photos are on the mantel. He still owes college loans and *damn you, don't cry*.

"What?" she says.

Jack is shoulder to shoulder with the man of God. "Charlee, this is Father Phil Sullivan. Father Phil, Charlotte King."

"Pleased to meet you," the priest says.

"My pleasure." Charlee offers her hand and is pleasantly surprised that he grips it firmly. Jack tops off their drinks. "Whoa!" the priest says. Charlee nods thanks. "Just doing my job," Jack says.

"Maybe too well," the priest answers.

Jack leans forward across the bar table. "They buried my brother today, Padre. You were there, remember?" Then he stands straight and raises his glass. The edge in his voice softens. "To Rory," he says, extending the glass and holding it until they both clink it with theirs.

"To Rory," Charlee says. She decides Jack reminds her a little of him after all.

348

"May he rest in peace," the priest says.

"May we all," Charlee says. She turns to Father Sullivan. "Do they give a course on eulogies at the seminary?"

Jack arches his eyebrows and flees with a pitcher of Manhattans. The priest sips. "Were you a close friend of Roark's, Ms. King?"

She winces at the name, sees his eyes notice; he is uneasy, and looking for a way out. One hand fidgets in his black pants pocket. She can hear Rory laughing, laughter she can't share.

"Intimate," she tells him. "We were lovers when he was in town, which was most of the time."

"I see."

Charlee feels sorry for him until she recalls the sermon. "Does that make you want to take back some of the pious things you said about him?"

It's a sincere question, not mocking. Father Sullivan runs a finger under his collar. Veins bulge on the back of his hand, like a tennis player's or a weightlifter's. He sips again, a big one, then clears his throat.

"None of us is free of sin, Ms. King. I prefer to believe that Roark saw his way clear before it was too late. Excuse me, please."

Saw his way clear. Charlee watches the priest's broad back cross the room to Rory's father. She likes Mr. White, though she dreads seeing him now; they get along fine as long as they discuss baseball, or maybe how much any right-thinking human detests the Dallas Cowboys, but today is no time to talk sports, and they have nothing else to say to each other.

"Rory threw a no-hitter against Newstead High, Charlee," he told her the first time they met, in this same living room. He tapped a framed photo of his son releasing a pitch. "You should have seen his stuff that day."

"How do you know, Dad?" Rory said. "You were at work."

That didn't faze the old man. "You don't throw a no-hitter without good stuff."

"Of course, you don't," Charlee said.

"You never saw so many line drives hit right at people," Rory said. Later he told her Newstead was a bunch of stiffs who only won two games all season, and one of them was against him the second time they played. Dad never talked about that one.

"Rory went three-for-four too," he said, and nodded wisely.

"Seeing-eye ground balls," Rory said.

Saw his way clear. Charlee smells perfume, lots of it, and boils inside. Perfume should be for happy occasions, or to impress someone, not for Rory's funeral. She whirls around. The perfumed woman is sobbing into a black lace handkerchief, a Manhattan in her other hand. For God's sake shut up, lady, Charlee aches to tell her. The props are spoiling your effect. Then: Shut up yourself, Charlotte King. She could be a saint for all you know.

If she's a saint, I am.

Saw his way clear.

I'd be all right if it weren't for that damn priest.

Sure. Say it enough times, maybe you'll fool yourself. Rory's gone and you're a mess.

But the priest makes it worse.

He didn't tell you anything you don't know. Open the letter. Just open the letter and find out.

Saw his way clear.

"Glad you could make it, Charlee." Mr. White is at her side—gray, tall, thick-waisted like a former fullback who keeps up the training-table steaks without the exercise. He plinks a fingernail on her nearly empty glass. "Jackie's letting down on the job," he says with a forced smile. "No tip for him. What'll it be?"

"Thank you, Mr. White, but I shouldn't."

"'Shouldn't' has no place in an Irishwoman's vocabulary—or even half Irish," he adds before she can correct him for the tenth time. It's their little standing joke, dating from that first meeting with the baseball photo.

"Put down that *girl's* drink," he says. "There's a heavenly single malt Scotch here you have to try."

Charlee likes it when he treats her like another son. To her own father she had always been his little girl, a paragon to be adored but never really taken seriously, even when she graduated from law school. He died the day after she took the bar exam and was buried without knowing she passed. He thought lawyers were crooks, anyway. I've always said that, he'd tell anybody who would listen, even if the anybody was Charlee.

"Please, only a little," Charlee says. "With ice."

Mr. White shakes his head in mock disgust but serves the drink on the rocks. She tastes. It *is* superb whiskey. But Rory is dead so what does it matter? Mr. White's creased, eager face hovers above her, waiting for a reaction, and suddenly she realizes that this is all an act, as much for his benefit as for anyone's, a concentration on the commonplace to deflect thought from a reality too painful to confront head-on. They still have nothing to say to each other, but that doesn't mean they can't talk. It's better than thinking.

Charlee nods like a wise judge, giving him what he needs. "It's wonderful," she says.

He beams and puts back the bottle. "It was Rory's favorite."

"I think I remember him mentioning it," she lies. Rory almost never touched whiskey, Scotch or otherwise. Said he'd rather drink Liquid-Plumr than the Brown Death.

Mr. White manufactures another smile. The conversation sags. Charlee watches her ice cubes melt. Somebody has put Tchaikovsky on the stereo, and Charlee notices she is slouching again. Rory's father is staring at the mantel, at his son following through off the mound. He swirls the whiskey around in his glass.

"Rory sent us a postcard from Becky's, Charlee. Said he had big news. Do you know what it was?"

"What?" She drinks quickly. Her stomach knots around the burn, hugging it tight.

"You don't understand." Mr. White's forehead is sweaty, glistening at the hairline, and he takes out a handkerchief to wipe it. "We don't know. He said it was a surprise for when he got back. You were his closest friend—I'm sure he'd tell you before anybody."

Saw his way clear.

The burning knot rises to her throat. Rory's father folds the handkerchief, meticulous as a fisherman tying a trout fly, then stuffs it in his pants pocket like a handful of change.

"We were going to get married," she says to the floor.

Mr. White puts a fatherly hand on her shoulder and gives it a squeeze. Their eyes meet and they both fight not to cry.

"Thank God you could at least give us a *little* peace of mind. Thank God for that much." He forces a crooked smile. "Congratulations, daughter."

Charlee stares at the plush carpet, remembering a quarter-century back to her grandparents' farm, to Grandpa Dolan in front of the fireplace, slapping a crooked poker against his palm. She cowered under his tirade about bearing false witness. Yes, Charlee had stolen eggs from the chicken coop, she wanted to save their lives, let them hatch into chicks and give them to her friends. Yes, Grandpa, I'm sorry, please don't hit me. Yes, Grandpa, I won't do it again, no, never. She feels the squeeze on her shoulder again. The whiskey is smooth fire on her tongue. Charlee smells perfume, and someone turns up the music.

She looks up at the pain in Rory's father's face. Almost sobbing from realizing how much comfort a lie can hold, she lies for him again.

"Rory and I didn't have any secrets, Mr. White."

Charlee has not had a martini for months. Rory was always the one to make them, and she kept gin and vermouth on her liquor shelf in case the urge hit. She mixes one and drops three olives in her glass. They're black olives but that's all she has. She sips; it's vile. Rory made good ones.

She eats an olive. No sun streams through the east-facing window onto the desk. It's sunny in the bathroom now, but that's no place to go. The bathroom is no place to go—how cute, King, what a punster you are, what a comedienne. The second sip is less awful. People were getting plowed when she left the funeral reception. Jack tried to convince her to stay, and she saw the priest watching her from across the room as she slipped out the door.

Drink in hand, Charlee walks to the desk. She had left the letter address-side down, which surprises her now. She edges a Bic pen cap under one top flap and rips it the length of the envelope. That works fine except for aerograms. With aerograms you have to be more careful.

"Who gives a damn about aerograms, Charlotte?" she says. "Who gives a damn?"

It *is* spiral notebook paper, with untrimmed border and folded about five times to fit into the envelope. The third sip is as bad as the first. Charlee sets the glass on the envelope, goes in the bathroom, puts down the toilet cover and sits in the sunshine. She holds up the letter but it's backlit too brightly to read. She smooths it on her lap, trembling knees clamped together. She realizes she is holding her breath, so takes a deep one. Her heart thuds in her chest.

Dearest Charlee:

Sorry, but this will be short—I'm writing on the porcelain throne while Becky's out for bagels. Weather's good, we're having fun. Becky's good. The minor league baseball game was a blast—all the hits, errors and beer you could ask for. We have to go sometime. Were you an all-star with my glove? Tomorrow Becky and I will have a long talk. Hope you had a great weekend. That's about all for now. I miss you like crazy. We have so much to talk about, honey, too much to fit in a quick letter. I'll see you Sunday. You'll get this after I'm back but that's OK, it's the thought that counts.

I love you big much. R.

Suddenly she can hardly recall Rory's features, but she refuses to look at a photograph. Instead, she is back at home, the Thanksgiving a few months before her father died, as he botched the turkey carving the way he always did, hacking off rough slices and piling them high on a plate. Without warning her mother pounded a fist on the table and burst out sobbing.

"I can't take it anymore! You're a failure, William. Why didn't you listen to me and take that job at *Time*?" Her fork flew against the wall, gashing the plaster. "Twenty years! Can you answer me that? Can you?" She ran from the table and up the stairs. A door slammed on the far side of the house. Then all was silent except for the clicking of her father's knife and fork, cutting again. Charlee gripped her wine glass.

Her father stopped and bit his lip. He had liver spots on his hands, and the flesh on his neck sagged like his shoulders.

"I didn't want you kids to grow up in New York," he said. "It's no place to raise a family." He looked down at the butchered bird. His voice quivered.

"Who wants dark meat? Charlee?"

The parakeet sings in his cage, music escaping through the bars without trying. Charlee looks up, into the sun, and has to turn away. The letter flutters to the floor. She picks it up and leaves the bathroom, re-folding it, as complicated as a road map. She holds it up to the bars and Terence pecks at it curiously, ripping off tiny inedible pieces. "Just like a man," Charlee says. She takes the news clipping off the table and holds it side by side with the letter, then drops them both into the drawer.

"Bastard," she says, "you bastard," wishing she really meant it, and slams the drawer shut with her foot. The parakeet panics at the sound, squawking and bouncing off the single round wall of his cage, until he forgets what he was afraid of and stands warily on his perch, waiting for the next time, assuming there will be.

ALTIPLANO[91]

The sun had set behind them. It was almost dark, and getting colder. The Chilean *carabinero* at the checkpoint, over 14,000 feet above the sea they had left only five hours before, sneered when he checked their passports.

"It's crazy to be up here at this time of day," he said in Spanish, then returned the documents without looking at the gringos and offered no assistance. He waved them away. They watched another *carabinero* stoke the coal stove and warm his hands, then zipped their jackets and stepped back out into the icy wind.

"Finding two frozen bodies will give them something to do tomorrow," Hatfield said.

"It's February," Maggie said. "It's the bloody middle of summer. How could I know it would be like this?"

"You've only lived in Arica for nine months. Did it ever occur to you to ask someone?"

Maggie stopped and glared at him. "Damn it, it'll be OK."

"I've been reading that for a year now."

"Well, isn't it?"

"I miss you," he said.

"God, don't start that again."

"Slow down, Maggie." She ignored him and strode hard across the packed earth to the Volkswagen. She was already behind the wheel when he opened the passenger door, panting.

---

91 Published in *The Chariton Review*, Spring 1989.

"Jesus," he said. "This altitude."

"I warned you to take it easy on the wine."

"Glad you reminded me." Hatfield pulled the cork on the liter bottle of Concha y Toro and took a swig. He held it up to the remnant of daylight: it was better than half gone.

"Brilliant," Maggie said. "The cops'll love that." She popped the clutch and spun gravel, sliding sideways for a second onto the washboard dirt road.

"That too," Hatfield said, and nestled the bottle in his crotch as they bounced north toward Bolivia.

They had a tent but no stove, having planned to cook over a campfire. But they discovered that the altiplano lay far above the timberline, and they found no wood, nothing at all to burn outside of some worthless scrub grass that somehow kept the llamas and alpacas alive. The road had no shoulder, nowhere to pull off to safety even if they saw a reasonable place to camp, which they didn't—nothing but tremendous plains stretching in all directions, cut by primitive hills, blue streams flowing like transparent ice, a pair of snow-crowned volcanoes in the distance. They shivered in their shorts. It was over 90 degrees when they left Arica.

Hatfield hugged the bottle between his thighs. "Maybe we should just turn back," he said.

"But we have to see the pink flamingos on Lake Chungará! Besides, I'm not sure we have enough gas."

"Great."

"You know, Kenny, you're not helping matters any."

"Not like Ernesto would, I know. Sorry I'm not a macho Latin."

"Check the map," she said, eyes on the road.

There was no moon. The VW's headlights were thin beams in the blackness. They had seen no other vehicle for hours, since they passed a rickety Bolivian transport truck loaded with bulging sacks and unsmiling people piled on top of them.

"That turn's got to be around here someplace," she said.

"Take a left at the next woodpile."

"This was supposed to be fun, Kenny."

"Tell me about it! Travel 9,000 miles to visit your girlfriend and find out she's with another guy. I'm having a blast, Maggie, time of my life. Fun is too mild a word for the pleasure I'm experiencing."

"I told you I *see* Ernesto. I'm not *with* him."

"No, you're *with* me—sorry to have bothered you. Watch out!"

Something thudded and squealed under the front bumper. It was a definitive impact, the kind when you know immediately things will not be the same. Maggie braked and killed the engine. She trembled and took deep, sucking breaths as if suffering from the altitude.

"Flashlight?" she asked.

"It's back at your place. In the same bag with the toothbrushes, oranges, Swiss army knife and your diaphragm."

"Can't you let anything drop? I said I was sorry—isn't that enough for you? I feel like I'm on trial."

"Here's matches."

She turned off the lights and they entered darkness as complete as a cave's. The car doors slammed but the night swallowed the sound. The wind was gone and its lonely moan with it, the night as silent as space until their feet scuffed the road. Hatfield cleared his throat. Maggie struck a match and it flared in her cupped hand. On the ground lay a crumpled creature the size of a fat woodchuck, half rodent and half rabbit, its sides heaving and one bloody leg pawing at the air.

"Vizcacha," Maggie said. They had seen a dozen of them during the drive.

"It's history," Hatfield said. "Poor bastard."

"I hate to see him suffer."

"Want me to crush his head with a rock?"

"No!"

"Then it's going to suffer."

"I don't care."

"I didn't think so."

"You know what I mean."

"Get in the car," he said.

"What're you going to do?"

"Get in the car."

To his surprise, Maggie did. Hatfield lit a match, found a rock as big as a football, lit another one, and lined up his target. He raised the stone with both hands over his head, looking up for a moment to the sky, and was still thinking how amazing it was, how he had never seen a sky so full of bright, uncountable stars, as he drove the rock down hard like an ax and heard a squishing crunch in the darkness. He almost vomited, but comforted himself that it was her fault. He'd tried his best to make it better.

Maggie started the car and in the red glow of the taillights Hatfield saw what he had done. He gagged as he kicked the stone off the road, then went back to the car without looking up.

"Drive," he said, and closed the door so tenderly it rattled as she pulled away. He yanked it tight.

"Did you do it?" Maggie was hunched over the steering wheel.

Hatfield hesitated, watching the little cones of light in the black everything. He sat on his hands. His stomach felt like old meat.

"It feels no pain," he said finally.

"I'm sorry, Kenny."

"Yeah," he said.

A dirt road, more primitive still, branched left and they took it. It had to be the way to Parinacota, the only village in the area, though in the darkness they saw no sign. The crude map showed no distances. Twice the road narrowed to hardly more than the width of the Volkswagen.

After five kilometers, Maggie stopped at a flooded depression. There was no way to skirt it—a bank on the right and a two-foot drop to the left prevented that— and no room to turn around. Hatfield got out to check. Ice was already crusting at the edges of the puddle. He couldn't see the bottom, but what could he expect in those dim headlights.

Maggie rolled down her window. "Well?"

"I think it's OK."

"Get in, then."

Hatfield went over, trying to rub some warmth into his hands. "Want me to drive?"

"Why, don't you trust me?"

"I used to," he said.

"Get in," she said. "Before I change my mind."

She gunned the engine and splashed through. The water was only a few inches deep. It was easy.

"In Maggie I trust," Hatfield said, hand over his heart. "I pledge allegiance. My Maggie right or wrong."

"Grow up, Kenny."

They rode in tense silence, slowly over the pitted road, rarely getting the car out of second gear. Hatfield mumbled something.

Maggie crawled around a blind curve. "What?"

"I said this is the loneliest place in the world."

"For someone by himself, maybe."

"That's my point."

Maggie's chin almost rested on the wheel. "Please, Kenny. We've come such a long way."

He leaned over and peered at the odometer. "About eight kilometers," he said, and the silence returned.

Creatures appeared on the road. Maggie braked slowly, easing against traffic into a small herd of llamas, branded with multi-colored ribbons on their ears. Their herder tapped their flanks with a stick and made clucking noises, and the llamas gave ground.

"Signs of life," Maggie said. "Like a seagull on the ocean. The town's got to be close."

"This guy's wearing sandals with no socks," Hatfield said. "These people are maniacs."

"Maybe they're just *men*," she said playfully, but got only frozen quiet for an answer. She rolled down her window.

"Excuse me, señor. Is this the road to Parinacota?"

"*Sí.*"

"Is it far?"

"No."

"How far?"

His broad, Indian face was barely visible in the night. He kept several strides between him and the car. "Not far," he said.

"Two kilometers?" Hatfield said. "*Dos kilometros?*"

"*Dos kilometros.*" His voice was like a shrug. He followed his animals. Maggie thanked his back. They drove two slow kilometers, then three, four. The first building was a surprise in the high beams. Not a single light shone in the tiny village. BIENVENIDOS A PARINACOTA, said white letters on a cinder block wall. Maggie turned a corner and they found themselves in a dirt plaza the size of a basketball court, in front of a crude stone-and-mortar church with a thatched roof.

"It's like a Spanish mission," Maggie said.

Hatfield finished the bottle, corked it for nothing and tossed it into the back seat.

"They could be cannibals," he said. "They could do anything to us they wanted to."

362

"Who?" she said, and she was right. No noise disturbed the deserted plaza. A dog barked a few times but stopped, as if it didn't have the energy. "Well?" she said, and opened her door. They got out.

Hatfield stood with head hung back, gulping the thin, cold air. Never had he seen so many stars, a glittering dome from horizon to horizon, so close and bright that they seemed real, a presence, not something far away and unimaginable like city stars. He walked around the car and hugged Maggie from behind. Heads together, looking up, they stood in silence, but it was a different kind of silence from the ride. Maggie's breath blew warm on his cheek. He hugged her tighter.

"I wouldn't trade this for anything," he said.

"Me neither," she said. Her hands gripped his wrists. "Kenny, I'm so sorry for everything."

"Forget it. Yesterday's history. It's what happens next that matters."

They were still watching the sky, breathing together, when the first door opened, then another. Sandals scuffed the bare earth. A dog howled; Maggie and Hatfield heard a curse and a kick, then a whimpering that died like an unplugged fan. A dozen people slowly surrounded them. A brave boy edged up to the Volkswagen and touched the bumper; a woman spoke sharply and he jumped back.

"Say something," Hatfield whispered. "Your Spanish is way better than mine."

"*Buenas noches*," she said. "Is there a hotel here?"

A man snorted. "No one comes to Parinacota, and if they do, they don't stay."

"We came from Arica and can't make it back tonight."

"Is it beautiful down there, in Arica?" the woman who'd scolded the boy asked.

"*Sí*," said Maggie and Hatfield together, holding hands now against the realization that this person's whole life had happened here.

"Someday I will go," she said.

"You should," Hatfield said, and felt ridiculous.

"*Qué pasa?*" said a voice with a thick foreign inflection. A burly man holding a kerosene lamp stood stiffly at the corner. When no one replied he walked toward them, limping slightly and leaning on a cane. No one spoke as he approached. There was no sound but the scrape of his boots, and the tap of his cane on the packed dirt. He stopped in front of Maggie and Hatfield, a cane's-length away, his broad face as lined and creased as his cracked leather jacket. He stared at the Volkswagen, then at them, then back to the car.

"*Sind sie Deutschen?*" he asked.

"No," Maggie said. "*Norteamericanos.*"

"Ah, good," he said in German-accented English. "Come with me. It has been years since I have had the opportunity to speak your language." He turned to the townspeople. "Go back to bed. These Americans will be my guests tonight."

"*Muy bien*, Doctor Schaffner," said a voice. The rest of the people dispersed without a word, slipping back into the darkness. Doors closed around them. Hatfield and Maggie gathered their stuff in the car.

"Should we lock it?" Hatfield said softly in the front seat.

Before Maggie could answer they heard, "Do not worry. I guarantee your safety."

The German stood at least fifteen feet away. Hatfield pulled Maggie to him and whispered directly in her ear.

"Could he have possibly heard me?"

"Does it change anything if he did?" she whispered back. They locked the doors.

The German was waiting, his face ghostly in the lantern light. He led the way with Maggie at his side, Hatfield lagging behind a step.

"It's dark," he said. "Always the generator is off at night. But at least now we have electricity."

"It must have been hard before," Maggie said. "Have you lived here long?"

He paused and looked at her blankly as if calculating, or maybe translating the numbers into another language. Smiling he touched her shoulder and Hatfield tensed.

"Perhaps forty years in South America," he said, walking again. "Perhaps ten years here."

"Here in Parinacota or here in Chile?" Hatfield asked from the shadows.

Schaffner gave no sign that he'd heard. "Here," he said, and pushed open a door covered with peeling blue paint. His cane bumped loud on the rough plank floor, the wood gray with age and grime. Maggie followed, then Hatfield. There was only one room. Two metal-frame twin beds, one with a tangle of bedding, one a bare mattress, extended from the opposite wall. A rickety table took up the middle of the room, a single unshaded light bulb dangling from the ceiling above a dirty plate and silverware. The only two windows were in the same wall as the door, to Hatfield's right as he entered, over a long workbench that stretched to the far corner.

Hatfield held his breath. On the bench and windowsills, lined up like soldiers, were jar after jar of things once alive, floating now in a pale fluid stained yellow by the lamplight.

"Please," Schaffner said, with a vague gesture at the open bed. "Make yourselves at ease."

365

They hesitated. Schaffner caught them staring at the jars. He smiled, slowly. Hatfield had never seen an expression take so long to happen.

"I am a biologist," he said. "Entomologist especially. I collect things to study." He smiled again, rubbing his hands together. "As you see."

"That's very interesting," Maggie said.

"We must study to learn how things work. We must experiment," Schaffner said. "I do not see any other purpose to this life."

"Where did you live in South America? Before Chile, I mean."

Schaffner glanced at Hatfield and held it an extra count. He lit a Belmont cigarette. The match reflected in his glasses like two torches.

"Paraguay for many years," he said. "Then Argentina." Twin trails of smoke drifted from his nostrils. The slow smile returned.

"My friends," he said, pointing with the cigarette. "Make yourselves at ease."

They realized they were still hugging their gear like shields. Abashedly they dumped the stuff on the empty bed, and stood wondering what to do next. Still wearing his smile Schaffner reached for a bottle among the specimens, half full of a murky purple liquid, and poured it into three glasses. He handed them each one. Hatfield dared to inspect the drink; it looked like burgundy with milk in it.

"*Pintatani*," Schaffner said. "Wine made only one place in the world—the oasis of Codpa, hundreds of kilometers south in the Atacama Desert."

"I've heard of it," Maggie said. "Someday I'll go."

"You would be one of the few," Schaffner said. "It is very isolated."

Hatfield gripped his drink. "Like Parinacota?"

Schaffner's smile withered. "Yet somehow we are all here," he said. "Together." He held up his cup. "*Prosit.*"

They clinked glasses, and Hatfield felt a twisting sense of complicity in something illicit. He couldn't explain it, but that first sip was like a handshake closing a deal, a seal of approval to an act he should be ashamed of, though he had no idea why or even what the act was. Prepared to detest the evil-looking *pintatani*, Hatfield steeled his taste buds to the inevitable bitterness, but to his surprise it was pleasantly tart and tasty. He enjoyed it, and drank deep the second time.

Maggie was smiling at both of them. "This is good," she said.

"It's like anything else," Schaffner said. "One becomes accustomed." He uncorked a second bottle.

Time passed quickly, or maybe slowly; Hatfield wasn't sure which when he looked at his watch and saw it was midnight. The only thing that matters up here, he thought, is that time doesn't. He watched Schaffner start to pour the third bottle. Maggie's friends in Arica had jokingly warned them that you get drunk faster the higher you climb. Now Hatfield felt giddy but clear, as if he had a head full of altiplano air. He looked at Maggie and his jealousy and mean remarks turned back on him, cutting deep and shameful. I haven't exactly been a monk since she left. Those women didn't mean anything.

Schaffner slammed his fist on the table. "What I wouldn't give for a good German lager! We are the only ones who know how to make beer!"

He left the chair and moved to his bed, walking overly straight despite his cane to demonstrate he wasn't tipsy. He sat down heavily next to Maggie, the two of them now facing Hatfield. Their thighs touched and Maggie tried to inch away invisibly.

Schaffner grinned. "The privy is outside, by the way. What do you expect from this bloody country? And Peru, Bolivia,

Paraguay—all worse! What do *you* think of a country where the trains do not run on time?"

Schaffner stopped, as if expecting an answer. He topped off his guests' practically full glasses and searched their faces in turn, but they didn't speak. Maggie's legs were pressed tight together. Hatfield glanced at her and remembered their morning in Dachau two years before. It's a short train ride from Munich, a popular side-trip.

"Our train to Dachau was ten minutes early," he said. "We got there before it opened."

"You think it is a joke!" Schaffner said. "You think it is a circus with clowns to be laughed at! Of course, you think that unless you are a clown too!" Schaffner pointed the bottle at Hatfield. "Well, I am no clown."

Caught in his stare, Hatfield nodded. "Yes," Maggie said, but her eyes were on the floor. Hatfield looked away to the specimen jars, standing like carnival targets for a softball throw, and thought of a child mummy they'd seen last week in an Iquique museum. It lay in a fetal scrunch with hands crossed in front of its face as if for protection, a few beads still braided in the ancient, matted hair.

"Hair," Maggie had said. "Jesus."

Afterward they sat in the square and licked ice cream cones. Maggie played with his hair, stroking it and winding it around her fingers until Hatfield brought up Ernesto again and they fought all the way to the bus station.

Schaffner nodded in what appeared to be satisfaction. "That is the trouble—we do not put ourselves enough in the place of another, to try and understand." He struggled to his feet, calm now, almost eerily self-controlled. He limped to the workbench.

Maggie reached to squeeze Hatfield's knee. He covered her hand with his, and felt new again.

368

"I'm sorry," he whispered.

"Sorry?" Schaffner said, his back to them.

"Nothing."

Schaffner turned around, beaming, a large jar in his hands. He held it up to the light and inspected it like a bottle of wine, then brought the jar to them. A tattered lump floated in the liquid.

"An alpaca's heart," he said. "Very much enlarged by disease." He faced Maggie. "The crucial organ, my friend. Without it your warm, silky sweater would not be possible."

He cradled the jar in one arm and touched the alpaca wool on her shoulder, slid his fingers almost to the bare skin of her throat. He grimaced and set the jar down. Slowly he flexed his fingers.

"Arthritis," he said. "I was a good flute player in my youth, but those days are gone. You give up much as you grow older, my young friends. But of course, you do not believe me."

Maggie and Hatfield sat with hands folded, not meeting his eyes.

"Tired?" he asked, leaning on his cane. He tossed back the last inch in his glass. "Yes, we are all very tired. I will show you the WC."

He walked them around the corner. Maggie entered the shack, and they heard the bolt slide. Schaffner and Hatfield stood with hands in their pockets, silent as two strangers in an elevator. Their eyes met, by chance it must have been, and a sad understanding passed between them, knowledge Hatfield could not define but knew had changed him forever. Schaffner shrugged and unzipped. Hatfield followed like an initiate, and back-to-back they urinated in the frozen starlight, their separate streams hissing and steaming as they spattered the frost, the only sounds in the utter stillness. Eyes to the sky, Hatfield saw the same infinity of stars that he had seen with Maggie, holding her close as the villagers tightened their circle around them.

I'm pissing on top of the world, he thought. And the stars couldn't care less. He wondered if Schaffner did, and shivered in the dead cold.

They slept in their clothes. Untying his sneakers, Hatfield saw his right toe smeared with blood. He remembered the dying vizcacha, the stone, the sounds of impact. He swallowed and slid the shoes under the bed.

Schaffner killed the lamp. "Good night, my friends. Pleasant dreams."

The bed springs creaked, and soon he was snoring. Hatfield hugged Maggie, hard, and she hugged back. "Good night, lover," she said, and in a minute she fell asleep.

Hatfield stared at the blackness. The jars were dim memories on the windowsills, contents invisible. He fought for sleep, but every time he came close his lungs begged for oxygen in the thin air, and he gulped deep breaths that snapped him awake. He burped and tasted *pintatani*.

Tomorrow, he thought. Tomorrow we will see flamingos in the dawn.

Hatfield rolled over and gently kissed the reason he had come to this place. Her breath was warm in the absolute darkness.

SCENERY STARK AND STUNNING SURROUNDS CHILEAN PORT CITY [92]

Chile is a vast string bean of a country, stretching 2,650 miles along South America's west coast, yet is only 225 miles at its widest point. Chile is California tipped upside-down—and even more wild, spectacular and extreme. California is green and rainy up north, desert in the south; Chile is the opposite. Its southern tip is part of fabled Tierra del Fuego (Chile also claims a disputed slice of Antarctica), including the treacherous Strait of Magellan. The central region is the breadbasket of the country, like California's San Joaquin and Sacramento Valleys, and is the source of Chile's excellent wines.

As you move north, the land gets progressively drier, until even cacti can't survive. This is the Atacama Desert, possibly the most arid place on earth. At Chile's far northern tip lies the port of Arica, *La Ciudad de la Eterna Primavera*—The City of Eternal Spring. Atacama Desert spring, that is, with no showers in April or any other time.

Only twelve miles from the Peruvian border, Arica takes a little effort to reach, but getting there will be a big part of your memories. On a domestic flight you come from the south, hugging the rugged Pacific coastline (think Big Sur without the vegetation) for a tourist-friendly fly-by of the city en route to the airport (sit on the right side of the plane). The flight from

---

92 Sunday *Hartford Courant* travel section, December 25, 2005.

La Paz, Bolivia is totally different, a half-hour hop over Lake Titicaca, the Andes Mountains, and an Atacama Desert Mars-scape. Take the bus from La Paz and you cross stunning terrain reminiscent of Zion and Glacier National Parks, the Grand Canyon and the Badlands—all in nine hours, with closeups of snow-capped volcanoes for good measure. From the south on the Pan American Highway you will never forget the three *cuestas* in the 150 miles before Arica, enormous ravines with oases at the bottom, each a precipitous drop from the road clinging to the desert hillside—and your vehicle clinging to the road. From the north you gradually emerge from pure desert and see the shimmering Pacific to your right, then Arica in the distance.

Or at least you see Arica's most famous feature: El Morro, a massive sandstone bluff overlooking the harbor. From this angle it looks like a huge bowhead whale, brow looming three hundred feet above the ocean. The Morro is not only the symbol of Arica, but also part of Chile's national history and mythology, like the Alamo is to the U.S.—with the difference that Chile won the battle as well as the expansionist war.

The conflict was the War of the Pacific; the year was 1880. At dawn on June 7, Chilean soldiers sprinted up the spine of the whale toward the Peruvian garrison. Fueled by *chupilca del diablo*, a devilish concoction of *aguardiente* mixed with gunpowder, and screaming a South American version of the Rebel Yell, they overwhelmed the defenders in less than an hour. Gallons of blood stained the sand, most of it Peruvian, and from that day forward Arica has been Chilean territory.

You can see photos and artifacts of the battle and learn a lot of history (if you read Spanish) at the museum atop the Morro. Take an inexpensive taxi or hike up from downtown if you're in shape and feeling energetic. Even if you skip the museum, the view from the Morro is easily the best in town. A bit higher up the hill is the Cristo de la Concordia, a large statue of Christ overlooking the harbor. It was erected in 1999 as a symbol of newly established amity between Chile and Peru (though people from both countries point out that the statue has its backside facing Peru.)

Look left (south) and you see a curving coastline and spectacular rugged escarpments. Directly below are beaches and the ex-Isla Alacrán (Scorpion Island). It's an ex-island because a short causeway now connects it to the mainland. Don't worry, there are no scorpions; the island was named for its odd shape. Fishhooks nearly 2,000 years old have been found there. Nowadays there's a Yacht Club, though don't expect to see any Russian oligarch-size ships.

To the north, nearly empty beaches fade into the misty distance toward Peru. Far off to the east are the Andes, snowy peaks visible on a clear day. Keep turning around to your right and you see Arica extending away from the ocean, its limits stark where the buildings and irrigation end and the desert begins.

Arica is a crossroads town steeped in history. It was Inca territory when the Spanish invaded in the 1530s, but people have lived here for millennia. The archaeological museum in Azapa (one of two fertile valleys leading from Arica to the interior) has 10,000-year-old mummies in astonishingly good condition. In a place as dry as the Atacama Desert, things get preserved. Catch a taxi from downtown and you can be at the museum in twenty minutes. Or save some pesos and take a *colectivo* taxi (the stop to Azapa is at the corner of Patricio Lynch and Chacabuco Streets).

Speaking of history and downtown (*el centro* in Spanish), definitely take a stroll around the center city. The main commercial street, 21 de Mayo, was rebuilt after a 1986 earthquake and its downtown blocks closed to through traffic. Shopping, banks, restaurants, sidewalk cafes—even a McDonalds and a Blockbuster as you get nearer the ocean. But why come to South America to eat a McPollo?

Instead, turn left onto Bolognesi, another pedestrians-only street. Walk one block and you'll reach the Iglesia San Marcos, a metal church designed by Gustave Eiffel (yes, architect of the Paris tower) when Arica was still a Peruvian city. Tour the church, and maybe relax under palm trees in the adjacent Plaza Colón. (The helpful tourist bureau is across the street near the ocean end of the plaza).

It's a short stroll to the downtown waterfront, featuring a small but thriving fish market. Vendors constantly filet fish and flip the carcasses into the water. This attracts seals, sea lions and pelicans looking for easy meals, and tourists looking to be entertained by the process. You can also sign up for a boat ride around the harbor and surrounding coastline.

Most visitors to Arica spend at least some time lounging on the beach, especially during the summer months (the opposite of ours, remember). From *el centro*, Arica's beaches to the south are accessible by foot or by vehicle. There are frequent buses all over the city, but for a few cents more you can flag down a much quicker *colectivo* taxi; they run set routes and carry up to four passengers. Beaches on the north side of town are also popular, but primarily for wading and sunbathing. Strong undertows make swimming risky.

January and February are high season in Arica, with more people and higher hotel rates, though prices are generally much lower than in the U.S. There's a full range of accommodations, from spartan backpacker *pensiones* to four-star hotels. The same holds true for restaurants. Basic eateries abound, many specializing in local seafood, but plenty of more elegant options are also available. Wherever you dine, taste the famous *aceitunas* (olives) from the Azapa Valley. Have a pisco, the national firewater, usually drunk with cola (piscola) or as a pisco sour. And it's hard to go wrong with Chilean wines.

For a day that you'll never forget, drag yourself away from the beaches and take a trip to the altiplano. It's amazing to leave sea level and in four hours find yourself in another world over 13,000 feet up in the Andes. Almost as amazing is that a 25-seat tour bus will pick you up at your hotel, provide breakfast and lunch at "real" (not tourist trap) restaurants in the mountains, and give you a full day of touring with a multi-lingual guide—all for less than $25. (Tipping the guide and driver is not expected, but very much appreciated.)

The road to the altiplano begins in the Lluta Valley (pronounced either YOO-tah or JOO-tah) and continues all the way to Bolivia. It used to be rough gravel at higher elevations, but now is a generally smooth two-lane highway for its entire length. The bus makes a number of stops that allow you to: 1) take pictures, 2) learn things, and 3) buy stuff. Highlights include the ridge overlooking the beautiful mountain town of Putre; candelabra cactus, which grow nowhere else in the world; and the Pukará de Copaquilla, a rebuilt Inca outpost with spectacular views and possibly the best echo I've ever heard. Encouraged by our guide Jorge, most of our diverse group (seven different nationalities among 25 people) gave a few good whoops and smiled to hear them reverberate through the valley.

Later the bus detours down a dirt road to Parinacota, a tiny Indian village in the middle of nowhere—a sublime, desolate nowhere. It's far above the tree line; there's no vegetation except scrub grass and moss. Evidently, it's sufficient grazing for the numerous llamas (the correct pronunciation is YAH-mah or JAH-mah). There's a small colonial-era church that had to accommodate the indigenous religion to be accepted: drawings on the ceiling depict a number of pagan gods and legends, many of them decidedly ferocious-looking.

Last stop is magnificent Lake Chungará, only ten kilometers from the Bolivian border. The lake is famous for enormous flocks of pink flamingoes, and snow-capped Parinacota Volcano, over 19,000 feet high. On sunny days the preternaturally blue water reflects the volcano in a stunning mirror image, the ultimate photo-op. Fortunately the weather is usually good there, although clouds and rain or snow can develop during the summer—the months ironically known as *invierno boliviano* (Bolivian Winter), because that's when precipitation falls at higher elevations.

Chances are you'll be glad to head back down to Arica. It's a fascinating day, but a long day, and high Andes air can be rough on bodies accustomed to sea level. To avoid altitude sickness—called *soroche* (so-ROE-chay) or *puna* (POO-nah)—bring water and drink a lot of it, walk slowly and rest frequently. Also consider ordering *mate* (MAH-tay) *de coca* in the restaurants, which is said to soothe the *soroche* and any stomach ailment. Besides, it just feels illicitly fun to order coca leaf tea. It's perfectly legal—and no, it doesn't get you high.

Why not buy a box of coca leaf tea bags in Arica to take home and offer guests at your next dinner party? Eyebrows will surely rise, and you'll have a perfect pretext to regale the group with tales of your unforgettable trip to the City of Eternal Spring.

DWARF OF THE DIAMOND [93]

I remember my first practice with his school.
He stuck his glove on the wrong hand and—
after I'd just corrected three kids for the same
mistake—tried to bat cross-handed.
About a week later an easy fly ball clipped him
square on the forehead. But he blinked back
most of his tears and refused to leave the game.
I ruffled his hair and he spun away, embarrassed,
determination glinting in his moist eyes.
That was just over a year ago.
He's grown a bit, but so have all the
other boys, and my favorite second baseman
is still usually the dwarf of the diamond.
His team played yesterday. He led off the game by
taking a called strike three that was almost
in the dirt, but after a quick, unbelieving glance
at the umpire he hustled back to the bench.
He cracked a double over third base in his second at-bat.
The next time up he caught the third baseman
playing deep and laid down a perfect bunt for
another hit, the first time I'd seen him dare to try
in a game the play we had practiced so many hours.
There wasn't even a throw to first.

---

93 First published in *Ideals* magazine, 1980.

His teammates yelled their approval,
and he grinned like the sun as he waved
to me, keeping score on the sidelines.
I saluted with clenched fist as something
welled up for both of us, spilling over,
but anybody looking my way would
have thought I, shielded by my sunglasses,
was just wiping some sweat off my face.

ABOUT THE AUTHOR

Tom Hazuka has published the novels *The Road to the Island*, *In the City of the Disappeared* and *Last Chance for First*, as well as over sixty-five short stories and two books of nonfiction, both co-written with C.J. Jones. He has edited or co-edited nine anthologies, including *Flash Fiction*, *Flash Fiction Funny*, *Flash Nonfiction Funny*, *Sudden Flash Youth*, *A Celestial Omnibus*, *You Have Time for This* and *Flash Nonfiction Food*. Tom is also a singer-songwriter; links to his writing and original songs can be found at tomhazuka.com. He taught fiction writing at Central Connecticut State University for many years, and now lives with his wife Christine in Sebastian, Florida and Berlin, Connecticut.